Twice
You burned your life's work
Once to start a new life
And once just to start a fire
—The Long Winters, "Be Kind to the New Girl"

So, this is important:

This is what I remember, and how I remember it—although I've changed some names, and amalgamated some people, and some places.

I'm certain that some people in this book remember things differently, or remember things I don't remember. Some people probably have no recall of events that are vivid, and crucial, to me.

I'm scared not just of subjectivity, but of losing people I love.

In life, I'm meticulously honest, but my default is to feel like a fraud. I walk through customs thinking I'll get busted for drugs I'm not carrying. I walk out of stores afraid to be caught with things I haven't stolen. So, of course, I'm terrified of a common scenario: a memoirist is dogged, exposed, and denounced.

I'm telling my memories with scrupulous precision, while scared that the mind is unreliable. Maybe every person on the planet is equally susceptible to errors and contortions of remembrance—whether or not they consider their minds to be suspect. Does that make memory itself an act of imagination?

I wrote my ideas on Post-It notes and stuck them on the wall by the desk. Lyrics, ideas for poems, ideas for newspaper pieces, preposterous diagrams for joysticks and wired-up boxing gloves that would work as sound-effects triggers. These are two notes I left for myself in November 1999:

I'm mostly writing drug stories. I have them. People read them.

I know a famous actor who was a regular on *Page Six,* going in and out of nightclubs, in the heyday of the Hilton sisters and the Olsen twins. He struggled with cocaine and painkillers but was embarrassed to talk about it. "Addiction stories are clichéd," he said.

You're a storyteller, I told him. You know how few essential stories there are. This one is *new,* how often does that happen? It's up there with Boy Meets Girl Boy Loses Girl, Man Challenges the Gods and Is Punished, Rags to Riches. Joking cynically with friends, I've called this book a JADN: just another drug narrative. We, the addicts, keep writing them, but nearly everything we have to say has already been expressed just in the title of Caroline Knapp's *Drinking: A Love Story.*

I can't renounce drugs. I love drugs. I'd never trade the part of my life when the drugs *worked,* though the bulk of the time I spent getting high, they weren't doing shit for me. I wouldn't be *here* if I didn't do the drugs first. This part of my life—even minus the bursts of euphoria—is better, sexier, happier, more poetic, more romantic, grander.

And if heroin still made me feel like I did the first time, and kept making me that way forever—kept *working*—I might've quite happily accepted a desolate, marginal life and death.

I've heard from so many people who got clean, then went out and got wasted again, that, bewilderingly, they were *exactly* at the same place they were when they left off, *immediately.* It's just the bizarreness of addiction, which waits patiently, no matter how long you go without drugs. Who knows, maybe I *am,* in fact, unlike the aforementioned relapsers, but I have no desire to try the drugs again, and see if things go differently. I don't want to test this life's durability.

None of this guarantees I won't go out and get fucked up. It happens, often to people who've made enthusiastic public declarations of recovery. I watch *Celebrity Rehab* and think: *My people!*

Caroline Knapp, it bears mentioning, was also addicted to nicotine, and died of lung cancer.

I loathe myself in a lot of these stories. I feel compelled to tell you now that eventually I turn into a kind, loving person who struggles to live the first line in Saint Francis's prayer: "Make me a channel of your peace." Not to demand peace, but to transmit it.

Maybe that's not what you're interested in—maybe you want salacious tales of the debased guy: the cleaned-up guy is intolerably corny. Maybe you just want to read *drugs heroin heroin drugs* over and over again. When I was getting high, that's what I read these books for.

My dad's dad was the town drunk in Tullos, Louisiana. In the mid-1950s, when everybody else's family had gotten a car, my dad's family still had a horse. Because the horse knew how to get home. My grandfather would get wasted at the bar, slump on the horse when his money was gone, and the horse would take him home.

He lost their house in a card game—I mean, he literally *lost their house in a card game*. He came home and said, get up, everybody, we have to leave.

My dad got into West Point. When he came back on vacations, his dad made him go to the bar with him in uniform so he could show him off, which my dad hated. He went to Vietnam, where he served as an adviser to a South Vietnamese tank unit, not with an American unit, possibly because the officers doing the assigning disliked him: he was too uptight, too intense.

I spoke to my dad about Vietnam just once when I was a kid.

Dad, what's that citation from the South Vietnamese government that's hanging on the wall of your study?

"Well, we were at _____, and we were surrounded by _____ of them, and there were only _____ of us."

So, it was a battle?

"It was a battle."

Did you win?

"No," said my dad. "But we killed a lot of them."

He was interviewed by the *New York Times* in 2000, about how the war's legacy is taught at West Point—a salient point, being that the Vietnamese were so fanatical, or so patriotic, that they leaped heedlessly, or courageously, into death.

"Lord, I saw them die by the hundreds," my dad told the *Times* reporter.

I think what he saw in Vietnam amplified, demonically, what he learned as a child: terrible things could happen, unexpectedly, at any time. His became a life of hypervigilance. He tightened like a fist.

He drank beer at night and on weekends. I don't remember him drunk—not in the way he told me my grandfather was drunk—but on the weekend, if you had done something wrong—(failed Algebra, neglected to mow the lawn)—you had to tell him early. At 11 AM, he would be disappointed. At 2 PM, he would be angry. At 4 PM he would leap out of his chair, red-faced, in a rage, and whip his belt out, threatening to finally beat me the way his dad beat him.

My dad never hit me. I waited, and waited, but he never did. He reminded me often how lucky I was; that he grew up in a house with an openly, constantly drunk father who actually beat him. I did feel lucky.

My younger brother, a matchless student who eased virtuously through school, began to have strange episodes when he went off to college. He stopped going to class, and, for reasons he found to be perfectly sensible, started sleeping only every other night. He's brilliant, and odd; when he turned thirty, I congratulated him. He shrugged: "It's only significant because we have a base-10 number system."

My mom had unpredictable manias when she'd yell at you for something someone else did. "Your brother doesn't have a plan he doesn't have a plan *he needs a plan a person needs a plan!*" she screamed. OK, Mom, I'm not him, so . . . "*How can you live without a plan he's an adult he needs a plan!*"

He moved home and spent his days hanging out in the garage playing chess on the internet. I gave him my old laptop when his died; he would drive his car to a riverbank and spend the day writing code on it, in antiquated computer languages like COBOL and FORTRAN. He got a job, at night, sitting in the basement of a bank counting things. She still yelled at him. "When are you going to get a job?"

"Mom, I have a job."

"*When are you going to get a job, you little shit?!*"

Eventually my brother was living in his car. It's harder, post-9/11, to live in your car—they won't let you just park and sleep just anywhere, anymore. So he'd come home for interludes.

He developed delusions. He thought somebody had broken into his car and moved things around. He stayed up all night gripping a kitchen knife, believing people were coming for him.

He was institutionalized and medicated, then got out, didn't take his meds, went back home, went out and lived in his car again, went back home, etc. He seemed better off when he was homeless.

I see my brother as the guy I should've been. I have the same disorder: I down four pills every morning to stay rational. But he's the guy whose illness was exacerbated to the point where he became homeless and delusional. He was once the family star and I was the fuckup.

I had something he didn't have: an obsession.

When I was eleven or twelve, I'd pull up a folding chair to the jukebox at the teen center and listen to the same songs repeatedly: "Tainted Love," by Soft Cell, "For Those About to Rock, We Salute You," by AC/DC, "The Stroke," by Billy Squier. Mostly older kids came there, to play pinball and that formalist masterwork of vector-graphic arcade games, *Tempest*. They taunted me, I think because my intensity scared them. An adult staffer saw me pulled up so close to the jukebox that my head rested on the grille, and said, encouragingly, "There's a piano in the other room, do you want to go play it?" What? What made her think, so mistakenly, that I actually had within me the capacity, the potential, to *make* music?

I lived with this desperate feeling: no access to anywhere that bands played, no friends who played guitar. When I should've been doing homework, I would be lip-synching to Thin Lizzy and Dio records. *"You don't think we hear you jumping around up there?!"* my mom yelled. *"You think you're gonna be a rock star? Well, rots of ruck!"* She liked the racist faux-Chinese put-down.

I tried to stop wanting it, but I couldn't. As life went on, I pursued my dreams, for sure, but not in joy: I was harangued by them. I pursued them in dread.

My mom told me she'd buy me a guitar if I got on the honor roll. So I did—by a tenth of a point, and I had to go and argue with a gym teacher for it. I got a guitar—an Aria Pro II, and a Marshall practice amp, from a guitar store in Paramus, where the Jersey-metal sales guy yelled at me for touching the instruments hanging on the wall—and returned to fuck-up-hood.

I picked up simple chords and coarse riffs here and there, and watched the British New Wave how-to show *Rockschool* on PBS. I invented a song every time I learned something new.

The army sent my dad to UCLA—also paying to send my mom and my infant self to California with him—after he came back from Vietnam, so he'd get a degree and return to West Point as a professor. He lived in L.A. when Joan Didion was writing screenplays there, when John Phillips and David Crosby were up in the hills chuffing mounds of cocaine. He went on to get a Ph.D. and became an authority on French history, particularly the period between World Wars I and II, and France's failure to stop the invading Germans. He's written books, including one called *The Seeds of Disaster,* which sounds to me sometimes like a dark joke about his sons.

He taught at West Point for a few years, was sent to Germany, where American tank divisions prowled moodily up and down the Iron Curtain, worked for a year as a speechwriter for a NATO general in Belgium, then came back to West Point and was made head of the History Department.

West Point was so orderly, it was in a chokehold: an enforced family atmosphere. Divorce was a scandalous rarity. Neighborhoods were segregated by rank, each subdivision of identical houses having its own strange name: lieutenants and their families lived in Grey Ghost, captains in New Brick, majors in Stony Lonesome, lieutenant colonels in Lee Area, colonels in Lusk. There was a tiny crescent of houses for members of the military band called Band.

This was the early '80s. Most of the adult men had been to Vietnam; essentially, everybody's dad. There was an undercurrent of stress and rage—sometimes barely controlled panic—which I thought was the nature of adulthood. Most of them joined the army in an America still in the glow of World War II's victories; many of them had themselves gone to the military academy, were inculcated in West Point's resonant motto, Duty, Honor, Country, and a host of other sacred words chiseled into the arches of the castle-like barracks and academic buildings. They came back, carrying the horrifying things they saw—having killed other people—to a country that disdained them. I subbed on a friend's paper route and was screamed at by a man in a baby blue bathrobe for being a half hour late; I was raking the yard and a man walked by, barking, as if it were my fault, "The leaves will always win! You try, but the leaves will always win!"

There were plaques on the steps of each house with movable letters telling the name of the officer within. Most of the nameplates said something like "LTC Matthew J. Jones," or "MAJ Simmons and Family," or sometimes "The MacDonald Family," which to me seemed manic in its profession of familial unity. I had a friend named Luke, whose dad was Mexican and taught Spanish to the cadets, a civilian; this gave him a certain liminal status, an outsider's authority. Luke and I would sneak out at night and change the movable letters in the nameplates around, so they said "Captain Shit" or "Fuck My Ass." Military police cars, painted pale green, cruised by every few minutes. We dove into bushes and behind cars, breathing fast, eyes bulging with delight at the danger.

I went to summer camp. There was an ostracized kid in my cabin called Jumpin' Josh MacIntosh. He wanted to be a comedian, and he told weirdly pointless stories meant to be jokes: his sister's bike hit a twig and she fell over the handlebars; one time he was walking to school and he was late; one time his cable TV went out. No punch lines. A cruel prank was started: whenever he told one, everybody in the cabin would burst out in fake laughter.

Jumpin' Josh exulted.

The ruse spread. Even the first-graders were in on it. At the camp talent show, Jumpin' Josh MacIntosh stood in front of the bonfire and told this joke:

> I got detention, and I was sitting alone in class after school. Somebody had drawn football goals on the blackboard. A teacher came in and said, "Did you draw those football goals?" And I said, "No, I didn't draw those football goals." [In falsetto] *"I think you did! I think you did! I think you did draw those football goals!"*

A hundred kids broke out in fake hysterics. The camp director stood horrified. Jumpin' Josh MacIntosh walked off, and we chanted, JUMPIN' JOSH! JUMPIN' JOSH! He came back and told another. The fake laughter doubled in intensity. The camp director walked up as Jumpin' Josh started another, turned to us with a glare and said, "That's enough!" He put his arm around Josh and said, "Let's go; come on, Josh, let's go." Jumpin' Josh MacIntosh burst into tears in front of the entire camp, struggling to pull away from the camp director, squawking, "But they want me!"

My parents expressed vicious grudges against each other openly, daily. We listened to them yowl at each other, and as years of shrieking fights passed, my terror that they'd divorce turned into *Will you please, please just get divorced?*

Much of the terror and the anger was focused on me. I was a fuckup for sure, but that's not why. It was because the awfulness needed a place to go.

My mom screamed at me until I broke down in tears. My dad would pass by, get a beer from the fridge, glare at me, and then walk back to his TV. I made a couple of pitiable suicide attempts. I tied a guitar cable to a shower curtain rod and jumped off the side of the tub, bringing the shower curtain crashing down; I chugged a bottle of completely benign medication. Instead of taking me to the hospital, my dad made me stick my fingers down my throat to puke it up. He didn't want to become the officer whose kid tried to kill himself.

He took me to a military shrink—all of our doctors were military, free to us because we were an army family—and loudly filled out my questionnaire at the nurse's desk. "Drug use? No. Homosexual behavior? No."

The military shrink told me my problem was that my parents were pushing my buttons.

I thought this was how it was everywhere. I thought everyone feared and hated their parents like I did. I saw TV shows with teenaged kids who behaved affectionately, and thought: *How weird that our society feels compelled to pretend that children love their parents.*

In the 2000s, after being demolished by a pitiless rant from my mom about what my brother was doing, I removed myself from my family. I told them not to call unless somebody was ill. My mom called anyway, and again yelled about something going on in somebody else's life. I changed my number.

My mom found me on Facebook seven years later. My parents have unquestionably changed. There's compassion there. My mom used to yell at me—as a man in his thirties!—about failing Algebra in the seventh grade, like it happened last week. In seven years, she learned how to live in the present. My parents love each other now, which is strange, nearly implausible. I have empathy for them. I know their brains a little, because I know how my brain is like theirs. We had a long talk about the grief and rage of my teenage years. "But did you know we loved you, Mike?" my mom asked, pleadingly.

Yes, I said.

I lied. I didn't want to hurt her. I saw on her face that, despite her cruelty to me as a teenager, what she remembered was loving me.

I remember my dad fixing my guitar after I dropped it on the kitchen floor and broke the headstock off. I was despondent, thinking my only hope of ever being a musician had perished. My dad meticulously applied wood glue and fashioned a brass plate to reinforce the crack. Days before, there had been some event of screaming and threatened violence and abrading blame for my nonfulfillment, but now I stood there, watching him in this very practical demonstration of love. I couldn't make my hate and fear go away, but how could I not be grateful? I stood there, bewildered at life inside and outside of me, watching him mend the guitar neck.

I can think of my parents as loving or I can think of them as crazy people. If I try to see the duality, I get disconcerted, disoriented.

There was a girl named Meredith whom Luke had a crush on; she was olive-skinned and beautiful; she wore prim pink sweaters and a tiny gold cross. He schemed up a pickup line for her that he never used; he would say, "How are you?" and she would say "Fine." He would say, "I know you're *fine*, but how *are* you?" Meredith asked me to dance at the Sadie Hawkins Dance; she came to visit me when I was in the hospital recovering from an appendectomy and happened to walk in just as I was getting a shot of morphine in my ass. Years later, Luke and I were looking through a photocopied yearbook. "Jesus, there's, like, a picture of you on every page," he said. "Who took these pictures?" He flipped to the last page. "Meredith Peterson. Wow, she was in love with you."

How many signals did I miss? Maybe if Meredith Peterson had sat me down and told me, my life would have been different. It would have shaved just a little bit off the corner of my self-loathing, maybe enough that I'd have had something to live for other than the despair of my obsession.

Self-loathing freed me to be weird. Outlandish smarts weren't a liability. I took tremendous pleasure in big fat words. At recess, I tried following the ebb and flow of a wall-ball game for a week, not actually playing, just running back and forth with the herd, trying to look like I was supposed to be there, but I gave it up, and from then on sat on the blacktop with my back to a brick wall reading books. I declared myself a Communist in the seventh grade—at West Point!—after reading a comic book about Mao. I wrote stories plagiarizing famous science-fiction movies that I was confident no one else had seen, and was praised for them.

I hung out with heavy metal kids, the younger brothers of the high school burners on skateboards. Some of them threw contemptuous jeers, but I think they actually found my angsty intensity—I shot them murderous glares over the top of my glasses when they mocked me—fascinating, and frightening.

Years later, a girl from a high school French class found me online. I quipped about my outcastness.

"I always thought you were one of the popular kids," she typed back.

I met Chad Ficus in the West Point cemetery, where General Custer, General Westmoreland, and General Daniel Butterfield, the composer of "Taps," are buried. We leaned on the mausoleum of Egbert Ludovicus Viele: a twelve-foot pyramid. Behind a barred door were the sarcophagi of Viele and his wife, and something on the back wall that looked like a light switch. It was said to be a buzzer, so that if Egbert were buried alive he could ring for help.

Chad was beloved by the girls on the first tier of cuteness. He was on the cross-country team and had fantastic grades. Like I said, I thought the world saw me as a peculiar no-hoper, and I was defiantly unathletic: when the gym teacher made us run 200 yards, I walked—leisurely, sullenly—I would've done it while smoking if I could.

We drank a mixture of spirits—two inches' worth of alcohol from each bottle in his dad's liquor cabinet—from a green plastic 7-Up bottle. I had a stillborn sister buried in the cemetery, a few yards from the pyramid. When I was a child, and my mom came to visit the grave, I climbed the sphinxes and tried to run up the pyramid's sheer walls. I had no idea what was going on. I showed Chad Ficus the grave of Catherine Georgia Doughty and told an elaborate lie that my sister was a teenager who killed herself, and that she'd owned all the Led Zeppelin and Van Halen records.

We walked down the road, passing the 7-Up bottle between us. We met up with a bunch of kids and became a procession. A girl had a boom box and a cassette with Madonna's first album on one side and Prince's *Purple Rain* on the other. We acted conspicuously stupid: the alcohol let us. The idea was to go to a public pool up in the hills, climb the chain-link fence, and set off fireworks from the high-dive platform.

My dad suddenly drove up in his white Volkswagen Rabbit, opened the door, and told me to get inside. I did a decent job of pretending not to be drunk. I talked him into letting me walk home.

My dad drove off. I started following our parade up the hill. They were moving faster than before. "Go home, Doughty," said Chad Ficus. "Your dad told you to go home. You have to go."

If I didn't, my dad would somehow intuit that I was up at the pool, and their party would get busted.

Chad ran away towards the pack, already getting smaller. He turned around, jogging backwards. "Go home! Go home!"

Some parents at West Point pressured their kids into going there for college. My dad wasn't one of them. I suspect that if he had the option as a kid, he wouldn't have gone, and without Vietnam, which I think made him need a structure in which to live, he wouldn't have stayed in the army.

Chad Ficus's dad did want him to go to West Point—he was one of the rare officers there who hadn't gone there himself, and he seethed with resentment about it. He told Chad that once he graduated, he'd buy him a Porsche.

Chad's dad owned a lot of guns. (Everybody's dad at West Point owned some guns—my dad had two hunting rifles and a double-barreled shotgun handed down from my great-grandfather, a knife-fighting youth who, upon getting a bullet lodged an inch from his heart, repented and became a pastor. Perhaps not incidentally, I look exactly like him.) Chad's dad actually made his own ammunition as a hobby; there were drums of gunpowder in the basement.

Chad showed his friends his dad's porn collection. It was a notebook into which his dad had pasted a profusion of box shots; that is, he cut out pictures of vaginas from porn magazines and made himself a disembodied vagina portfolio. Page after page of them.

Chad did end up going to West Point. I saw him the summer before he entered, and he was cynically blithe; he said he didn't care about serving his country, he was going for the prestige (it's roughly as difficult to get into Harvard, but at West Point you also need a congressional recommendation to go with your grades and athletic bona fides). He was going to parlay it into a Wall Street job. Not to mention the Porsche.

Before your sophomore year at the military academy, you can quit, no questions asked. After that, you owe the government five years in the army. If you flunk out, or mess up, you have to enlist as a private. Chad called his dad at the midpoint of his West Point stint, in tears, begging his dad to let him drop out, he didn't want the car. His dad said no.

Chad Ficus came to a gig of mine twenty years later. After his service, he had become a snack food magnate. He gave me one of the warmest, most loving and kind hugs I have ever received.

There were, like, fifteen black kids, total, at my high school, but one of them owned the only sound system. DJ DRE IS ASSKICKING! was stenciled on the side of a speaker cabinet. At the dances in the cafeteria, he spun twelve-inch rap records that he got in New York; a dozen black kids danced, did the chants—"The roach! The roach! The roach is on the wall! We don't need no Raid, let the motherfucker crawl!"—on a nearly empty dance floor, while the white kids stood at the walls. Then, a blonde cheerleader from the senior class took Luke—we were freshmen, so it was shocking, but Luke was, even by then, the star of the school musicals, *Guys and Dolls, Damn Yankees*, etc.—by the hand, as Kurtis Blow's "Basketball" played, and pulled him out to dance. The white kids trickled out after them, reluctantly.

I was fourteen, listened to Judas Priest—I probably wouldn't have danced to the music those white kids liked, anyway, Billy Idol, The Outfield, Kenny Loggins, whatever—and would have had no idea what a great rap record was, were it pitched like a throwing star and lodged in my head. It was 1984. I can't imagine how good those records must've been.

(There are two lines in the song "Rapper's Delight" that fascinate me: one is, "Guess what, America? We love you," which has to be the only time that sentiment was expressed in a hip-hop song. The other is, "Now what you hear is not a test: I'm rapping to the beat." Because it was necessary to say, I know you're out there thinking, hey, that guy's not singing, he must be just making sure the mic's on, but, in fact, what I'm doing is called *rapping to the beat*.)

(Another moment in the history of rap's emergence: Stanley Ray, whom I'll tell you about later, went to see George Clinton in the early '80s—Stanley Ray was flying on LSD—and Grandmaster Flash and the Furious Five opened. A lady behind him sputtered, "He's just playing the record! He's just *playing the record!*")

I talked my parents into sending me to Simon's Rock, a tiny experimental college in Massachusetts that admitted students after their sophomore year in high school. It was half kids who wanted to be in med school by age twenty and half fuckups like me who wanted to play guitar and find out what drugs were like. I talked to the admissions guy about Sartre; I told him that I also thought hell was other people. I didn't really think hell was other people, but it was a fantastic teenage pose. I had, however, actually read the play, which wasn't the case with most of the literary and filmic works I stole my poses from. My grades were wretched, but my precociousness quotient got me in.

(Again, the baffling ambiguity: my parents berated me nearly to suicide the same year, but they paid for this weird school in full.)

I sat at the punks' table my first day at Simon's Rock; everybody had a piece of their hair missing. That was the identity I was most interested in adopting. I didn't meet orthodox punk standards. "I'm a goth, and _____'s a punk, but you're not *anything*," said a girl they called Laura Morbid. I was in love with her. She had seen *Pretty in Pink* the summer before, and, in her head, wrote a goth Molly Ringwald script for herself; she'd have a Ducky figure, hip but geeky, chasing her, while she crossed clique lines to be with a rich kid. The rich kid turned out to be gay—not to mention deranged: he had weekly dorm-room-trashing fits—so she ended up with me. She was mean. The first snowfall came in November, and I said it was beautiful. "You're so immature!" snapped Laura Morbid.

She left the school, and I fell in with a gentler group of goth girls. They were cheerful, and into building their own working versions of Brion Gysin's dream machine out of stereo turntables and poster board. One of them was obsessed with the German industrial band Einstürzende Neubauten, and the New Jersey Devils; her bedroom walls were papered with pictures of Blixa Bargeld, and hockey players.

I papered my own walls with pictures of Keith Richards and Lou Reed. Heroic junkies.

I had a lovely beer binge. We drove to a bar just past the New York border, to elude the Massachusetts blue laws; I went in with somebody's brother's ID to pick up a case of Rolling Rock and emerged giddy, arms laden. We drank the beer, and I transformed into some kind of magical celebrity-roast emcee. We wandered the dorms having magnanimous exchanges with everybody; I chatted amiably with people to whom I'd previously been scared to speak, shook hands with the hippie dudes skulking around the girls' dorm, flirted with girls in sweatpants sitting in the hallway doing homework.

Beer, I thought, *is the ANSWER.*

The next day I awoke with my first hangover, and swore off liquor. If you hang around twelve-step types, you'll hear tales wherein an alcoholic wakes up with a hangover, swears off booze forever, and then is drunk later that same day; a bleak joke repeating itself throughout her or his drinking life. But when I swore off booze, it took. I knew alcoholism was rampant in my family, and that I didn't want to become a drunk. It was weird for youthful rebellion, to give up drinking as a fuck-you to your family. I got snooty about it, and when kids who were drinking asked me if I wanted a beer, I'd tell them, theatrically, that due to genetic misfortune, I was an alcoholic.

I started smoking weed. I realized that I'd found the solution to my genetic dilemma: I could satisfy that innate urge to get messed up by using something that, as every honest person in America knew, wasn't addictive in the least: wholesome, in fact. I was writing songs and hating them; when I was stoned, they sounded amazing to me. I could love my own mind.

Weed, I thought, *is the ANSWER.*

I discovered cigarettes. I got two packs of Benson and Hedges that I smoked in one night, one after the other, staring at my sexy, smoking self in the mirror. Soon I was shoplifting cartons of Marlboro from the Price Chopper. Smoking rings that little bell in your head that the rat in the clear plastic tank, with the wires in his skull, is compelled to ring when he gets that signal, *use use use use.* But it doesn't enact fucked-up-ed-ness. It's using-lite. And it makes you look incredibly cool.

When I was nine years old, I read a comic book meant to scare kids away from drugs. One panel showed a kid looking, in terror, at trees and houses with scary faces.

That looks amazingly great, I thought.

I'm reminded of an ad campaign against meth: teenagers are shown with scabby faces going into motel rooms to prostitute themselves with sinister middle-aged men, robbing elderly people, overdosing hideously. I find the campaign inherently cynical, because it's specifically targeting one drug. If the guys at the ad firm have any awareness, they must know that a kid prone to meth addiction is prone to addiction in general and might very likely end up, say, an alcoholic. Meth is a tremendous societal drain; the ad campaign isn't about why a kid would become an addict. It's designed to mitigate that one particular civic problem.

The tagline is: NOT EVEN ONCE. If you use meth once, you may end up one of those scabby-faced wraiths. In some of the ads, the humiliated, sick addicts return, like the ghost of Christmas future, to the very party where their past selves are about to get high for the first time and beg them not to start towards this inevitable fate.

They're pretending not to understand that what they're really saying is: *Don't take this, you'll love it.*

Here's a message I prefer: *If you try meth, it'll feel amazing. You've been in emotional pain for a long time, and you don't know it; you won't know it until the drug makes the pain go away. You'll feel like you've solved the essential problem of being alive. But sometimes this leads to an unthinkably gruesome humiliation. Be aware of that.*

We, the adults in authority who are concerned about you, want you to know that other ways to deal with emotional pain certainly won't provide the sudden cure that a noseful of drugs will. They take more time, more effort, and you may be extremely discouraged along the way. But they may be worth it, especially considering that drugs can be a form of suicide.

I took acid on Halloween, and I ended up in my room with this black kid I barely knew, who had painted his face white to look like the moon. The acid came on stronger and stronger and I became deathly afraid of the moon-faced man: I hadn't met many black people in my life, and the face paint seemed to be bubbling on his cheeks. He left. A roommate gave me a giant rubber band to play with; I tangled myself in it for a few hours. Then I became seized with an idea: the universe was a fabric. Everything was a fabric. My life's key moment of enlightenment. I fumbled for a cassette recorder.

I listened to it the next day and heard this manic voice intoning, half laughingly, "The universe is a fabric. Everything. Is a fabric. A fabric. A fabric."

So of course I realized that I had had one of those ridiculous moments one has on drugs, those embarrassing epiphanies that are really stupid and meaningless. I didn't even remember what I meant by that.

Years later, my friend the rock legend kept hipping me to all these quasi-Buddhist, quasi-Hindu nebulous spirituality guys, as a means of grasping for a power greater than myself. One of them—and I can't for the life of me locate the text—wrote something like: The entire universe and everything in it is kind of a *fabric*, where everything is stitched to everything else, and nothing is a truly independent entity.

"You are a function of what the whole universe is doing in the same way that a wave is a function of what the whole ocean is doing," Alan Watts wrote.

I had a friend named Peter Mack. Peter Mack's version of being a punk was to dress like a middle manager, circa 1960. He wore grey suits, skinny ties, and a fedora. He actually owned a pair of *jodhpurs*, the kind worn by British officers of the Raj, with the weird wings sticking out by the hips. Everybody called the teachers by their first names; Peter called them Professor _____ and Dr. _____.

Peter Mack and I would get high in his dorm room, then put on a recording of the chimes at Notre Dame. We'd blast it and yell, "THE BELLS! THE BELLS! THE BELLS!"

The next Halloween, Peter Mack and I went to a different college for their famous hallucinogen-fueled Halloween shindig. We took acid. We got separated. He got into what he thought was a bathroom line, and kept following it, his mind zooming every which way at once. Suddenly he found himself on a stage, in a spotlight, and a guy in a vampire costume thrust a mic in his face.

"So what are you supposed to be?"

Peter Mack paused. "I'm an art fag," he said.

The crowd erupted with cheers, and Peter Mack won the Halloween costume contest.

I got a funny haircut—a semi-Mohawk-mullet, shaved on the sides. I dyed the floppy front part black. "You look like a queer," my dad said to me one holiday I had come home for, as he opened a beer can.

I told people I was bisexual. I identified intensely with being gay; I felt ostracized, disparagingly feminized. I tried making out with dudes, and I didn't dig it, but I kept trying. There was this one guy named Alfred. He was a black kid, from Bed-Stuy, Brooklyn, where life couldn't have been easy for him. "Are you bisexual? I'm bisexual, too," he said. He was fake-bisexual in the other direction; he was gay, and was very slowly admitting it to himself. I kissed him once, and from then on he'd come knock on my dorm room door every now and then, sit on the bed, and say things like, "Have you ever thought about blow jobs? I mean, hmm, isn't that interesting, blow jobs? Hey! I just got an idea! Why don't *I* try giving *you* a blow job?"

I never let him. But I always let him kiss me goodnight. A soul kiss. One day we lay around spooning, cuddling each other. He nuzzled my neck. I wished somebody would've come in and seen us—I wanted my bisexuality proven. I also felt a strange peace, even though I was uncomfortable—I was receiving real affection from a man. I didn't know how I yearned for a man to show love for me.

(I met one other guy who said he was bisexual. It was when I was working at a McDonald's on a summer vacation. He had just gotten out of prison. He kept asking me if I wanted to hang out in his car and listen to Kraftwerk.)

In the room next door was this short, pig-nosed guy from Westchester who played metal guitar: he did that *wheedly-wheedly-wheedly* superfast Eddie Van Halen stuff—in fact, he wanted to start a band also named after his last name: Ruckman. He wore big square Cazal glasses in the style favored by members of Whodini. He had a butterfly knife, and did tricks, spinning and flipping it. "Better keep my ass turned to the wall around you," he said, like anybody at all would want to fuck him. When he discovered weed, he became one of those guys so indebted to the profundity of stonedness that he wrote songs called, "Stoned Again," and "Getting Stoned," and "Get Everybody Stoned Again."

We were sitting around, high, and I asked Ruckman the Cazals kid if I could play his guitar. He said, "Nobody touches my axe but me. My axe is like my woman."

Somebody told me Paul Simon was sitting in the admissions office; his kid was thinking about applying. I went, shamelessly sat on the couch across from him, and bothered him for an hour. He asked me if I had a notebook; I didn't. He chided me. He gave me a list of poets to read—the only name I remember was Seamus Heaney. He meant this list as a take-my-wisdom-and-begone thing, but I didn't take the hint. I asked him if he'd heard the band Firehose. He hadn't. I told him that all good songs had to be political, which is a pretty fucking brazen thing to announce to Paul Simon. He mentioned Lou Reed.

I like his work, I said.

I wrote some plays. I was desperately searching for something I wanted to be, other than a rock star. I was OK at it, so I applied to the NYU dramatic-writing program—I thought my clumsy junior-avant-garde stuff would compel them to take me in and teach me to write for sitcoms. It didn't. Bitter at the rejection, I ended up at Lang College at the New School. I just needed to be in New York, where there was music.

I met Mumlow in an acting class. We were supposed to bring in monologues; she brought an American flag as a prop. She folded the flag deftly while doing her monologue in a Southern accent. She was clearly brilliant, but the shtick was irksome.

There was another guy in the class named Seth. He had a lazy eye. The gaze of his good eye was bracing, while the other eye shot off to the periphery. He did a monologue taken from a layman's physics book, standing on two chairs, leaping between them, talking about the constant stream of molecules or light waves or something like that. We shared a glance of mutual annoyance at Mumlow's flag shtick.

Mumlow's apartment was called the universe. She called it that because her downstairs neighbor, an aged flower child, had come up to ask her to turn her music down, telling Mumlow that she knew that she created her own universe and thus the problem wasn't really Mumlow's loud music, it was that she created a universe wherein this music was disturbing her.

It was a studio apartment on the eleventh floor of a building overlooking Sheridan Square, bigger and cleaner than anything anybody I knew could afford. She lived alone. So she was a rich girl. Seth and I ended up at the universe doing something for the acting class: Mumlow's energy was crazy but alluring. I wasn't attracted to her, but her eyes were gigantic and blue.

I wrote a script in which two people sat across from each other in a diner, arguing in fake David Mamet language:

MUMLOW: I came here. From space.

SETH: From *space*.

MUMLOW: That's RIGHT.

SETH: So you say you *came here* from space.

We ran the script competitively. They wrote down who they thought won each scene. At the end of the play, the winner got a dime bag of weed. Seth added a comparison to fabric: "I won. Give me the weed. Wet gabardine."

Ani DiFranco went to Lang. She had her thing utterly together. I was half formed as a songwriter; her songs were acute, her deployment of them wickedly agile. She made me want to get good.

She came to New York from Buffalo, where she was packing clubs. New York was a jungle of shitty bands; she gained no audience except us kids listening to her, astonished, in the dorms. She went back to Buffalo, discouraged and aggrieved. *Oh well,* I thought. *We'll never hear from her again.*

Ani and I were in a class called "The Shape and Nature of Things to Come," taught by an African American poet named Sekou Sundiata. He taught us to cut our writing pitilessly. We pleaded the purity of our precious compositions as he cut words, cut whole verses, and as we sat there dazed, beaten up, he'd pause, and say, "Is it soup yet?"

He would press the poet in question until he or she mumbled what the poem was supposed to be about. "That's great," he'd say. "Why isn't that in the poem?"

He taught me not to pretend to be black. "They call it soul because it's the truest version of yourself."

We read *The Autobiography of Malcolm X* and Joseph Campbell's *Hero with a Thousand Faces*, and Sekou analyzed Malcolm's life spellbindingly, using the paradigm of the universal hero's journey as a lens.

He asked one kid where he was from. "Outside Boston," the kid said.

"Outside Boston *where?*" Sekou asked.

"Uh, the suburbs?"

"No, no," Sekou said, "where are you *from?*"

"Town's called Braintree?"

He wrote BRAINTREE in huge letters on the blackboard and spent the rest of the class speculating on the roots of the name. Often, we didn't even get to our poems; we sat, transfixed, as he zoomed off on rapturous tangents.

Some things Sekou said in class:

"Do you talk to yourself? You should."

"You speak to the poem, and sometimes the poem says, 'You're trying to build a house, but I'm not a house, I'm a bird.'"

"This poem is a life-support system for one killer line. Lose the poem, use the line somewhere else."

I walked in the graduation ceremony, but never got my diploma: I owed the library $11. I thought it was more poetic to not get your diploma for being $11 short. Plus, I needed the $11. My bank balance was usually under $10, which meant I couldn't get money out of the ATM, so, humiliatingly, I had to go up to the teller's window and withdraw $4.50. At least once a week I had to decide between a pack of cigarettes and a container of hummus. Usually I chose the smokes and stayed hungry. I figured out that if I could just fall asleep, I wouldn't be hungry when I woke up the next day.

Sometimes I gave in and bought a sandwich, but when I was sated I would be overcome with buyer's remorse.

Seth and I considered doing the dine-and-dash at a tourist trap known for its tub-sized blue drinks and signature charred mass of onion rings, but we argued for an hour about which one of us would get to stroll out of the restaurant first, and anyway, we got lucky, and were taken out by a girl from school with a credit card. She bought us Indian food and two packs of Marlboros; she wanted friends.

I fell in love with a girl named Betty with a superabundance of red curls. She was my idea of perfect. It wasn't so much ardor as a feeling that I'd arrived. At last, I was with an unimpeachably beautiful girl! I meant something in the world! But there was something about the keenness of my love for her that freaked her out; she dumped me the night before we went on a trip to Jamaica with her two roommates.

"Thanks for the great sex," she said, offering a handshake.

The four of us went to the evil little tourist town of Negril; me and three beautiful girls. We were broke: what we didn't spend on marijuana and a windowless one-room, two-bed shack we spent on a single shared plate of french fries each day. The two roommates slept in one bed, Betty and I in another. Lying there, blasted on the cheap weed, it was torture to feel her presence. I felt as if every tiny budge I made in the tiny bed was followed by a tiny budge from her, shifting away from me, as if it disgusted her to brush against my hip bone.

We spent the days drinking mushroom tea, tripping, wandering the beach; hustler dudes came up to the three girls and me, singsonging to me in gorgeous Jamaican accents, "You have t'ree! Give me one!"

Negril ran on two grey economies; one involved selling stuff on the beach to people who were too high to protest. They'd grab you by the arm and pull you towards their little stand selling shell necklaces. Fat ladies on the beach would grab the hair of passing white girls, starting to braid Bo Derek braids without a prompt. If the girl tried to pull away, they'd cry something like, "You have no respect for the Jamaican people!" There were a lot of white girls wandering around the beach with Bo Derek braids.

Dudes with intense gazes would block your path as you were strolling and say, "I come from the hills. I got the good bud." The weed was generally terrible—dry, yellow, and stemmy. We smoked a lot of it anyway, rolling massive spliffs of shitty pot that we told ourselves was the world's greatest, we're in *Jamaica*, right?

The other industry was kids who came down from the hills to fuck middle-aged tourist women. The women rented them scooters and bought them clothes. These were less pure sexual transactions than sham romances; you'd see a flabby German tourist walking hand in hand with some washboard-abbed, nineteen-year-old guy pretending to be a Rastafarian. How desperately did they need this, that they'd buy into the fantasy?

(Years later, I came back with my friend Sally. We told everybody we were brother and sister, despite the fact that we looked nothing alike, so she could fuck Jamaican dudes without suffering questions. She charged everything to an American Express card that her mom had gotten her strictly for emergencies. Every morning at 7 AM a girl claiming to be the sister of the fake-Rasta she was sleeping with—and renting a scooter for—would knock on the door, claim that she worked at the place they ate at the other night, and will you please sign this AmEx slip again, I messed it up again, please sign the slip again or I'll lose my job?

Blearily, Sally always signed. She discovered a month later, when she got the bill, she'd been taken for five grand.)

I had gotten a job driving an ice cream truck. It started on Monday, so I came back a Sunday earlier than the three girls. I decided to smuggle some of this terrible weed back in my sock.

At JFK, we deplaned into a hallway. The cops told us to stand single file. A flight from Lithuania landed right behind us, and its passengers ambled down towards customs unmolested. In the furthest reaches of this endless corridor, a door opened, and a cop with a tiny dog came out. The panting terrier scuttled down the line, stretching the leash to its utmost. The dog passed me. Stopped a few feet behind me. It barked.

"Good boy!" said the cop.

The terrier bounded a few yards ahead of me and barked again.

"Good boy!" said the cop.

They let us through. I was almost tearful with gratitude. I went to pick up my guitar at baggage claim and went up to a cop to ask where the luggage for the Air Jamaica flight was.

The cop was leaning against a wall. When I said, "Excuse me," he straightened up with a start. He pointed towards a carousel, looking me directly in the eyes.

I was chatting with a middle-aged lady about where I went to school when a fat guy in a black t-shirt, flanked by uniformed cops, walked up to me holding a badge. They took me into a side room.

Good vacation tale for that tourist lady, I thought. *The teenager she was chatting with turned out to be a drug smuggler.*

I envisioned myself getting raped in jail.

They opened my rucksack and shook the contents out. My guitar case was bound with silver duct tape; they took a box cutter and cut through the tape, slicing the clasps off with it. The fat guy in the black t-shirt patted me down, grabbed my balls. As his hands moved down to my ankles, my sight went blurry. The bag of weed had gathered in the arch of my foot.

"Take off your hat," he said. He shook it out, smelled it.

"Take off your shoes," he said. Banged them against a table to shake whatever was in there loose.

A long blank space of fear. Then:

He didn't ask me to take off my socks.

"The dog makes mistakes," he said.

Delirious with my luck, hugging the guitar case with the sliced-off clasps so the guitar wouldn't fall out, I went back to Betty's place, where Seth was crashing. She lived on East Tenth Street, which at the time was an open-air market for dime bags of weed. On every stoop were four guys whispering: *smoke, sinse, smoke smoke, sinse, smoke.*

Seth demanded the weed. We packed it into Betty's roommate's bong and allowed ourselves to believe it was the best weed we'd ever smoked.

That summer, I'd get up at 5 AM and drive the delivery truck, heading up First Avenue as the sun came up, listening to the Stone Roses, or Toots and the Maytals' *Funky Kingston.* I was bringing gourmet ice cream to restaurants before they opened.

Heartbreak, new to me, was surreal. I was in tremendous pain, which I regarded in disbelief. *How can this be happening to me? Can something really hurt this much?*

When Betty got back, she and Seth split on a bus trip, traveling through the South, then the Midwest, then over to California. Seth called from Wichita to tell me that the yellow terrain was so flat you could see the rain coming from miles away. They called me from a pay phone on the grounds of Graceland and left a jovial message. I was sitting at home, staring at the answering machine, stoned, too paranoid to pick up the phone.

The other record I favored in the ice cream truck was Elvis Costello's *My Aim Is True*. I identified intensely with his vindictiveness. I read somewhere that the working title was *Revenge and Guilt*.

My aim was not true. I fantasized about beating the shit out of Seth, though I had never thrown a punch. I fantasized that I'd go to the Port Authority bus terminal, pick them up in the ice cream truck, and as they fell asleep in the shotgun seat—she on his lap, his head lolling on her shoulder—I'd take them through the Lincoln Tunnel to New Jersey, push them from the moving vehicle, abandon them in the reeds of the Meadowlands.

I was supposed to meet somebody at the Knitting Factory. She stood me up, but the bartender knew me and said they needed somebody to bartend that night. I said I didn't know how to make any drinks. She said if I didn't know, I should ask, "What's in it?" As it happened, the bartenders at the Knitting Factory had the least professional aptitude of those at any bar I've ever been to.

The band that night was a trio: Joe Lovano, Bill Frisell, and Paul Motian. I strolled through the club in a trance, amazed by the music, though I didn't know anything about jazz. The next night Bob Mould played acoustically; he let the audience sit Indian-style around him on stage. The night after that the Lyres played, with the Jon Spencer Blues Explosion opening—their first gig ever.

The sound guy got me high every night. Then he'd complain for hours about how he wanted to be a recording engineer and nobody appreciated him. There was a tiny recording booth upstairs from the stage that he'd go into, get baked, and twiddle with the knobs while the band played, leaving the mixing board unmanned. Feedback howled every night.

The bartenders were mostly dope fiends, and the customers foreign tourists. Japanese jazz nerds would wander in, stunned that the legendary club was a dive, run by surly malcontents. Europeans would pretend they didn't know they were supposed to tip in America; as they walked away, the bartenders hurled fistfuls of change at them, cursing.

The Knit was a magnet for a certain type of dissatisfied upper-class Japanese girl—there was a steady stream of them showing up at the club, having moved to New York seeking gritty adventure. One by one, they were scooped up by one of three guys—an avant-garde saxophone player, a drummer, and a guy who worked at record companies, doing some kind of job I couldn't fathom. "Oh, she's with D_____? I thought she was with T_____."

They took me off the bar and made me the doorman. I did two nights a week, then five, then the freaked-out dope-fiend rockabilly guy who did weekends quit, and suddenly I was working seven nights a week. Naturally, I began to hate the job, but in my half-cocked military-bred mind I didn't think it was my place to tell the owner he had to get somebody else for Mondays and Tuesdays. So I started stealing.

Nearly everybody in the place was stealing. The bartenders would put the dough for two beers in the register and the third in their tip jar. The beer was always running low before its time, but nobody got fired. The would-be recording-engineer sound guy would order Chinese food at the ticket desk and stare at me incredulously when I called him down to pay for it. He expected me to take the money from the till as a matter of course.

I seethed with frustration—when applying the hand stamp that audience members got in lieu of a ticket, I'd bang the stamper down on their wrists so hard they'd yelp in pain. One night a saxophone player known for his assholery—an '80s icon due to some suave roles in black-and-white indie movies—had packed the joint. He called up and said petulantly that he was considering canceling the gig. My guess: he wanted to hear the club plead with him.

Do it, I said. I want to go home.

And I slammed the phone down.

Mumlow was in love with me, until I started hanging out at her place constantly, because I was desperately lonely, at which point her love blended with contempt. Then I moved in. Mumlow kept the door unlocked; we'd come home to find random friends sitting on the bed, smoking cigarettes. One of these was our friend Sally. We treated her like a pedigreed dog. Mumlow would stroke her sandy-blonde hair. Mumlow had a video camera; we'd get high, videotape ourselves having a conversation, then watch the tape and laugh and be fascinated by our own conversational nuances. We'd beg Sally to stay; she'd sleep on the couch. She stayed for four or five days at a time; when she finally left, we nearly clung to her legs.

Sally's father was dying of AIDS in North Carolina. As he got sicker, dormant mental illness stirred in her. She called from our friend Dottie's parents' house, deep in Queens. She was having delusions. She wasn't sleeping for days at a time. She was planning a party, with cheerless determination, for which she was writing a ten-page guest list of rappers and movie stars.

Dottie was a committed party girl. Despite having flunked out, she somehow walked in the NYU graduation ceremony; she paid a guy who could do calligraphy to forge a diploma for her parents' wall. Her mom looked like Peggy Lee—just shy of elderly, with platinum wig and gigantic sunglasses that covered half her face.

In Queens, Sally sat on Dottie's mom's ottoman, by turns motionless and creepily agitated. Dottie's mom brought Sally crackers and cheese on a platter with sweetness, "Do you want another snack, honey?" Then she went back into the kitchen and barked in a stage whisper, "What's the matter with this girl, what's wrong with this girl?"

I called a car service to get Sally back to Manhattan. En route, she kept hallucinating family members on the streets of Rego Park. Back at the universe, Mumlow was calling Sally's mother.

We went to her apartment to pick up her things. She whirled around on the steps. "I'm Madonna," she yelled, "and you're all going to be in *my movie!*"

My friend Luke, from West Point, came down to Manhattan to audition for some drama schools and stayed with us. We had removed the cable (telling an incredulous cable company guy that, no, we weren't in fact moving, we just *didn't want cable anymore*) and had just a VHS tape of *Goodfellas* to watch. We put it on every night; Ray Liotta pistol-whipped Lorraine Bracco soundlessly, flickering in the corner like a fireplace. The other VHS tape we had was called *Taste My Juices.* We never watched it. We got Luke high—he was unaccustomed to it—and left him alone in the apartment. Paranoid and agitated, sitting on the bed, he put it on; the opening scene was a man fucking somebody in a rainbow wig, with a dubbed voice—Japanese-monster-movie style—going, "Aw. Aw. Aw. Aw. Aw. Aw. Aw. Aw. Aw. Aw."

I never wanted to fuck Mumlow. I stayed because her mind was so wonderfully strange, she was so much fun to get high with, and because I was broke. The old joke: What do you call a musician without a girlfriend? *Homeless.*

She paid for the Domino's pizza we ordered twice a day ("How many ICE-COLD COKES do you want with that?" the Domino's guy would yell enthusiastically, on every call. How about *no* ice-cold Cokes, thanks), and my contribution was to get the weed, the funds for which I embezzled at the Knit. Every tenth ticket, I'd put the cash in my pocket, rather than input the money into the computer.

I was meeting girls at the club, getting them high, and fucking them in their living rooms while their roommates slept. They'd ask for my number and I'd say I didn't have a phone.

Mumlow was getting churlish and horny. She binged on porn, buying stacks of gruesome magazines with titles like "Black Plungers," "Preggo Sluts," and "Shaved Asian Snizz." She spread them out in a porn-rainbow fan on the bed and plied her vibrator on herself for hours, grunting, never having an orgasm. I kept my back to her, typing lyrics on her beige, boxy Macintosh.

My friend Wind-Him-Up-and-Watch-Him-Go Joe introduced me to a weed source. He called the proprietors Smokey and the Toastman. They worked out of a shop on East Ninth Street, onto which they had painted, in shaky letters, RECORD-A-RAMA.

Smokey stood behind a glass counter inside of which maybe four or five dusty twelve-inch singles—vinyl records—lay. There were a few nailed onto the walls, too. The Toastman would be sitting a few feet behind him, staring blankly. Both were Caribbean dudes in Hawaiian shirts, with red, slitted eyes.

"What do you want?"

Um, a $50 bag?

"Who are you? I don't know you."

I bought from you last week.

With a wary gaze, Smokey walked backwards towards the Toastman, who handed him something, and then Smokey palmed it to me. I put it in my pocket.

"Put it in your waist, man! Put it in your waist!" he hissed.

I stuffed it down by my cock, embarrassedly.

Smokey looked side to side, as if there might be cops suspended from the walls of the Record-A-Rama. "Take this." He handed me one of the dusty twelve-inches. I walked out with the record, ostensibly looking like I'd bought it.

There was a collection of misbegotten twelve-inches leaning against the wall in the universe. All these third-rate reggae and house singers, their dreams of fame having resulted in being the decoy record for Smokey and the Toastman.

Mumlow had a bunch of heroin friends she knew from the arty-groovy Northeastern college from which she'd dropped out the previous year. One of them abandoned a cat named Big Bunny in the universe. Big Bunny radiated angst. We'd throw a stuffed duck on the floor and Big Bunny would hump it—obediently, bleakly, neurotically—while we cackled.

The heroin friends came down for the weekends; one of their parents had a pricey loft in the West Village. I looked down on them. One of them came over and, without asking, ripped open a bag of dope and cut lines on a CD. I kicked him out, yelling.

I got a terrible fever. Mumlow wanted me to take a bath to cool off, but the water, though lukewarm, was icy to me. She had a bag of dope that had been sitting in her purse for weeks, after an evening with the heroin kids. "If you take a bath, I'll let you have this," she said.

Wrapped in towels, I sniffed the dope.

Wonderful. Peace. Warmth.

"Another one of the heroin faith-healed," Mumlow said.

(I loved the Stones' song "Gimme Shelter": "Rape, murder: it's just a shot away." Rape and murder? Heroin imparts a *soothing warm and fuzzy feeling*.)

After that, I got excited when the kids from the arty-groovy school came to town on a heroin excursion. I still disdained them—they were *junkies*—but I always connived a bag of dope out of them. Mumlow didn't like it. She forbade me to use heroin in the universe. I myself thought it was better for me to avoid it; I had so much I wanted to *do*. I figured that I could get high every other month or so. I wouldn't go where the groovy-liberal-arts-school kids were going. Their faces were a little greyer each time they came to town.

I was going out and doing open-mic nights, doing poetry at the Nuyorican Poets Cafe's Friday night slams. I was a desperate and ambitious kid; at twenty-one, I felt like I was almost too late for stardom. I slogged through my notebooks of club bookers' numbers and record companies' addresses, sending demo cassettes, repeatedly calling the gatekeepers of New York nightlife.

The most feared booker was Louise from CBGB. CBGB let unknown bands play on Sunday and Monday nights; the sound guys, who could be relied upon to not give a fuck, would write down what they thought of the band—and if the band had brought a significant number of beer-buying friends—and maybe you'd get a real gig after that.

I played a Monday night, then anxiously waited. The call never came. I called up Louise, nearly hyperventilating.

"Call me next Wednesday at 3 o'clock," she said, and hung up the phone.

Next Wednesday I called promptly at three.

"Call me next Wednesday at five." Click.

Next Wednesday: Hi, is this Louise, this is M. Doughty, I . . .

"Call me on Tuesday at noon, on this number." She gave me a number different from the one I called on. I fumbled madly for a pen and took it down.

Tuesday: "Call me next Tuesday at one."

Next Tuesday: "Call me on Friday at this number: _____."

I called dutifully on Friday. An unfamiliar voice answered. "CB's."

Hi, uh, I'm looking for Louise . . .

"She's not here right now," he said, "but you're calling *the right number.*"

Louise wouldn't book a solo guy in the main room—massively disappointing—but she gave me a gig at the space next door, CB's Gallery. I lugged an amp all the way up the Bowery—I was skinny as hell, it took forever. A car pulled up—a bunch of drunk girls from out of town looking for Bleecker Street. I told them I'd show them the way if they gave me a ride. I put my amp in the trunk, and they drove me—just a few blocks—to CB's. They were incredibly impressed that I was a musician, in New York, no less, who wrote his own songs, no less, and actually *had a real show to play.*

There were two guys at the bar. I played some songs. Another guy showed up. Another guy left. Then the other guy left. It was just me, playing to the bartender. What do you do? I had a meticulously conceived set list at my feet, and I couldn't figure out anything to do but stick with it.

The bartender went out front and brought down the steel grate over the big window. She came and stood in the center of the empty room. "I think I'm gonna close down now," she said.

Years later, she was the manager of a big band on the hippie circuit. I bump into her at music festivals and tell everybody near us the story of her shutting down the club on me. I'm trying to be good-naturedly funny, but she winces.

We took acid and went to a dance club. It was me, a couple of friends, Wind-Him-Up-and-Watch-Him-Go Joe, and another, a cute blonde girl who had played the ingenue in this cult movie that everyone had seen.

We spent the night jiggling and wobbling wildly in front of a speaker. We knew we looked like idiots.

We left as the sun came up, and sat on the curb. Wind-Him-Up-and-Watch-Him-Go Joe ate a piece of pizza; the slice devolved into an indistinct mass of cheese that he held in both hands and gnawed at like a dog. We went back to another friend's place. Everybody went up to his roof, and I lay in bed with the blonde ingenue. She started telling me intimate things about her life, how she'd fucked a creative-writing teacher and read the stories she wrote about it aloud in class, how she gave a lighting guy on the cult movie a hand job every night after shooting ended. I kept waiting for the moment that I would kiss her, but she bolted up and went to the bathroom. I heard her puking, and crying.

Wind-Him-Up-and-Watch-Him-Go Joe burst into the room behind his fuming girlfriend, pleading, trying to placate her. She stopped in the middle of the room, heard the ingenue crying, turned on her heels, and went to the bathroom. She knocked on the door lightly, saying, "Honey, are you OK? Are you OK? Honey?"

I stayed on the futon for an hour, hoping the ingenue would come back to get cozy again. Eventually, I got up and walked home in the ashen daylight.

The Knit's manager yelled at me that I'd get fired if I didn't do a better job sweeping up at the end of the night. Then Wind-Him-Up-and-Watch-Him-Go Joe showed up telling me he had some Ecstasy and had found a Discover card lying on the ground someplace—he and some friend of his were going to drop the E's and call a whore. I gulped the E as I closed up the desk and left without touching the broom.

(I once found a credit card on the street; I would've bought stuff with it, too, if it hadn't been in the name of Yuka Kaneko. Instead I sent it to the address in Tokyo printed on the back, promising REWARD. Four months later, I got an embroidered towel in the mail.)

Joe's credit card was in the name of Ann Hill. How are we going to convince an escort agency that your name is Ann Hill?

"I'll tell them I'm from England," Joe said.

Wind-Him-Up-and-Watch-Him-Go Joe was intent on getting a black girl. "I don't want a *black girl,* why would we get a *black girl?*" whined the friend. Mumlow was out of town. We went to her place.

"Hello? Yes, how much does it cost? Yeah. Do you take the Discover card?"

Nobody took the Discover card.

Ten calls later, somebody finally did. "The name is Ann Hill." Pause. "Yes. Ann Hill. I'm from England." He said this in his regular, suburban-Illinois accent.

They bought it. "We're young and handsome, so send somebody really good," he said.

I drew second. So I went out into the stairwell and waited. I was coming up on the drugs. The stairwell was a cold, hollow chamber, painted institutional pale green. Every fidget echoed eleven stories down. I don't think it was really E—actually, I think every E I took was not in fact E until roughly 1996.

I puked a rainbow on the landing.

I sat there, staring ahead, getting paranoid, hoping nobody would come up the stairs. A ring in my ears became an insectoid buzz. Years passed. I stared at the pool of rainbow puke. Finally Joe came out and knocked on the stairwell door.

The whore wasn't beautiful. She spoke with an elegant accent that suggested she was from somewhere like Côte d'Ivoire. Her frank gaze scared me. I didn't get hard. "Have you been doing cocaine?" she asked pleasantly.

In the end I rubbed my soft cock between her ass cheeks as she lay there placidly. I came, she pulled out a massive credit-card charging device, and suddenly I was alone.

Joe's whiny friend got nothing.

I was paranoid for weeks. I didn't dare to look in the stairwell; I didn't know whether the puke had been cleaned up. It was a fancy building, who took the stairs? I feared a knock on the door from a wrathful superintendent, and then Mumlow would kick me out.

I feared lupine pimps nabbing me as I left the building. I feared Pinkerton men sent by the Discover card people. I feared Ann Hill, whoever she was, and whatever she made of that unexpected $400 charge.

There was a Rollerblading German cocktail waitress named Ilsa. She thought herself a soul singer, and when she went down to the basement at the end of the night to replenish the beer—she carried the heavy cases on sturdy shoulders—she sang flamboyantly in a faux-Memphis Germanic accent. She Rollerbladed from the bar to the tables by the stage, the Rollerblades slamming on the wooden floor during the band's gentlest passages.

I saw her on Avenue A on a night when I was going to cop dope for the first time. I was always afraid to go there—every time I got high, somebody else went to buy it—but I resented being beholden to them. Mumlow had told me she'd kick me out if I got high in the universe, but she was in Texas seeing relatives. Ilsa was walking in a stream of people towards a place called the Laundromat, where you'd stick your money through a hole in the wall and get heroin or cocaine in return. There was a guy placed near the corner trying to mitigate the very obvious flow of customers, "They're gonna take you off the line," he sang gently, tut-tutting. "They're gonna take you off the line."

I gave Ilsa my money. Ten bucks. "Just one? Really?" she said.

I stood there thinking she'd stolen my money, but she returned and gave me the single bag of heroin, an envelope an inch and a half long, the size of two razor blades held together. We walked past her place, a storefront on Seventh Street with futons on the floor and tie-dyed sheets hanging on the walls. There were a couple of other Germans there, who looked like they were just beginning to tip into real junkiedom; they looked like tourists in shiny European clothes, but there was something drawn and desperate in their faces. They were surprised that I didn't want to hang out and get high with them.

The bag of dope was tiny, but I felt its every contour in my pocket.

I had started moving the furniture around the universe earlier in the day, wanting to change my brain by rearranging the physical world. So the place was a mess; it didn't suit my visions of effete drug use. I tapped the little quantity of powder onto a book anyway. I sniffed up a line, sat there, decided I wasn't high yet, sniffed up another line, thought the same, and suddenly had sniffed the whole bag within five minutes. The high walloped me.

I nodded out, then came to. I had bought a Charlie Parker tape—some live recording. I put a Walkman on and lay back on the bed in the jumble of shoved-about furniture. I didn't know much about bebop, except that I wanted its sophistication. I wrongly thought that Charlie Parker would be a soothing, heroingenic drug soundtrack. I passed out again.

I had some kind of frenetic nightmare that I can't remember. I sat up in a panic. The wild music was shrill in my ears.

Sun Ra's Arkestra played the Knitting Factory soon before Sun Ra died. He'd recently had a stroke. The band wheeled him onstage for sound check, then left him there, alone, as they all went to dinner before the show. After the first set, they left him onstage again. I walked up with my notebook and Sun Ra signed it with a shaking hand, his autograph like that of a third-grader just learning cursive.

The guitar player Marc Ribot was a regular; I idolized him for the biting, bitter leads he played on Tom Waits's *Rain Dogs*. Somebody said that he'd been at the bar speculating that the next musical revolution would be led by a band featuring the white-rapper version of Kurt Cobain. I buttonholed him. *I am that kid!* I said. *Let's start a band!* He politely declined.

A fellow doorman named Gordon and I started an improvised-music band called Isosceles; we grabbed slots from the boss on off-nights and asked twenty musicians to play. Seven or so would show up, hopefully a drummer among them. We played to stragglers who hung around after the night's first set. Gordon bawled on a tenor sax; I bayed poetry out of a notebook. Once, all twenty players showed up. We literally couldn't fit on the stage.

They say if the band could beat up the audience, cancel the show.

I heard the free-jazz prophet Charles Gayle every Monday. The same fifteen people came every week, so after they'd all gone in, I'd shut down the desk, get high with the sound guy, and watch. The sound was exquisite pandemonium. I learned how to *hear* this music; it was like seeing through the Matrix. Minuscule changes would flip the whole sound over.

John Zorn's game piece "Cobra" was performed on the last Sunday of every month. It's an ingenious system for structured improvisation: twelve players in a semicircle face a prompter at a table who administers multicolored cards that stand for various musical acts. The musicians signal their desired operation, using hand gestures, then the prompter picks up a corresponding card, bangs it on the table, and a musical change happens: players enter or exit, volume goes up or down, tempo goes up or down, players imitate other players, players trade phrases between each other.

A different avant-garde luminary picked the cast every month. (One month, there was a Cobra done by a bunch of layman avant-garde enthusiasts. They were given the night because they were the ones keeping the scene stoked; record-store guys, flyer-putter-uppers, habitual attendees. The show was wretched. The sampler pioneer Anthony Coleman was there. "It's now proven that there's such a thing as *can play* in this music," he said.)

In March, it was all sampler players. There were a bunch of musicians pioneering new approaches to playing the sampler: they were playing it live, as an instrument, as opposed to chaining the sounds in a pattern using a sequencer, as hip-hop and techno producers did.

I was a solo acoustic guy in a magical time for hip-hop music. You heard it everywhere, booming from passing cars. It was before SUVs were called SUVs, so they called them *Jeep beats*. The bass Dopplered down Broadway. I tried to replicate the rhythms on guitar, and failed, but in an interesting way. At the Knit, I heard all this atonal, outside, beautifully messed-up music, and connected it to the dissonant textures and flourishes on the rap records. I saw LL Cool J's glorious version of "Mama Said Knock You Out" on MTV, with a band instead of a DJ. In my head I heard huge rhythms, played live, shot through with surreal *information*.

The show was wonderful: unearthly noises, volleys of mayhem. You could barely tell who was doing what, as it was twelve guys standing next to machines. Post-show, I cornered them one by one. Each gave me the same spiel: there were two ways to play the sampler—either to trigger sound effects or as a more conventional keyboard. I hoped for something *in between*.

I was asked to do Cobra and felt like I'd arrived. The doorman takes the stage! To an *audience!* This one was all singers. One of them was this guy Jeff Buckley.

Jeff had been playing with the guitar player Gary Lucas, a jocular psychedelicist of Zorn's generation. Gary had, incidentally, been a publicist at Columbia Records in the '70s and came up with the Clash's slogan, *The Only Band That Matters*.

Jeff's dad was Tim Buckley, whom I'd never heard of but who was apparently notable in the '70s. (Everybody thought this meant Jeff was rich. From where I stand now, that's hysterical; I've had a couple songs on the radio and receive a negligible check a few times a year. Everybody thinks I'm rich now, too.)

Alone among the Cobra singers, Jeff had presence on the stage. The show was quasi-disastrous: singers don't like supporting roles. We fought to bellow loudest. Jeff soared over our ruckus.

Gary Lucas was quickly realizing that Jeff was en route to something spectacular. He tried to corner him, but he ditched Gary and began to play his own shows, accompanying himself on a Telecaster—that brittle, tight guitar sound. Jeff had a fantastic ear, could pick anything out. I saw him mostly play covers: Van Morrison, Edith Piaf, Morrissey, Shudder to Think, Nusrat Fateh Ali Khan. Yeah, that's right, *Nusrat Fateh Ali Khan.* He grew up on Kiss and Led Zeppelin and could play anything of theirs. "Detroit Rock City!" I yelled at him during his shows, and he'd doodle a bar of it, smiling.

Jeff happened to call me on the day Luke and I were moving from Brooklyn to an East Village tenement. "I'll meet you there!" Uh, Jeff, it's a *six story walkup.* He came anyway, ebulliently humping furniture up the stairs with us. We sat on the back of the U-Haul afterwards, eating plums and a bucket of Kentucky Fried Chicken.

A year later, Luke bumped into him in front of the Second Avenue Cinema, a gorgeous indie-celebrity songstress trailing him. He was snooty and aloof: "I'm sorry, what was your name, again?" Didn't introduce Luke to the songstress.

The cutest girl in the room always beelined to him. So I hated him for that. We did a gig together; I shorted him his cut of the door money. "Thanks, this is my rent!" he said.

He was conscripted into playing the title role in a cheap production of Georg Büchner's *Woyzeck* by a friend of mine who saw him at that gig. It's the story of a soldier forced to be the subject of cruel experiments. Woyzeck loses his mind, suffers terrible hallucinations, murders his girlfriend. In the last scene, he walks into a lake to wash the blood off, and drowns.

He did a weekly show at a bar on St. Mark's Place. Even crazy people flocked to him; he played by a window, and this renowned maniac called Tree Man—he adorned himself in branches, looking like he was scowling from inside a bush—would come and glower. There was another guy, Camera Man: fake cameras made out of plastic bottles hung from his neck. He'd stop passersby and coax them to turn their chins in flattering directions as he pretended to take their picture. He'd lean over Jeff's shoulder to frame the audience of enraptured girls.

Soon St. Mark's Place was lined with black Lincoln Town Cars. Jeff signed with Columbia Records. Columbia was a Sony subsidiary, run from a tower on Madison Avenue with a crown shaped like that of an antique cabinet. The label was renowned for ruthlessness, not for carrying out its artists' creative impulses. There was a marketing person there who brought a big cardboard box into her office and sat in it with her phone for a month, not leaving until Alice in Chains's "Man in the Box" was in the top ten. This was artistry as Columbia saw it.

Jeff was utterly crushed-out on Sony. He called it Sony, never Columbia. Before CBS sold it off, Columbia had been famous for its stable of iconoclasts—Dylan, Leonard Cohen, Bruce Springsteen. Sony, on the other hand, was a bloodless monolith. Jeff's lust for a conglomerate's approval wasn't uncharacteristic of the times. There were a lot of artists—myself included—who longed for acceptance by the entities of commerce. (Why? Being an artist wasn't good enough? We chose bohemian lives and now needed to be patted on the head by somebody respectable?)

We saw each other on the street just as my band was being courted by labels. "Sony!" he enthused. He walked away backwards, yelling, "Sign to Sony!"

Years later, when I myself was on a big record label, my band toured America, opening for Jeff. He snapped, as ever, between eager self-deprecation and haughty self-regard. His managers had hired Soundgarden's crew. They gave Jeff princely treatment—Jeff would walk to the side of the stage, playing guitar, and a tech would put a lit cigarette in his mouth; he'd puff once or twice before the guy took it back. But they hated being on a rinky-dink tour of clubs and took it out on my band. During our sound check, their stage guy rang out the monitors, discharging shrieks of feedback at us. They set up Jeff's band's amps so close to the lip of the stage that we barely had any room for our stuff; my spastic, outburst-prone sampler player pushed them back and nearly got punched.

We were playing the Great American Music Hall in San Francisco, a place that looks like a mirrored bordello in France. "Detroit Rock City!" I yelled from the crowd. Jeff obliged with a titter of the riff.

He had been selected as one of *People* magazine's Fifty Most Beautiful People. He wasn't happy about it. He went into a monologue about how he didn't want to be *People* magazine's idea of beautiful, and all the black movie stars they'd skipped over.

Jeff played a snippet of The Smiths' "I Know It's Over":

> *If you're so very entertaining*
> *Then why are you on your own tonight?*
> *If you're so very good-looking*
> *Why do you sleep alone tonight?*

Then Jeff sang:

> *And since you're Jeff Buckley*
> *Why do you sleep alone tonight?*

I muttered acridly: *Poor you.*

I was standing with a friend. "You should show up at sound check tomorrow with his page from *People* duct-taped to your chest," he said.

Later he enthused about Jeff's hotness. "How old is he?"

Twenty-eight.

"Twenty-eight!" he said. "No way. I'm no chicken hawk, but that's a *chicken.*"

Jeff and I sniffed dope in the Great American's basement dressing room. It was powder heroin. You get black tar in California—it must have been a bitch to find this stuff. We walked back to the hotel together; a girl who looked like a Modigliani painting traipsed along. He kissed her on the cheek and she walked away.

?! I said.

"I can't go spreading myself all over the country," he said distastefully.

If you don't want to *spread yourself all over the country* with a hundred different girls, what the hell are we doing here?

Really? I said.

"I've got a plan," he said. He winked. *Winked.*

Yeah? What's the plan?

He gave an agitated frown, and didn't answer.

We played the Urban Art Bar in Houston, a tiny place with a decrepit sound system. Jeff's crew parked their huge purple bus in front and obscured the whole building.

I talked to this beautiful Texan Indian woman. She was a doctor. I thought we were flirting; she just wanted me to take her backstage to meet Jeff. Devastating.

"He speaks French!" she said.

No, he doesn't, I said.

"You haven't heard his version of 'Je n'en connais pas la fin,'" she said, imperiously. "Edith Piaf. His accent is *impeccable*."

I don't think so—he's a really talented mimic, I said.

She huffed.

Eventually, she figured out that all you had to do to get into the dressing room at the Urban Art Bar was push the door open.

The next day Jeff said he'd been accosted by a crazy woman who said she was a doctor; she babbled at him in French. "I don't speak *French*," he said, exasperated.

I didn't speak to Jeff again. I heard stories about Jeff nodding out in bars, deliriously high, and thought, *Figures*. I wanted him brought down.

My band played the WHFS *HFStival* at RFK stadium in D.C. Vivian from Luscious Jackson told me that he had walked out into the Mississippi River with his boots on, singing, was pulled under by the wake of a passing boat, and washed up dead at the foot of Beale Street in Memphis.

A perfect fable. *You fucking cunt piece of shit asshole fucker,* I thought. *You'll be a legend now.*

Years later, I met a committee of producers at a coffee place. They had bought the rights to his story. I expounded about Jeff, and the '90s, and my grievances, and how, at some point, it had occurred to me that it was better to stay alive and make music than to be a dead legend; long past his death, I realized it was a horrible fate, and that he had once been my friend.

They told me about Jeff's journals, that he wrote something about me, how he admired my drive, and how hard I worked, and how he wanted to emulate me. I was shocked.

I told them my dubious theory that he'd gotten clean before he died. For one thing, a musicians' recovery organization was thanked in some liner notes. For another, there was an article written by a Memphis acquaintance who said he'd found him walking around a shitty neighborhood in the rain; nonresidents mainly go to shitty neighborhoods to get drugs, but Jeff apparently wasn't fucked up. Where there's drugs, there's twelve-step meetings.

I wondered if he was aping *Woyzeck* when he walked into the river. I gave them my friend the director's e-mail, maybe she'd show them the VHS tape of the show.

I told them that on our tour together, my sampler player had put a pebble in the air tube of a tire on his bus, twisting the cap on over it; the air slowly leaked out as they drove. They were stranded on the roadside for twelve hours. They could've been killed. His other notable prank was re-arranging some letters on a marquee to read JEFFY O'BUCKLE.

I told them that I thought Jeff wasn't a songwriter; I had asked him once if he wanted some songs that I wrote and he reacted indignantly—I'd touched a nerve. Few mention the songs he wrote when they rhapsodize about him; they adore his covers of "Hallelujah" and "Lilac Wine." I thought he just got lucky with "Last Goodbye." In Memphis, making his final album, he was repeatedly pushed back to the drawing board by Sony; he journaled about how it made him feel cheap and crazy. The songs on the slapdash compilation of demos that Columbia released postmortem were weak, unmemorable. His enormous gift was interpretation, I told them. The problem was that the only real source of income if you're a major label artist is publishing—songwriter's royalties. The label makes sure you don't recoup; you spend more on touring than you make. You write the songs on your albums, or you're broke.

Walking away, I hated myself for how I pontificated. I nurtured a fear that when the movie was made, I'd be in it, cast as Jeff's Salieri: Jeff played by some celebrated young movie star, and I a clown.

The place where Luke and I lived, after I broke up with Mumlow, was in the East Village at a cacophonous intersection. A hundred truck horns thundered every day at rush hour; the screen of the living room TV was filmed with a layer of exhaust soot. Our telephone number spelled out (212) CAT-BUKS.

CAT-BUKS became the destination for everybody we went to school with who lived outside the city. In the evening, the buzzer would ring, and a few random friends would climb up the steep six flights with beer and hang out doing bong hits until they had to take the Long Island Rail Road home. "What are you doing tonight?" "I don't know, just going over to CAT-BUKS, I guess."

Nobody ever brought women over.

Luke kicked me out of CAT-BUKS. We were both slovenly post-collegiate stoners, but I was just slightly more slovenly than he was, and it drove him spittingly unhinged. The night he sat me down and told me I had to go was the last time in my life I cried, openly, in front of a man.

I was replaced by a succession of roommates who lasted a month, two months, six months, nine months. I started arbitrarily showing up at CAT-BUKS, myself. I brought over a thumbnail-sized bag of Ketamine that I bought from a guy outside of Wetlands—I'd never had it before, and the moment the bag was in my hand

I thought the guy had ripped me off—we sniffed it, and sponta-
neously, did a mirthless single-file parade, room to room, around
CAT-BUKS, radiating that Ketamine *whoom-whoom-whoom-whoom,*
like aliens had seized our bodies.

They never changed the phone book listing; it was under my
name for years after I left. A French girl who was quasi-stalking
me left messages on the machine. One of the replacement roommates told me, and I asked if she'd called before. "Yeah, like six
times in the past four months, maybe."

I started cadging off-nights, Mondays or Tuesdays, from my boss
at the Knit and playing gigs as "M. Doughty's Soul Coughing" with
different guys I heard at the club. The saxophonist Tim Berne
played once. I called him up cold, and he had no idea who I was. A
friend asked what he was doing that week, and he apparently said,
"Monday night I'm playing with this African cat—Emdodi."

I booked the 11 PM slot on a Tuesday night five days after my
twenty-second birthday. A month before the show, I had no band.
I was worrying about it, talking to a bass player who worked a
day job as a sound-effects guy on a soap opera. "Don't worry,
Doughty," he said. "We'll find you a band."

I called him up two weeks before the show. He had forgotten.
He couldn't do it, because that week there was a fictitious hur-
ricane in the soap opera's fictitious town, so he had to work
overtime.

There was this one amazing drummer around, an Israeli guy
who could sound like a hip-hop record. There were drummers
who could play those beats, but nobody who could *sound* like that.
My only interaction with him was that he'd once walked into the
Knit's office and asked me to send a fax for him. I told him that I
didn't work in the office and didn't know how the fax machine

worked. He stayed silent for a minute and then asked me again if I'd send a fax for him.

I had nothing to lose, why not call up this amazing player at random, for the hell of it? He had nothing to do on a Tuesday night at 11 PM. Who would? He said yes. I was astonished.

I wanted an upright bass player; the record I wanted to emulate was A Tribe Called Quest's *The Low End Theory,* powered by upright bass lines, some sampled, some played live by the master Ron Carter. There was this one upright player who was unsettlingly corny: he had long hair, wore pointy Night Ranger at the Grammys boots, and was often seen in the sort of pajama-like sultan pants associated with M.C. Hammer. But the drummer said he was good. I got his number from somebody; he, too, had nothing booked on a Tuesday at eleven. I learned later that he had no idea who I was; he showed up for the rehearsal, and thought, *The door guy?*

There was a sampler player who had done both the all-sampler and all-vocalist Cobras—he was brought on to the latter along with some other nonvocalists because he knew the piece. He was less intimidating than the other sampler players; they tended to be mavericks, but this guy was timid and high-strung. He was constantly wide-eyed, like the proverbial animal in headlights. He said yes, too.

Rehearsal studios in New York went by the hour. It was something like $12 per; insanely expensive for me. It was my gig, so the assumption was that I was hiring them, that it was my deal. They were, in fact, so busy that this was the single rehearsal I could grab them for.

Half an hour late, the bass player and the drummer arrived with bagels and coffee. I stood there with my guitar plugged in, gawking at them, as they joked and ate their breakfasts.

Can we play? My money's running out, I said.

They laughed at me. A half hour later, they had finished their bagels.

"Yo, G," said the drummer, who spoke a thickly Hebrew accented, broken Brooklynish, "it is time to pump. It is time that we must pump now."

I was floored from the jump. I had tried to explain to other rhythm sections how to do the grooves I wanted. With these two, it was just *there*. That huge sound.

I started one tune by explaining I wanted the rhythm to be something like James Brown's "Funky Drummer."

"Yo, G," said the drummer, "nobody want to play that there beat. Everybody done that beat already."

We blasted through a bunch of songs in an hour. I was half elated, half panicked. Suddenly the sampler player walked in.

Where's your sampler? I said.

"I brought this," he said. He held up a video camera. "I'm going to record audio and practice to it later."

To promote a gig, I'd call 200 people; basically, everybody I'd ever met in New York. I sat down at 3 PM, with a notebook with names and numbers anarchically scribbled in it, and made calls until 11. Every third person asked to be on the guest list.

Seventeen people came. One rehearsal wasn't enough to really know the tunes, so transitions were sketchy, but I was dumbstruck. The bass player and the drummer seemed not to give a fuck that I was standing there, but they filled the room with an extraordinary rumble.

The sampler player didn't start playing until about the last verse of each tune; it took him that long to load his hard drive. He clearly hadn't listened to his videotape, but I loved his sounds. Peals from space and spectral voices.

There wasn't much, but I divided the money four ways.

"Yo, G," said the drummer. "This is not right. This isn't enough. You pay for my cab. That's how it's done, G."

After paying for cabs, I had lost the precious (for me) sum of $25. But I was sold: if I could hold on to them, this was my band.

They showed up for the gigs I booked, usually looking sort of bored, sometimes en route to other, more profitable gigs later in the evening. Their lethargy was a little contagious. For one gig, I didn't call those 200 people beforehand to hawk the show. Too exhausted. Fuck it, if seventeen people was the norm, what difference would it make if it was ten?

Fifty-five people showed up anyway. *Fifty-five people.* Something was actually happening.

"There's two ways to play the sampler," the sampler player said, "as a conventional keyboard, or to trigger sound effects." I hoped I could convince him otherwise.

I brought some CDs over to his house. There were a bunch of sounds I wanted him to use: Howlin' Wolf, the Andrews Sisters, Toots and the Maytals, The Roches, Raymond Scott, Grand Puba, a cast recording of *Guys and Dolls*.

His house was so organized, it made me feel weird. He had a master's degree in composition from an uptown conservatory and was well inculcated in the conservatory mind-set—he called rock drummers "percussionists" and used terms like *sforzando* when discussing how best to approach a rhythm that I'd ripped off from Funkdoobiest. There was an oddness to his look; it was as if he only wore those clothes that middle-class moms buy at department stores and lay on the childhood bed when their kid comes home for Christmas. Which, it turned out, was exactly the case.

He was a protégé of Anthony Coleman, who brought him into the messier world of the Knit and at whose goading he switched from writing jokey orchestral pieces with scatological titles to electronic-collage pieces, stitched from recordings of his own music school recitals.

The sampler player got me high. Despite his square look and academic pedigree, he was a gluttonous stoner. He had a job editing radio commercials in a windowless studio; he stayed up all night mousing and clicking at a monitor, getting high (next to the computer was a briefcase-sized hard drive with an utterly impressive four gigabyte capacity), alone but for his boss's yellow canary. The weed made the sampler player so jumpy that sometimes he seemed deranged.

He played me a thing that he'd done with a few horn notes from a recording of his chamber-music pieces. He played sloweddown and sped-up versions of it simultaneously. It was aching, and cyclical, and it was gorgeous. I recited a poem over it, and it became the Soul Coughing song "Screenwriter's Blues."

The repetitions of dance music were foreign to him. "You mean, you want me to play this *over and over again?*" he asked in rehearsal.

"Yo, G," said the drummer, "just hold down that there key with some duct tape."

He was too proud for the duct-tape maneuver, but he became OK with the repetition. He bought a copy of Parliament's *Chocolate City* and practiced to it. He learned how to load his hard drive faster. He idolized the bass player, who had wizardly ears—he could hear what you were going to play before you played it, and could complement or contradict your part with a bass line, concocted on the spot, of great force and ingenious simplicity.

After a rehearsal, we ate at a diner. The waitress took the plates away, and the check was passed around. I got some change and put down $12. The sampler player got out his wallet, pulled out $10, put it on the table. The drummer got out his wallet, took out $20, put it on the table, took the $10 back.

Then the check got to the bass player. He held the check in his hand, and took out his wallet. Opened his wallet. Then he put the check down and put his wallet back.

The guy had just *mimed paying the check*.

When the sampler player counted up the money, we were short exactly what the bass player owed. The check was passed around again. The drummer put in a couple extra bucks. He gave it to the bass player. The bass player rubbed his chin, acting stumped by the discrepancy.

The sampler player saw it, too. We didn't confront him. The sampler player was too in awe of the guy; I couldn't believe somebody would actually *do that*.

At that moment, the bass player was thirty-four years old. I didn't occur to me until I was myself thirty-four that this kind of trickery wasn't something most adults did.

I was twenty-three, the drummer was thirty, and the sampler player, thirty-one. My idea was that guys older than me would know what they were doing. Musically, I was correct. On every other level, I had no idea what I'd stumbled into.

I talked Louise at CB's into giving us a Monday night residency at the Gallery. There was a club night—clubs were not buildings but branded parties that migrated between venues—called Giant Step in New York. It was a cauldron for the sort of stuff that Pete Rock and CL Smooth and DJ Premier were doing: old jazz records, cut up and played over big beats. They had saxophone players and trumpeters come in and play along with the records. I envisioned a Knitting Factory version of Giant Step, with more strangeness: a tinge of the avant-garde. It would be us and a DJ. I invited some Knitting Factory types to come in and jam along.

It was mostly a bust. We played a decent set, but the Knit guys just lingered for a minute at the bar and then left, confused. While the DJ spun a Beatnuts instrumental, I went to the mic and yelled: SLAW! SLAW! SLAW! SLAW!

(I should've called the band Slaw. Soul Coughing is a wretched band name.)

A guy named Joel, just out of film school, showed up and wanted to do a video. A mere five grand, he said. Yeah, great, but unfortunately I left my wallet in the penthouse. Undeterred, Joel told me that he was going to call up a bunch of major labels; one of them would sign Soul Coughing and pony up the five grand. I listened in amused disbelief.

They showed up.

As I left the stage, a woman came up and introduced herself as being from a record company. Yeah? I sneered. Want to put out my record?

"Yes," she said.

I went to a luxuriously wood-paneled office on West Fifty-seventh Street, next door to Carnegie Hall. Huge black-and-white photos of the label's stars, broodingly lit, loomed in the reception area. I met the label's tanned, British president in an opulent office. We sat on couches made for a pasha. A lavish platter of sushi was brought in—but it was his lunch, he wasn't planning on sharing it with me. He lectured me, in the tones of a loony, upper-class limey, about how I should fire the band—saying this without having seen the band—use the band's name as a brand, continue alone. No, no, I said. The band is important, the sound is important.

He was a rich, tan fool. But he was right.

There had been an awkward pause in the show, for the sampler player to load sounds onto the tiny hard drive of his sampler. "You should tell jokes or something there," he said irritatedly.

I heard that he appeared in Bob Dylan's *Don't Look Back;* he was the bespectacled student whom Dylan goaded, "Why should I get to know you, *maaaaan?*" The bespectacled possible-future-label president: "Why, because I'm a very good person!"

I went back to the band, agog, and told them.

"Why didn't you invite us?" they asked.

Slaw became just a weekly Soul Coughing show. I had posters made, with a slogan I meant to emulate The Who's inspired descriptive phrase "Maximum R&B." It was "Deep Slacker Jazz." The manager of the venue, CB's Gallery—CBGB had annexed the stores flanking it, making one a pizza parlor and the other a gallery/performance space—knew this junkie guy who put up posters for her. I gave him a stack of posters and some cash.

The bass player came in the next week complaining he never saw posters. Fine, I said. Here's the posters—you put them up. For the next show, there were even fewer posters. The bass player had hired the very same junkie guy, on the same manager's recommendation.

"I see my posters all over the place!" he said, outraged, when I brought it up.

I divvied up more responsibilities; the sampler player agreed to advance a show. When we got there, there was an art opening; the place was jammed; there was no way to do a sound check.

"I can't believe this," said the sampler player, showing a glimpse of the juddering rage under his frightened surface.

Huh? I said. This is your fault!

"My fault?!"

Yeah, I said. That's what 'Call them up and ask if everything's OK for us to show up at 4' means.

The drummer refused any other duties. "I play the drums, that's enough, G," he snorted. But soon, in what I took to be a sign of surprisingly deepening engagement, he started arranging the rental of a supplemental speaker—just one, a big subwoofer, that's all we could afford—every week. Two sketchy-looking dudes would come in a hatchback, load the thing into the club, and I'd pay them $100.

Eventually I figured out that the drummer had set it up so the only thing in that subwoofer was his kick drum.

People from labels kept coming. We got a lawyer. His assistant called up and left on the answering machine a sprawling guest list of A&R execs, which we ignored. Admission was $4, who could kvetch? The lawyer called up, apoplectic. "These people need to feel *important*," he said.

We went, all of us together, to offices and had magnificent lunches. There were certain business-y phrases that every exec at every label used. "At the end of the day," and "bring to the table." "It's about _____ at the end of the day." "_____ is what _____ brings to the table." "At the end of the day, it's _____ that we bring to the table."

We went to meet the head of Columbia Records—Jeff Buckley's cherished Sony—at his office. He looked like a longshoreman in beige Armani.

"GENTLEMEN!" the president of Columbia yelled. "YOU—CAN DO—ANYTHING!—YOU WANT!—ON—COLUMBIA!—RECORDS!" This must've been his pitch to artist-y type artists. Even as many of us yearned for corporate love, it was barefacedly uncool to want to be on a major label.

"ISN'T THAT RIGHT, MICKEY!"

"That's right, Johnny!" smarmed a henchman.

"You look like serious young men!" Johnny yelled. "Look behind you!"

We turned to see a monumental burnished-sterling Columbia logo on the wall.

"COLUMBIA RECORDS!—IS THE BIGGEST!—LABEL!—IN—THE—WORLD! Isn't that right, Mickey?

"That's right, Johnny!" Mickey said.

"Now look at this!" Johnny said. "This is the new Sony mini-disc player!"

He slammed a minidisc into a desk-side console.

"Look! The title is RIGHT THERE ON THE L.E.D. DISPLAY!"

"Thunder Road" scrolled across the console in digitized yellow letters. Bruce Springsteen blasted at enormous volume. In the din, Johnny beamed, shaking his head up and down like an over-stimulated dog.

We played on Halloween. The Jon Spencer Blues Explosion played the main room at CBGB; their show was packed. Ours was nearly empty. An A&R guy from a small label attached to a bigger label, tired and sweaty, wandered in, sat down, and fell in love with me. He was an obese, closeted-gay guy named Stanley Ray.

The tale of the '90s is sometimes told as the tale of underground bands thrown into the mainstream and showered with integrity-threatening lucre. This is partially true—certainly true in the case of the imperial grunge bands—but in general, artists' advances were sucked up by recording costs, and the best they could seek was a reliable source of tour support—that is, somebody to pay for the van rental. Real money was made by people who worked at labels.

Labels were selling shitty CDs at insane markups. It was cheaper to manufacture a CD than a vinyl record, but, on a pretense of technological sophistication, CDs cost more than twice as much.

Many contained just one good song. There were CDs by bellicose hardcore bands with one lilting lounge-y sing-along tune, CDs whose song played on the radio was the lone song written and sung by the bass player, funk-metal bands with one incongruous acoustic ballad. The job of an A&R person—it stood for the antiquated description "artists and repertoire"—had transmogrified into mostly just trying to nab bands and sign them, abandoning the repertoire part entirely. Nobody's job was to say, "Hey, guys, why don't we take another six months so the bass player can write more tunes like that one."

The labels stopped selling singles, in the traditional radio-song-plus-a-B-side format; fans, assuming that the rest of the album would be in the same vein of the song they'd heard on the radio, had to shell out for the whole CD. Nobody saw this as a con.

So the labels were drowning in cash.

(The tanking of the labels, en masse, circa the 2000s, messed up my career a little. I might've been richer. Maybe substantially so. I still don't feel sorry for them.)

Alternative music's popularity meant the labels were trafficking in a genre in which they were almost wholly nonconversant.

So they went on a hiring spree. People who worked at fanzines, people who ran "labels" out of apartments and sold only seven-inch vinyl oddities, people who booked bands at dive bars, friends of bands, people who just *went out a lot* were flying first class—not business class, *first class*—and being paid executive-magnitude salaries.

Many of them embraced end-of-the-day-bring-to-the-table-ese; others fooled themselves into insouciant contempt for the bosses signing their enormous paychecks. They signed band upon band upon band.

The story of Nirvana—the band that wrought the cultural sea change—was perceived like this: Nirvana was friends with Sonic Youth, asked them which label was best, and Sonic Youth said, "Our label!" Bands were signed because *they might be friends with other bands,* or they carried a whiff of prestige that might attract more profitable acts. Some bands were pursued as trophies by the labels, pelted with cash in bidding wars, and shrugged off nonchalantly when their CDs tanked.

Nobody worried. They were tax write-offs for companies with much tax to write off. Plus, who knows what this stuff is, what it means? Any of these bands could fluke into a hit.

A hit! What major labels *did*, above all else, was seek a *hit;* a song that gets played on the radio, and then, once MTV was assured by radio of its hit-ness (MTV's reputation as a tastemaker being altogether undeserved) on cable TV. The fanzine-bred label people didn't know what hits were, or how to get bands to make them; many of them were unaware that hits were the heart of the enterprise at all. Eventually the bands-that-were-friends-with-bands, the bands-with-artistic-merit—and, alas, that new guard of A&R people, who couldn't just go play in bars and thus had to find other ways to make a living—discovered that they had wandered into a car dealership and sniffily announced they were shopping for boats.

Corpulent, delicate Stanley Ray used to work in the stockroom at his label but was promoted to A&R when another guy quit. He got the job because he went out to clubs every night, compulsively (if he spent a night at home he'd jabber neurotically about how he must be missing out on something). He was bald on top, with two dirty-blond dreadlocks tied into a ponytail.

He met with us in the revolving restaurant atop the Marriott in Times Square and charmed us comprehensively. He hinted at stories about bands getting fucked by labels, said, "No, I should stop, I can't tell you that story." We begged, and with a theatrical sigh, he said, "I shouldn't tell you this," then told the sordid tales, with names coyly omitted.

His boss was an ex-football player who'd fluked into putting out singles by L.A. punk rock bands in the '70s. He was a grey-haired man in big glasses—sort of Harry Caray–looking—who liked to wear a sport jacket over cutoff jeans. He flew out to New York, met us at a Japanese restaurant, sketched out a diagram on a napkin of how his label meshed with its major label parent, Warner Bros. Then he told us, at length, about how he was going to leave the record business and build a house, in a cave, powered entirely by turbine engines.

(This guy told a story about once having signed James Brown, incongruously, to his then-minuscule punk rock label. He said that James's contract specified that he be given three Cadillacs; one went to a woman in Kentucky, another to a woman in Ohio, and one was for James. The sessions were wretched. Having given up on finishing a usable tune, the guy told James, sarcastically, "Why don't you try something New Wave on the chorus?" When the chorus came around, James shrieked, "New WAVE! New WAVE! New WAVE!")

Stanley Ray had a pattern: he'd fall in love with a singer, pursue his band, sign them, then hate him. His charm was powerful. The other side of it was a whining, griping passive-aggressiveness that snarled out if a singer expressed some measure of positive self-regard. His stories invariably went back to how _____ from _____ had once been so rad and they'd been close and he'd told Stanley Ray all his secret hopes, but then suddenly the singer had changed, had only hard-hearted interest in his career, and hadn't called him, in fact *actively avoided him, can you believe that?*

I saw this immediately, and made, half-consciously, a resolution: I was the guy who would *never* let Stanley Ray down.

We were flown to Los Angeles so Stanley Ray and the turbine-cave guy could further woo us. They put us up at the Mondrian on Sunset Boulevard; our suites looked out over twinkling Hollywood. I'd never stayed somewhere so posh, and they were paying for *everything*. Remembering the nights I had to decide between spending my $3 on cigarettes or food, I opened the minibar and ate all the candy. They took us out for dinner, and when I got back to the room, stoned and stuffed, I immediately ordered a pizza from room service that I could barely take a bite of.

I called the front desk and asked if I could call a dominatrix and charge it to the room.

"Uh, no sir," the front-desk guy said, contemptuously.

"Dude!" said the turbine-cave guy the next day. "Let's go to the Bu!"

The Bu?

"The *Bu!* Malibu!"

He drove us there in his black BMW, enthusing about the frozen margaritas at some seaside restaurant. We passed a pipe around. I put on a cassette of A Tribe Called Quest that I'd brought along. It came to the song "Show Business," on which five rappers take turns denouncing record company executives. Q-Tip calls them fakes, snakes, shady, says the business is a cesspool; Sadat X talks about smarmy, "palsy-palsy" A&R people that materialize when you're riding high; Phife kvetches about "bogus brothers making albums when they know they can't hack it"; Diamond D tells the listener to get a good lawyer, and a label that's "willing and able to market and promote."

Lord Jamar's verse is the most devastating. "You're a million dollar man that ain't got no dough," he says. He describes being at a restaurant with a label guy, asking him when he'll get paid. Just as a label guy tells him he won't get paid, because he hasn't recouped his advance yet, a waitress arrives. "More soup with your meal?"

"All you want to do is taste the fruit," Lord Jamar says, "but in the back they're making fruit juice."

Turbine-cave guy laughed and laughed.

Nonchalantly, Stanley Ray lived in peripatetic luxury. He came to New York a few times a year and stayed at the Rihga Royal Hotel, on Fifty-fourth Street, for a month, taking me or some other friend out to dinner every night. When I briefly lived with (and, perhaps, off of) a girlfriend in London, he came out and stayed in a cushy place he called the Disco Arab Hotel for three weeks.

In the '70s, Stanley Ray was the obnoxious guy at the L.A. punk shows, getting in people's faces and telling them off. (Maybe, says your armchair shrink friend Mike Doughty, he was preempting mockery for his fatness by cutting everybody else down first?) Somebody at Warner Bros. complimented him for niceness and he was glum. Seriously.

There were cards made for A&R guys to send out with CDs. He had his altered from "with compliments of . . ." to "with complaints."

He called our manager incompetent every time we spoke, and then said, "No, no, I shouldn't talk shit about your manager, he's *your* manager, after all," and we'd say, No, Stanley, please, we want to hear it, then he'd talk about how insulted he was that we hadn't asked him to quit the label and become our manager, but he didn't *want* to be our manager, he was just insulted that we didn't want him to be our manager. If I pointed out that perhaps management, involving math and planning, required skills other than alternately charming and alienating people at nightclubs, he'd say, "What, like it's hard to manage a band or something?!"

He didn't do anything a traditional A&R guy was supposed to do; he didn't help bands find producers, though he often complained, "Your manager isn't doing *anything* to find producers," and he didn't help us to develop songs, other than alluding to his displeasure at them. He did sign bands, but after signing Soul Coughing, in 1993, he barely signed anybody for the next seven years—he signed bands that he openly said he didn't take seriously. He was eventually bumped up from the smaller Warner Bros. imprint to vice president at Warner Bros. proper (not so impressive: every other person you met there was a vice president) and was making a quarter million dollars a year. His key mission was to make Soul Coughing feel too guilty to break up.

We sat tensely at brunch. A deranged Frenchman in a clown wig wandered between the tables playing the accordion. Our lawyer had gotten us a publishing deal—that meant songwriting. I had exhorted the guys in my band, when they were disinterested, that they should think of it as *their* band, as well as mine. It didn't really work at the time. But now it became clear that they expected every bit of money to be split even-steven.

I'd spent eight hours the night before typing out a screed explaining what I thought I had done, how it was significant that I put the band together; twelve dense pages of loopy argument. When I woke up, I realized I was just typing the same thing over and over again, in fact barely saying anything at all. I deleted it. My head spun, trying to devise a way to state my case.

Let's think about what songs actually *are*, I said.

They sat scowling.

The drummer spoke: "Yo G, you don't write the beat. *I* write the beat. Just because you do the vocal doesn't mean you're better than me. Listen to them hi-hat parts there. Nobody told me to do that, that's my hi-hat part, G."

Could I disagree?

"Don't be greedy," the drummer said.

"We were all doing something else, and then this came along. So this is like a side project for each of us," said the bass player.

I thought, but didn't say: *This isn't a side project. This is my life. Everything I've ever written I've poured into this band. You feel like this is just some fluke you fell into, because for you it is.*

But I was ten years younger than these guys, and they were much better at their instruments than I was.

The sampler player pulled out a sheaf of papers. "Look at this," he said. It was sheet music, with notes, actual super-fancy

Western notation *notes*, written on staves with clefs and the whole respectable-composer package.

"This," he said, "is music."

I thought, but didn't say: *You've contributed basically one keyboard part, brilliant, amazing keyboard part though it is, around which a song is based—and I put it together, laid it out, I made it into a song.*

But I was ten years younger than these guys, and they were all much better than I was.

"I'm not saying we don't have good lyrics, G," said the drummer. "Everybody's going to know we're one of those bands with good lyrics."

One of those bands with good lyrics? As if to say, we're one of those bands with interesting art on their CD covers?

The sampler player pointed at the bass player. "He's been playing for *years*. He's played in so many bands, he's played with _____" and here he mentioned an ornery avant-jazz legend. "Do you think that guy would even *think* of playing with you?"

"You act like you're the only one whose dream it is to be a rock star," said the bass player. "It's my dream, too."

But, I thought, *what did you do about it? In your entire life, what have you done?* I paid for those rehearsals when I barely had a dime—booked those gigs with those spiteful club people—called everybody I'd ever met in New York to gather a measly crowd for our gigs—

"You play the same riff over and over again, *Doughty*," said the bass player, putting a cruelly condescending emphasis on my name.

Yes. Just as some of the great rhythm guitarists and songwriters do, having a style that they modify and return to for their entire careers, I'm not great, but I live by the example of the greats, I could've said.

But I was ten years younger, and they were all much better than I was.

Finally, I said, You all sound like yourselves, and you're all amazing, but I knew what this band was going to sound like before I got you guys together.

They threw up their hands and scoffed, but it was true. I'd sat and imagined it for years, and it sounded as I intended it to. I could've said: It doesn't occur to you that I'm better than you think I am, that I have a vision that you'll never give me credit for—maybe you do know it, and you don't want to admit it to yourselves, because this would mean accepting that your future lay in following this guy, this annoying skinny kid from the suburbs with the weird lyrics, who can barely sing, and is such a primitive guitar player he might as well be a novice. Admitting this guy was a whiz kid meant admitting you were never a whiz kid yourself.

I wasn't going to say it. Because I didn't believe it. In my early morning stonedness, writing songs, bass lines, dreaming up rhythms, I thought myself a genius. But in the light of day I had no confidence.

"That's just *boring*. That's really *boring*," said the sampler player. "I *studied* music. And this man"—motioning to the bass player—"is the most talented musician in New York, and this man"—motioning to the drummer—"everybody wants to play with. You're lucky that he's playing with you. Do you have any idea how lucky you are?"

"You have to ask what key you're playing in, you don't even know the names of the chords you're playing, *Doughty*," said the bass player.

Long silence.

"We should split the money equally," said the bass player.

"That's what we'll do. That's the right thing to do," said the sampler player.

"Nobody should be more important than anybody else," said the drummer.

It was as if the solution suddenly occurred to everybody. They smiled these *Eureka!* smiles.

"Great! We've decided! What a relief."

Our food came. They chatted; I sat there stunned.

Something occurred to me, fifteen years later. Since I had actually written the songs, I owned them. As we sat there, those songs belonged to me. Legally and actually. If we went before a judge, and the judge was told, He wrote the melody, and the chords, and the rhythm, and the lyrics, but I wrote the hi-hat part, the judge wouldn't split up the songs even-steven.

I didn't realize this *for fifteen years.*

"You think you chose us, *Doughty,*" said the bass player, observing my dazed state, "but after you chose us, *we chose you.*"

I wanted each of my bandmates to have a big cut of the songwriting: what I wanted was 40 percent. The idea was that splitting it four ways was 25 percent per man; I wanted it split *five* ways, because I was doing *one extra job.* A five-way split meant twenty per man. Twenty for me as an equal band member; another twenty for me as songwriter. I had no problem divvying up the proceeds from ideas I prodded them into actualizing when they were barely participating in the band. I had no problem giving each of them a sizable, permanent stake—*ownership*—in the songs. I thought I was being modest. One extra job.

I tried one more time. We had a meeting after hours in our manager's office. The sampler player showed up drunk, with an open can of Guinness, and unbuttoned his shirt to his belly. His head lolled back like he'd been punched. "You stabbed me in the back," he said.

My request for 40 percent—everybody's got one job, but I've got two—was met with howls. That meant I was making *double* what each of them would!

I got whittled down to 33 percent.

"But that's a third," said the sampler player. "That number has too many implications for me."

It became clear that if they felt the slightest bit unequal, these guys would actually *walk* on this, the best opportunity that had ever showed up in their faces. I had a terrible feeling that even as I conceded this, this huge thing, it wouldn't be enough; they'd never really be happy. I'd always be a little bit too elevated. They'd always be aggrieved.

I got 31 percent—an extra 6 percent—but only on the first album. It'd be 25 percent each on the next one. All for one and one for all, huh? Some of these were songs I wrote a couple of years before I laid eyes on any of them—songs about Seth and Betty and my post-teen grief.

They told me that they'd give me a little extra money from our publishing deal. It was a six-figure sum—initially quite exciting-sounding—that would pay our lawyer, our manager, a long list of commensurate expenses, and provide a very little bit of income to live on for the next two years or so. "It'll be more than you think it will be," the sampler player reassured.

This reward turned out to be—the sampler player told me, smiling magnanimously—that I wouldn't have to pay my share of a $5,000 fee for a demo we'd done a year earlier, which meant $1,250.

I called the lawyer and told him about the deal we cut.

"Are you *sure?*" the lawyer asked.

Yes, I said, very quietly.

I'd try to convey to the drummer the beat I wanted for a song by referencing a hip-hop tune. I was totally green, so I had no language to express it otherwise. When I hazarded musical jargon, he and the bass player laughed.

(Sometimes I'd ask what some musical term meant, and they'd look nervously at each other, doing a higher-pitched, more nervous version of the laugh. It appeared that they didn't *want* me to learn anything. Years later, I went through a torturously complex explanation of a beat, and the drummer I was working with said good-naturedly, "Oh, you want the snare on the two and the four." Yes! Exactly! If somebody had taught me the language, maybe I wouldn't have felt helpless at rehearsals.)

He'd sneer, "Yo, G, that beat is played" (*played* meaning used up, out of style). I'd cajole him, and *maybe* he'd play it. Early in the life of the band, he'd roll his eyes and do something kind of in the neighborhood of what I'd asked him for, like he was thinking, *Whatever, who cares about this kid?* As the years went by, he would gravitate towards something self-consciously complicated, rarely funky. Uniqueness was more important to him than making the song better.

I stopped trying to tell him what to do. At rehearsals, I sat in the corner, reading the newspaper as he played permutations of these beats he found acceptably original, but were never particularly good. I waited him out. At some point, almost despite himself, he'd start doing something that was along the lines of what I needed for a song. I leaped up and began strumming the chords, and it would all start falling into place. I'd stop and say, Let's play that again.

We took it from the top and suddenly the beat was different.

Stop stop stop, I said. Hey, could you play the beat you were playing before?

"It's the same beat," he said.

Bewildering. Maybe I'd heard it wrong. We began again. I started in with my chords, and the beat would be even further removed from what I wanted. I stopped playing.

Hey, that beat that you were doing when we first started this—that was really great—could you try that again?

"Yo, G," he said, "It's the *same beat.*"

One time I insisted with a little more intensity, and he stood up, threw his sticks, and left the room, cursing at me, telling me he's a drummer, and I can't even play guitar, and he's played all over the world, and what the fuck do you know?

It'd be cool if you played something a little less space rock, a little firmer, I said, one time.

"You stole that there from Mary J. Blige, don't think everybody don't know you steal from other singers, G," he replied.

We were playing a college festival at a track stadium. I was way up in the bleachers, watching the drums get sound checked. Suddenly he played a beat that I had wanted in a song for years; this kind of shuffly hip-hop beat with a buoyant triplet in the kick drum part. I ran down the bleachers. I ran like hell. All my songs ran through my mind, which one do I start playing when I get there? Because once a song was played to a beat, there was no way to say, Hey, that doesn't quite work there, can we try a different song with that beat? "We already have a song with that there beat," he'd say.

I bolted down the bleachers to the field, I madly ran across it, ran up the stairs to the stage, pushing tech guys out of my way. I grabbed my guitar—it wasn't plugged in—I untangled the cable, frantically, ran to the amp—

He stopped playing the beat.

I saw him rehearse with a singer-songwriter; a song for a benefit show. There was a line that went, "I'll play the drums for you."

"Hey," she said, "when I sing that line, could you play a little roll on the toms?" A very corny idea, indeed.

They went through to the end; he didn't play the roll.

"Hey," she said, "that was great, but you forgot to play that roll after I go, 'I'll play the drums for you.' OK?"

He nodded. They went through it again; again, he didn't play the roll. Again she told him. Again they played, and again, no drum roll.

I left.

Once I got together with the drummer and Jeff Buckley. I had a notion that maybe we could form a band together. (In retrospect, it would've been hell for me to be second banana to a man I envied so bitterly.) Jeff wasn't interested, on account of the drummer. "He *lags,* man," said Jeff. He was right. When the drummer got excited, he hit the drums harder, and the effort made him slow down. In rehearsal, if the drummer lagged too much, the bass player would shut off his amp and stomp away, without explanation, muttering.

Rehearsals were dreadful when the bass player was in a bad mood. I'd sing a part to him, and he'd play back, looking me straight in the eyes, something different than what I just sang. "You think that works, huh?" he taunted.

His moods were ruled by food intake. "I have low blood sugar," he told us one day. He was telling us that, from then on, it was our responsibility to make sure he ate. If not, dark brattiness would come over him, and he would sit sulking. He had the sort of darkness that could stink up a room.

I'm going to get a bag of apples, so I can give one to you when you have low blood sugar, I said, once, when he was brooding.

"I hate apples," he replied imperiously.

Rather than communicating his feelings, he'd frown exaggerated frowns, and do these violent exhales until somebody noticed he was angry about something; he truly expected that somebody would be obliged to do something about it once they heard him puffing.

I'm sick of your blood sugar, I said, after enduring months of his blood sugar's reign.

"Do you *know* what it's like to have low blood sugar, Doughty?" he said, as if conveying a lesson in tolerance towards the handicapped. No, I said. Why don't you just *deal,* and *eat?*

There was some event that he took to be a crisis; he wanted Stanley Ray to intervene. "Somebody better call Stanley Ray! Somebody better call Stanley Ray!" he kept saying. He was ignored. "Somebody better call Stanley Ray!"

The drummer wanted to be the loudest thing in the mix. To accomplish this, he'd play quietly during sound check, so the sound guy would turn him up, and then bash the hell out of everything during the show. This infuriated the bass player. Playing the upright bass is difficult with a loud drummer; the boom of the drums would shoot straight into the F holes of the bass, causing hoots of feedback. If he hadn't eaten, he would throw his bass down and stalk out of the room. I noticed something—though I can't be sure I saw it—usually he'd play facing the audience directly, but sometimes, when he was in a mood, he'd rotate just a little bit towards the drummer, causing feedback, creating an excuse for a tantrum.

We made our first record in Los Angeles. I landed there on the day Kurt Cobain died. We stayed in the Hollywood motel where John Waters's transvestite muse Divine had died a few years earlier.

The producer was this wild individualist named Tchad Blake. He's the closest I've ever seen an engineer come to really being an *artist*. He put vocals through a big bullhorn on a stick that he'd bought in India; put microphones in old mufflers and recorded sounds through them; ran sounds recorded with $10,000 microphones through effects pedals he'd bought for $10 at garage sales. He had this spooky grey plastic microphonic head mounted in front of the drummer, staring at him; it had a brow, a nose, and ears, and microphones mounted in the spots where they'd be in the human skull.

He really didn't give a fuck about how the music sounded anywhere other than the beat-up '60s-vintage pickup truck he drove between home and the studio. It always sounded amazing there.

I loathed my fucking voice. Some of the tracks sounded amazing—that song with the looped horns that I mentioned earlier, "Screenwriter's Blues"—but hearing the vocals, I swelled up with enmity for myself.

The other guys used to take the rental car out at night, smoking weed and listening to Duke Ellington. I stayed in my room, clutching my head in my hands, obsessed with the record, hating my voice. Then I'd get high and my head would fill with fanciful ideas, and I'd feel better.

I used to write record reviews for the *New York Press*. My old editors there were overjoyed that their scrawny music critic kid had done good; they put a cartoon of me on the cover. They faxed the cover—my giant head—to the studio. The assistant engineer Scotch-taped it to the studio wall. The next day, it had been ripped down, scraps of ripped fax paper still hanging on the tape.

While we were mixing the songs, O.J. Simpson rode in the back of a white Bronco, moving at a steady, deliberate speed, followed by a formation of cop cars, through the streets of Los Angeles. The TV reporters said he was holding a pistol to his head. People gathered on street corners and overpasses, cheering and waving signs. We watched the helicopter footage of the stately pursuit, just a mile away from where we sat.

The record came out on the same day as REM's *Monster;* there was a line outside Tower Records of REM fans waiting to buy it at midnight. Stanley Ray and I went in. I found our CD stuck in some non-glorious spot at the back of the new releases rack. I was crestfallen.

"What, you think you should have a line of people waiting to buy *your* record?" sniffed Stanley Ray.

I bought a copy and listened to it at home. It sounded like shit to me.

I got high, and listened again. It sounded better.

There were some good reviews. Four stars in *Rolling Stone.* I was eager to read to the review in *Spin,* because I actually read *Spin.* The *Spin* critic talked about the psychedelic production, the depth, the texture, the robustness of the sound. "In fact, *Ruby Vroom* might have been one of 1994's most inviting sonic spaces."

Paragraph break; next paragraph was one sentence long:

"If it weren't for the vocals."

It went on to call me white; a kind of irredeemable whiteness, white without consciousness, not the arch whiteness of Beck or the Beastie Boys. They're doing something interesting, but this guy, he's just *white.*

I felt it. I took it into my heart. At last I knew I was right; my band was a great band, and I was a lowly thing attached to it.

We played a big Warner Bros. showcase at a ballroom on Thirty-fourth Street. There were four bands from the label, and in between they projected clips from Warner Bros.–produced sitcoms. A guy in a Bugs Bunny suit wandered in the crowd. Backstage, they had me do a chat room thing, which I'd never done before. There were three or four chatters, and they all wanted to talk to the lead singer from Saint Etienne: *hello? is this sarah? sarah are you there?*

(Chat room appearances became faddish. Usually they wanted you to call somebody sitting at a terminal somewhere, and they'd read the questions to you and type your answers out. I refused to do them, because I was snooty about my spelling and punctuation, which they always bungled. It's an abuse of the medium, I told the stupefied publicists.)

I met a dark haired, quasi-goth girl from Hackensack with fishnet stockings and an elaborate Italian name. We ended up backstage with my hand up her dress. We sniffed some heroin. I got her number but never called her, because I knew she'd come back with heroin every time, and I had too much at stake to become a junkie.

It was the advent of the dial-up modem, and our manager had gotten us an AOL account; each of us had a screen name we could sign in under. One day my phone rang; I picked up, and heard *click*. I dialed *69, a recent innovation in prank-call prevention; you'd dial it and it'd connect you to the number that just called.

The bass player picked up. "Hello?" he said, with a kind of exaggerated casualness.

Um, did you call me?

"No? . . ."

I just dialed *69, I said.

"That's weird," he said.

It seems like you called me to see if you got a busy signal, to tell whether or not I was online and you could use the AOL account.

"Doughty," he said, "you're so *paranoid*."

The AOL account was mostly for fan e-mail. I checked the sent messages and found a response to a German guy's message suggesting an alternate guitar tuning for me.

"Thanks," the bass player had written back, "but Doughty doesn't know how to tune his own guitar."

It seemed to me that strange things would happen if he was mad at you. Things would go missing; I'd come onstage to find that my guitar was suddenly out of tune, even though I hadn't touched it since sound check; the little foam-whatsits on my headphones would be ripped out and tossed on the floor; in the dressing room, somebody's bottle of red wine would have mysteriously fallen off the table and shattered; my takeout lunch that I had left on my amp while I went to grab a napkin would suddenly be gone, reappearing in the room he happened to be practicing in.

What the *fuck?* I said.

"Hmm?" he said. "What's the matter?"

There was a tape of Bollywood wedding music, *Vivah Geet,* that I'd bought in a bodega and treasured—Bollywood was a mystery before the 2000s, something you heard emanating from cab radios and nobody could help you find. I left it in the van, and when I went to retrieve it, it had vanished.

Anybody seen that Indian music tape?

"I packed it," said the bass player.

You *packed* it, I repeated. Can you grab it out of your bag and give it to me?

"Aren't you going to *thank* me for making sure you didn't forget it?" he said.

It took me a month to get it. When he gave it back to me, it was just the case—the cassette was missing.

We were in France. I walked into the hotel after a gig and saw the bass player in an alcove, on a hotel phone. He had a grim, secretive look on his face. An hour later, I walked out; he was still on the phone. I came back a couple hours later; he was *still* on the phone.

In the morning, I was sitting in the lobby, groggy, as the tour manager was checking out. He motioned me over.

"Zair ees a long-deestance phone call for Room 210," said the desk guy.

I had called the States the night before, dialing up the AT&T long distance to punch in my calling card number. It must cost something to call even a toll-free number. These greedy hotel fuckers.

I looked at the bill. It was something in the hundreds. I had no idea what the number meant. This was before the euro; every country had different money. English roadies had a charming tradition of mocking the confusion of currencies by calling every country's money *shitters*. In Germany, a cup of coffee cost five shitters; in Denmark, fifteen shitters; in Belgium a hundred and fifty shitters; in Italy, astonishingly, three or four *thousand* shitters; in Holland—and I must point out here that the Dutch guilder was once the world's most magnificently psychedelic cash—twenty or thirty shitters. So, whatever it was, I wasn't paying attention—I was just going to pay it and worry about exchange rates when I was broke. I pulled out a multicolored fistful of sooty bills.

The tour manager looked over my shoulder at the bill for the phone call and his eyes bugged out. "That's *seven hundred francs!*" he said. "How long was your phone call?"

Ten minutes?

"Ten minutes! That's not right." He began to argue with the front desk guy. I was just standing there wondering where I could get coffee.

The front desk guy was yelling at the tour manager. He picked up the phone. "He's calling the employee that was working last night."

Holding the phone to his ear, the desk guy repeated his description; long hair, striped shirt, pointy boots, long grey coat.

We turned to the bass player, dressed in precisely the same clothes as last night.

"What's the matter?" he said.

My interpretation: before he made the call, the front desk had asked for his room number, and the bass player had given them mine. The bass player *got on the phone with the guy and pretended to be clueless.* I believe that I've never known a man so committed to his lies; somebody who could serenely look you in the eye while he told you something that clearly, unambiguously, wasn't true.

And you know what? He got away with it. Nobody paid anybody seven hundred francs. We got in the van.

He was often on the phone—no, that's an egregious understatement. He was on the phone at every truck stop, in every hotel lobby, every restaurant. I think he had a network of women he badgered into talking dirty. It seemed that in every city, he met a woman but never actually brought them back to the hotel, and they were all of a type; none of them were attractive. I cringe as I type that, but I don't know how else to put it. He liked women who didn't have options.

He didn't have a phone, only a voice mail number, the kind that used to be common for struggling actors in New York to have, so they could call in obsessively and see if they'd scored auditions. He saw himself as super-erotic-man, and his outgoing message, accordingly, was so smarmy that I recoiled from the receiver every time I called him. Sometimes I held the phone at arm's length until I heard the beep.

"Leave me a message," he said in a porn-star voice. "A *detailed* message."

We did the radio sex advice show *Lovelines* once, with Dr. Drew and the hair-metal gadfly Rikki Rachtman. It was the policy of the band that for any media appearance, all four members had to be there, even though it was customary for the singer to go, because otherwise somebody might think that I was more important than anybody else. (Once, on the French iteration of MTV, an interviewer directed the questions to me, but when I began to speak, they'd all yell answers at the same time, to drown me out; when we showed up for photo shoots, somebody would loudly say, two or three times, pointedly, "We're not the kind of band where the *singer stands in the front of the picture.*" Though the magazines would always use the ones where I managed to be in front, because people look at any picture of any band and think, *Which one's the singer?*)

But *Lovelines* was done from a studio with only two microphones.

"Please let me do this," said the bass player. *"Please.* I'll never ask for anything again if you let me do this."

The sampler player and the drummer assented, possibly because they knew it would make me supremely uncomfortable. The bass player and I had done an interview in D.C. with a tiny Korean girl from a college paper, and he boasted at length about not wearing underwear.

We were on the show, and there was a call from somebody talking about a threesome and how watching her boyfriend fuck another woman had messed up her relationship irrevocably.

"I've been in a threesome!" the bass player piped in. Like he'd been waiting to say this.

"What was your experience?" asked Dr. Drew.

"It's nice work if you can get it!" said the bass player.

A discomfited pause, and then Dr. Drew moved on from the dead joke. "Many people in relationships experience blah blah blah something something something," he said.

"It's nice work if you can get it!" said the bass player, loudly, as if the joke, repeated, would be funny.

He often spoke in cartoon voices. When he was nervous, he would *only* speak in funny voices. It made for history's most excruciating conference calls. He would do it in interviews, too. He seemed to believe that somebody would think, "Oh, I love that band! The one with the bass player who does *impressions!*"

The very saddest thing about the guy was the way he smoked weed. He said that he had once smoked prodigiously, completely giving his life over to stoner's limbo; then, he had actually given it up for years. But, one day, the sampler player and the drummer and I were smoking in rehearsal, and he took the pipe and said, quite gravely, "If I get really messed up on *something serious*, you're responsible."

From then on, he smoked near constantly. Before and after shows; just offstage right before we played the encore. Before and after eating. Before and after watching a movie. Upon waking and before sleeping. He'd smoke and do interviews in cartoon voices, as I cringed. I invited him over to go through some songs, and he showed up too stoned to play, and without his instrument. We'd land in Copenhagen or Frankfurt or Manchester, and he'd whip out a bag of weed, leading me to believe he'd risked the tour by smuggling drugs across a border. He had a tiny wooden pipe. When he smoked, he sucked at it so hard that his body shook. Literally.

I was backstage in France, talking to somebody about the bass player. "I just have absolutely no respect for the guy," I said.

Then I saw that he was just outside the door.

That night he played the best show I ever heard him play; on every song, he abandoned the usual bass lines and improvised something fierce, you could say *persuasive,* seizing the music, flipping keys upside down, bashing around in weird spots in the rhythm. He didn't always play like this. Sometimes he showed up without his talent—sometimes he seemed to be trying to tell us about his blood sugar by playing badly. At this gig, he *killed.* Wholly in control.

"You think you write songs?" said the sampler player. "If you want people to know your poetry, *stick with us.* We make something out of your *naïve musical explorations*."

There's an old interview out there that I can't find on the internet in which he says (I'm paraphrasing, but you remember insults near verbatim, don't you?): "Doughty's not a musician. He's a *wordsmith*."

Not a musician. On my worst days, comparing my rough guitar scribbles to my bandmates' mastery, I believe this myself. I brought in the chords, the rhythm, the melody, the form, but still: not a musician. Years later, despite a preponderance of evidence to the contrary, I still beat myself up for not being a real musician.

There's another interview out there that I can't find: the interviewer mentions the Howlin' Wolf sample, the Andrews Sisters sample, the Raymond Scott sample, and then asks the sampler player what makes for a great sample. The sampler player answers at length, and quite pedantically, about how he selects and manipulates them. But wait—though certainly the guy's fantastic at what he does, no question—the interviewer guy's talking about *samples that I came up with*.

There's a difference between the sampler player and the other two, in terms of how I had my songwriter's rights hustled out from under me. He really *believed* that on every single song—every one— he's just as much the author as I am. There's certainly a lot of songs that began with loops or parts that he came up with, but that's not the full gist of it. Later in the same interview, he was asked about the songwriting process. He said that he plays samples in the rehearsal room and it *does something* to us. Does something to us. Puzzling. Like I said, sometimes he brought gorgeous loops into rehearsal and songs were derived from them, but that's not what he's saying. In fact, most of the time in rehearsal, he was playing so quietly we could barely hear him; we were always asking him to turn it up. Between songs, he'd be hunched in the corner playing near inaudibly.

At some point I came to believe he was saying he *provoked us subliminally into making music.*

I'd bring in songs that I'd written completely, and he seemed to believe, quite innocently, that I'd improvised them in the room, as he'd improvised his accompanying parts. Like you'd walk into a room, see a lamp, and think: I saw the lamp, *therefore I created the lamp.*

He was prone to tantrums. He'd throw chairs, turn over tables. Once he was driving and the tour manager said he'd accidentally told the sampler player to make a wrong turn; the sampler player went into a rage, swerved immediately, sent the van jolting over the island in the median and into oncoming traffic.

The sampler player's wife worked in a corporate accounting department; she harangued him about money. She would travel with us sometimes. I'd find her with the tour manager's briefcase open, going through our receipts. The sampler player would show up at meetings with our manager and say perplexingly random things: we have to make some obscure financial move; we have to incorporate in Delaware, for instance, because they don't tax companies. But we're not *from* Delaware, we said, how do we justify it to the IRS, if we don't, like, have an office down there or something? He'd sit there blinking, in a panic, and answer in fragments he didn't really understand. His wife had made him memorize something to say in the meeting that he'd recited verbatim.

There were people who disgusted his wife, and she couldn't—or didn't try to?—hide it. Our manager, for instance. In his presence, she'd wear a face, looking like he'd just puked on her.

The sampler player believed himself to be in a psychic death-war with me, with no incident too petty to be part of the struggle. We did a radio commercial, and I remarked that I was surprised that the ad lady made me do so many takes. "That's because you're *naïve!*" he yelled. "You're *naïve,* you're totally *naïve!*"

At the airport, I stubbed out a cigarette on the lid of a trash can and left it there.

"*Litterbug!*" he hollered.

We were in the back of a limousine, headed from a radio show in Queens. I said something innocuously arrogant.

"Do you need me to *wipe your ass for you?*" the sampler player asked. My face went slack. I told him once that this was something my dad used to yell to embarrass me. The sampler player was using it as a psyche-obliterating emotional weapon.

If I disagreed with something, he'd yell at me that I was afraid. "You're *afraid!* You're *so afraid!* Just admit you're *afraid!*" And if I remarked that something he did was unusual, he'd yelp that he had *always* done it, as if I were trying to catch him in an inconsistency and damn him. Late in the band's life, he stopped wearing the mom-bought polo shirts, bleached his hair, and wore an opulent Prada overcoat everywhere, even indoors.

You've really changed how you dress, I said.

"I'VE ALWAYS BEEN A CLOTHESHORSE!" he yelled.

We were having an argument on whether the personality was encoded in DNA. I believed mostly in nurture rather than nature. "That's because you're *afraid! You're afraid!*" the sampler player yelled at me. I tried to say, No, I just think that . . . "Why are you so *afraid?!*"

Laughing, I put my arm around him: Now why won't you let me answer you? He shrank, trembling, as if I were going to punch him.

He believed himself to be a wise patriarch among us. "Doughty, sometimes I'm afraid that the *only* things you're *learning* from me

are about music," he said, solemnly. Once I had yelled at the bass
player onstage, and he issued Solomonic punishment in the van, the
next day, raising his index finger. "Doughty, you can't speak between
songs at the show tonight."

Doing some preproduction, he punished me for an incident I'd
be smarter not to recount. It had something to do with the difference between smoking weed and smoking cigarettes. I had just
quit smoking, and he chain-smoked—he wasn't a smoker—for the
entire session. "Doughty, this is how I'm going to teach you a lesson," he said. I didn't say that it might behoove him to help me quit
smoking, as the entire band was sick of me fouling every dressing
room, every vehicle, every studio with noxiousness.

Our first tour manager was this guy Gus. He was massive and
tall—a high school linebacker who blew off football for punk
rock—with thick black glasses. His left eye went a little funny; he
told me later that a stepbrother had attacked him in his sleep with
a hammer.

The first gig was in D.C. How far is it? I asked.

"Two hundred miles," he said.

Yeah, but, how *far* is it?

If you don't spend a lot of time driving, you measure travel in
hours. If your life is spent mostly on the road, you think in miles.
I was new.

How far to Austin? I asked.

"You're soaking in it," Gus said.

First thing in the morning, at the airport check-in desk.

How are you? I asked.

"Pretty horny!" Gus yelled.

After his stepbrother took the hammer to his face, Gus had no sense of smell. When asked what he liked to eat, Gus said: "I like orange food. Sometimes I like brown food."

"She's *soft*," Gus said, describing his girlfriend. "She's *small*. I like her parts." His shorthand for finding girls was, "Let's go look at some shirts."

Gus drove the van, and I sat shotgun, for most of the tour. We had a two-man pop-culture retrospective. There was an M.C. Hammer song sampling the old ballad "Have You Seen Her?" that began: "Aaaaaww yeah, I'm glad I put this tape on."

"Aaaaawww yeaaaah, I'm glad I ate that sandwich."

Aaaaaaaawww yeaaaaaah, I'm glad I read that local alternative weekly.

"Aaaaaaaaw yeaaaaah, I'm glad I wore that Green Day shirt."

Aaaaaaawwww yeaaaaaah, I'm glad I bought that Trapper-Keeper.

We had this prank call tape that we loved. A guy called the numbers in the classified ads, seeking musicians for metal bands, in the back of an L.A. paper. The prank caller got drunker and weirder as the tape went on. We quoted the nonsensical lines endlessly. *"Don't be all high and mighty just 'cause you're from Illinois, Chris!"* and *"I just want to get my cock fucked and play some guitars with some strings on 'em!"* and *"That's what I want to rock about!"*

At one point, the guy is asked for his phone number, and he says, "My number is seven." This became our answer for everything. What time is sound check? "Sound check is at seven." The stylist for the video called, she's buying wardrobe, what's your shoe size?" "My shoe size is seven."

I was standing outside the 40 Watt Club in Athens, Georgia. There was a tattoo shop next door; I was looking at the flash in the window.

"You're not gonna get another tattoo, are you?" said Gus, disparagingly.

I'm gonna get a seven, I said.

He reached into his pocket, grabbed a hundred dollar bill, and slapped it in my hand.

"Get a receipt," he said.

The seven, in a blue-black circle, is on my left arm, between some Khmer script and a Dahomey image of a bull.

We rode to the Frankfurt airport with a cabbie wearing an ur-German walrus mustache. "Vair are you from?" he asked.

America, I said.

"OH! AMERICA!" he said. "I LOVE AMERICA! Cowboys! Montana! Giddy-up!"

"I can tell you really know how to party," Gus said.

Gus and I could feel the hate burning into our backs from the eyes behind us in the van. We bonded over a mutual childhood in punk rock, and played cruddy punk tapes to annoy them. We'd search out whatever the local alternative rock station was—music so rote and featureless it might as well have been air-conditioning—and blast it.

The first time we toured Europe, it was without Gus. I didn't speak in the van for the entire three weeks of the tour.

The first tours were continuous slogs. The record label was too stingy to pay for a trailer, so the instruments and amps and drums crowded us. We stayed at Red Roof Inns on the outskirts of town, sometimes so close to the airport that the landing-signal lights strobed in our room windows.

One morning I got into the back bench of the van, where the sampler player usually sat.

"That's *my seat*, Doughty!" he said, sounding unstable.

I looked at him.

"It's *very important* that I sit in *the same place every day!*" he yelled. "My *routine* is *very important!*" He elbowed in beside me, and sat on the wheel well, jammed in between me and the window, arms folded, grimacing with tremendous agitation.

The sampler player drove the van sometimes. He'd get particularly stoned for this. Nobody paid any thought to it, because we all assumed that you drove better high. People still believe this. I have friends in their late thirties who believe, genuinely, that weed makes you more perceptive at the wheel. I read about some study on some blog the other day presenting data that, at the very least, it was just as safe as driving not-stoned.

OK. So. I remember this one time doing bong hits with a girl. It was during the first Gulf War. The media were jazzed about there being a war—first real one in twenty years, right?—so they had canceled all the shows and had three anchors talking about the same unchanging information, sans commercials, until two in the morning. Eventually we tired of it; we turned the sound off and listened to CDs, loving the moments when the lips of the anchor synched, almost-kind-of, to the music.

I lit a cigarette. (I smoked three packs a day. A morning pack, an evening pack, and then another pack rationed through the intervening hours; I had ashtrays placed at five-foot intervals in my house.) I put it in the ashtray, then got down on the floor to pick out a CD. Flipping through the rack, I decided I wanted to smoke;

lit a cigarette; put it in an ashtray on a speaker as I got out my copy of *Sign 'O' the Times*. The girl I was getting high with asked if I still had those Pringles from before. Sure, I said. I walked to the kitchen, lighting a cigarette on the way. When I got to the kitchen, I put the cigarette in an ashtray by the sink and opened the fridge. Blinked at the fridge's innards for a second. I got out a grape soda and walked back towards the couch.

Want some grape soda? I asked the girl.

"The Pringles?" she asked.

Oh, right, right. I went back to the kitchen, got the Pringles, came back, handed the canister to the girl, sat down, then decided I wanted to smoke, lit a cigarette, and, upon ashing, discovered the first of the four cigarettes I'd lit in the past three and a half minutes still burning in the ashtray on the end table.

There are a number of people in the world who believe that in this state I could *drive better.*

Weed was sustenance. We were never without it. Really and truly *never.* My bandmates were high constantly, and I resented the hell out of them for it, because weed fucked up my singing, thus limiting my intake. We had terrible days when all we had was shitty weed, shwag weed. Dark agitation would come over us; the other three would actually fight among *themselves.*

Purportedly, weed isn't what people call *physically* addictive—the expression implies bodily withdrawal when you stop using—but to me, the distinction is more or less superfluous. To me, addiction is mostly a state of being inherent in the addict that can translate to things that stimulate the brain's pleasure centers which most people can pick up and put down at will, like sex, sugar, gambling. I have no expertise in the biology of weed withdrawal. I do know that just having *bad* weed discombobulated us in the extreme.

Weed addicts are alone among drug users in that they think their shit is cute. I heard an anecdote once about a guy working in a studio, and there was somebody sleeping under a blanket on a couch; the guy whips off the blanket and gets up, and it's a legendary outlaw country music star. The storyteller goes on, like, "He fired up a joint and whoohoo! Wake-and-bake! Whoohoo awesome!" I don't think that story would go, "The first thing he did when he was awake was chop out a line of blow!" Or, "He downed a shot of tequila when he woke up, 'cause he had the shakes!"

We pulled into New Orleans at 3 AM, and it took the indifferent desk person half an hour to check us in. The drummer and I were rooming together. We went up to the room; the key didn't work. We called downstairs; it took twenty minutes for the maintenance guy to get there, and all he did was jiggle the doorknob and shrug. We went down to the desk to get another room, which took another half hour.

Finally we got into a room; I flopped on the bed. The drummer sat in a chair. "I think I might go to Café du Monde," he said. "For some of them there beignets."

I got under the covers.

"But then, I think, no, it's so late, maybe I'm tired, I should sleep."

Uh-huh, I said.

"But, those there beignets are so good, and I didn't eat almost nothing for dinner."

Yeah, sure.

"But then I think, no, we got the show tomorrow . . . "

OK, I said, through gritted teeth. Whatever you decide to do, I'm shutting off this light and going to sleep.

"Yo, G," he said, genuinely affronted, "there's *two people* staying in this room."

Later I roomed with our sound guy, Lars. His name wasn't Lars, but Gus thought he looked like his name was Lars, and we called him Lars so often that he had to start introducing himself to club staff as Lars, lest they get confused. Lars would go out and get drunk every night, then stumble in, sounding for all the world like he was going around moving absolutely everything in the room a foot to the left.

Lars had this thing about Asleep at the Wheel, the Texas swing band. At the beginning of every tour, he'd find a greatest-hits cassette in a truck stop, and listen to it every time he drove. "I've got miles and miles of Texas!" and "I'm going to boogie back to Texas!" and "Texas something, blah blah something Texas." He'd slip the tape surreptitiously into someone's luggage at tour's end.

(There was this piece of graffiti, by some astute band guy/ existentialist, that you'd see in the dressing rooms of shitty rock clubs all over America—Madison, Des Moines, Lawrence, Champaign, Tucson—expressing perfectly that feeling of dislocation you felt on tour: "I hate this part of Texas.")

The band didn't drink beer—we just smoked weed, and were insufferable snobs about it—but clubs always supplied it in the dressing room, so Lars hoarded it. Eventually we were traveling on a sleeper bus; Lars filled the fridge with beer. Annoyed that he was hogging all the space, we made him take it out; he started storing it in his bunk. He slept on piles of cans.

I journaled in the van to kill time. I left my notebook under the seat. Personally, when somebody I know has a journal, even if they left it under my pillow, I wouldn't read it. The sampler player, however, would take it out and read it when I wasn't around. I'd get in the van, and he'd confront me, saying, intensely, "How dare you say that we _____?"

We did a photo shoot. The bass player had slipped my journal into his pocket when I wasn't looking. In the photos, he was standing just behind me with the journal open, holding it up, with an exaggerated look of fake shock on his face.

Warner Bros. gave us a small budget for gear—new amps, etc. I used my cut to buy a laptop—circa 1995, about as thick as a Tolstoy novel. The sampler player wanted to borrow it for some reason. I blew him off. He kept asking. Finally, I said: That's kind of like asking to borrow both my guitar and my journal, isn't it?

Somebody chided him for not answering an e-mail. "I would have, but Doughty won't let anybody else use that computer that *we bought for him*," he said.

I slept with a girl in Amsterdam who refused to tell me her name. We played a place called the Melkweg—the Milky Way. The crowd was sparse. She was leaning on a column near the front. Her brown eyes floated upward to me as I sang.

Stanley Ray was following us on tour, riding in the same vehicle but staying at cushy hotels. We went back to his room after the show and got high. She followed us.

What's your name? I asked her.

We were walking along a canal. Lurid light was reflected on the water.

"I'm not going to tell you my name," she said, with a tight smirk.

We sat around a coffee table, passing the joint around, but she sat at a dining table just outside the perimeter. I kept looking at her, and she looked back with that same frank, sexy regard. She cocked her head a little, as if to say, Why aren't you taking me by the hand and walking me back to your hotel?

I was scared of the judgment of everybody in the room. I felt ludicrous. I pretended to follow the conversation, but my heart was pounding and I was desperately scheming for a way to get out of there with her. Maybe suddenly everybody would get absorbed in something, and I could escape unnoticed.

At last I said something stupid about having to leave. Stanley Ray looked at me with daggers in his eyes. He hated it when I went off with a girl. I managed to get up, walk over to the Dutch girl, whisper in her ear, and leave. Feeling burning eyes on my back.

So what's your name? I said as we crossed a footbridge.

My head was spinning from the weed. I kept stumbling into the bike path, and I'd hear jingling bells and think, *How pretty*, but they were the bells on bicycles, ringing at the idiot in their way.

"I'm not going to tell you my name," she said.

We came to our cheap hotel. I didn't know how to say, Hey, want to come upstairs? I coughed up some topic, Did you like the show? Or, What's up with the weird breaded cheese sticks you can buy at automats here?

"I think I will come up to your room," she said.

We made out in the elevator, and tumbled into my room. I had her blouse off and was trying to remove the beige bra from her plump, drooping tits, fumbling with the hook. Her pale skin was constellated with dark moles. I unbuttoned her jeans and slipped my hand beneath the beige panties—*What is this old-fashioned underwear doing on such a sexy girl?*—and my hand grazed the soft hair on her pussy's mound. She sat on the bed—a tiny twin bed facing a tiny television set, in a room half the size of a starlet's closet—and pulled me down onto it. She had another joint in her purse, and we smoked it, and then I was just utterly obliterated. My tongue was puffed up, filling my mouth.

Look, I said. Tell me your name. You have to tell me your name.

"It's ugly," she said. "It's Dutch, and you won't like it."

Dutch has a kind of *mish-mish-mush-mush* quality to it, punctuated with long, phlegmy, rolling consonants in the back of the throat. But how bad could it be?

"My name is Breggggggkkkkkgggggggggya," she said.

We fucked for a long time, an hour or more. I got that oceanic feeling of being extremely high; she became just a notion of femaleness. My cock was barely hard. It kept slipping out of her. Finally I came inside her, risk be damned.

I was staring at the ceiling, following the floaters in the liquid of my eyes, and she was talking. And kept talking. She went into a long and dull description of a dream.

"Don't you think that's funny?" she said. "I find this dream to be very funny."

I mumbled something, but I was entirely disinterested.

The sampler player caught a semipermanent fake Dutch accent with which he spoke to everybody he met in Europe, haltingly describing mundane things as if they were American phenomena. "In my country? We have? Something which is called? *Cable television?* We have? Many channels? And some of them? Show what are called? *Music videos?*"

I fell in love with a picture of a singer named Dusha Arangu, from a second-string British band, in *Spin* magazine. She looked like an alien, with long arms and huge black eyes. Her brown skin looked silver in black-and-white photographs. I wrangled a chance to meet her, and sometimes when her band would tour through New York I'd see her.

She had a night off and was staying at a hotel up on Lexington Avenue. It was one of those faceless, beige hotels. I went up to her room; she was lying on her bed. Her shirt rode up, and I could see a sliver of her back above the belt loops of her jeans. I asked her if she wanted to go downtown and eat, see some of the actual New York, but the idea unnerved her—New York's storied scariness? Distrust of me?

Suddenly Dusha Arangu was talking about how she needed a shag, really that's all she needed was a shag, a shag would mitigate her blues, sometimes you just really need a shag, you know?

I rolled up a joint and we smoked. I brought the weed because I thought we might have sex. I could shake off reality and be *there*. Why fuck a goddess not-stoned?

That's probably just a part of it. There's something about me that when I experience an intense feeling, any feeling, good or bad, I have to do something to mitigate it. I have an innate urge to smother exhilaration with medicine. Were I to get a phone call right now saying that I had hit the Lotto, I would immediately need to eat a gallon of sorbet and drink four cups of coffee.

The weed gnawed my confidence. Is that what she meant, shagging me? That's what she meant. But how could she mean that? Look at yourself, Doughty: like somebody could want you? I was saying all the wrong things as fast as I could say them, and then trying to backpedal and saying more wrong things, and I could have flopped onto the wide beige bedspread and kissed her—probably I'd have missed her face on the first two passes, that's how high I was—but I stayed in the chair, and when the long silences had erased any trace of a vibe in that hotel room, she suggested we go out to eat with her manager.

I ate tasteless Tom Kha in a nondescript Thai restaurant. I tried not to look at her. Baffled that I didn't make a move. Thinking that the waitress, the manager, every person in the place was thinking, "Look at this creature. We hate him."

Dusha and I stayed in touch with biennial e-mails for a while; in the last one, she joked about the record company dropping her band. "I've discovered what I was put on this Earth to do, and nobody's trying to help me do it!" she wrote, cheerfully irate. I knew that her band was neither good nor famous enough to survive the cultural sea change. It terrified me.

There was a lull as I typed this, during which I clicked from the word processor over to the browser, and typed her name into one of the social-networking sites: I found five Dashu Garangas, a Shusha Malangu, and a Dasu Ashangu.

I fucked somebody every time I got the chance. The sheer range of women I slept with on tour is striking to me, now: breathtaking women, and women that a desperate man on a lot of speed wouldn't consider as the bar closed at 4 AM.

I fucked an acne-scarred Irish girl in a Nashville Radisson for two hours straight.

I fucked a Danish girl, so fantastically beautiful that I was dumbfounded to be with her, for two minutes.

I fucked a woman from Milwaukee who described her job as "homeopathic oncologist."

I fucked a sandy-haired, pudgy woman who sold t-shirts for reunited classic rock bands; she cornered me at a club in New Orleans, fed me mushrooms, and we fucked, tripping; as I hotfooted out, she cried, "Don't you want to go fuck in the City of the Dead?"

I fucked a hirsute, angular Frenchwoman whose enthralling moans sounded for all the world like an oboe.

I fucked a fat Canadian journalist with a pin-up's face on her obese body.

I fucked another French woman who wore a rubber dress, had a full back-piece tattoo of *The Scream*, called me "zee byoo-tea-fall blond-uh angel," and had a notebook of pencil sketches of the other guys from bands she'd invited home.

I fucked a woman in Boston who, to turn herself on, spoke Russian the entire time.

I fucked a stewardess in Seattle who wouldn't take off her motorcycle boots.

I fucked a black woman nearly half a foot taller than me—I'm six foot one—backstage at a hockey arena in Minnesota; when I complained I was blind wasted, she took me by the wrist and led me to the bathroom, where, kneeling across the toilet from each other, we stuck our fingers down our throats and puked together.

I fucked a gangly, dazzling woman whom I recognized from an episode of *The X-Files*. Though insanely gorgeous, she spoke with the nerdiest voice I've ever heard.

I fucked a girl in Pittsburgh, in the back of a bus, with a boyish seventeen-year-old's body and a middle-aged senator's jowls.

I fucked an Italian woman in Paris who was almost but not quite beautiful enough to be a model; she kept talking, brightly, pathetically, about her future on the runways, and later became the traveling concubine of one of the Backstreet Boys.

I fucked a strawberry-haired girl in a billowing hippie skirt with a *Fargo* accent who, afterwards, pushed upon me a cassette tape of her terrible sludge-rock band.

I fucked the hostess of a country-music video countdown show, whose shoes I complimented; thus, she thought I was a foot fetishist, and mailed me snapshots of her feet for months after—

poolside, with "My Feet on Vacation" written in red marker on the back.

I fucked a publicist for hip-hop acts who wept as I went down on her.

I fucked a curvy goth princess who made squeaking noises.

I fucked a gamine Iowan; I begged her to wear her green-framed glasses while she went down on me.

I fucked a radio programmer who could've dashed my career, but I never called her again, anyway.

I fucked a girl with a high-school-pep-rally sort of personality who ten years later was managing a band with the number one record in America.

I fucked a serene Native American girl who smiled, noiselessly, as she rode me; she made me come, then she made herself a cup of tea and split.

I fucked a woman in a broom closet at the Paramount Theater.

I fucked a girl who picked me up with a friend at an after-party in London; the three of us went back to my suite, drank shitty champagne, then each said, "Yawn, time to go to sleep," then one went and feigned slumber on the couch, the other feigned sleep on the bed, and I had to choose which one to fake-wake-up and have sex with.

I fucked two girls in stairwells within a single week—one in a hotel, one in a mall. When I was with one of them, a pair of stoic tourists passed us as they headed down the stairs; I had my entire hand shoved up her pussy.

I fucked a woman in a limousine in Miami; we swigged tequila, mid-fuck, as the driver lectured us on the social history of Coconut Grove.

Mostly, though, I didn't fuck anybody. The above litany is uninspired compared to that of the average singer of a band that had a video on MTV in the '90s. I was usually too high to pick up girls. Every night that I spent alone, cotton-mouthed, in a hotel room, I loathed myself for loneliness itself.

On the scarce occasions where there was sex without weed, my disappointment was such that I felt I wasn't having sex at all.

In the last days of my drug life, I was unable to fuck, and uninterested besides. When I got clean, I started up again. Immediately, the stripe of women improved markedly. But I was itchingly dissatisfied, dogged by unfamiliar self-reproach. Flippant sex is a wasted man's pastime. At least, I was unable to do it without a basic desire to want to talk to, hang out with, the woman I was with.

I got through it, unaccountably, without an STD, or a vengeful boyfriend wielding a lead pipe outside a motel room.

We did our second record with this producer named Saul Mongolia. Weirdly, he had been the engineer on the James Brown session with the turbine-cave man, where James yelled "New WAVE!" He was a reserved man who wrote his own Zen koans, but he emitted a thorny, gloomily stubborn energy. He looked like a Botticelli portrait of Richard Nixon.

I liked him because he produced pop songs with weird stuff in them—odd sounds and expertly deployed discordances. He had a bunch of tunes all over the radio and MTV, strange and funny songs riding on big, wobbly bass parts, crisply produced and buoyant. He liked to mix things in mono, which I found rakishly eccentric. I met with him before we hired him, and enthused, tangentially, about George Jones records. "Oh, that's what you like," he said. "Drama." He said the way I sang reminded him of a soul singer—my phrasing, my approach. By saying this he won my heart forever.

My band didn't say much; the sampler player spoke of him with resentful deference, like he was talking about a hated, but talented, rival. "The most important thing," he said, "is that Saul Mongolia doesn't play piano on any of our songs." Cryptic portent that I didn't catch.

The other guys mumbled, frowning.

We recorded at the Power Station—I saw Russell Simmons on the street before the first session, and I wanted to ask him where the Power Station was, because Russell Simmons would *actually know*—in a massive room, wooden and vaulted like a Scandinavian church. Somebody told me that Michael Jackson had recorded in another studio, down the street, and had rented out this room just for his dinner break; they installed a circus tent and a banquet table. Currently, in the studio next door, guitar overdubs were being recorded for a Meatloaf record. Meatloaf was not in attendance.

We were loading amplifiers into the studio and the sampler player turned to me with his rattled-animal eyes. "Here we are," he said. "I can't believe we're making a second record."

I gave him a bewildered look. What? Who wouldn't make a second record? Who cares about hate and wretched time spent in a van, *this is the most important thing in the world.*

We tracked everything as a live band, playing all at once. Saul would stop us, and we'd go to the lounge while he tried to get the drummer to play the same beats he'd played in rehearsal. The drummer was changing them—of course—on a whim. Not telling Saul he was changing them—of course—and, as usual, pretending he was playing the same thing as before. Saul complained, when the drummer was out of earshot, that there was no forward motion to his beats. "That weird up-and-down feel that he has," Saul said. In fact, he talked copious trash about each guy when they weren't in the room—sometimes when they were overdubbing; behind the glass in the studio, where they couldn't hear him.

Couldn't tell you if he talked trash about me, too.

Saul spoke incessantly about singles. "I hear this as a single," he would say. Initially this was exciting. *We're cutting a hit record, at last!* I thought. But he said this about every track. He'd want us to play an overdub, and we'd be skeptical; "But I hear this as a *single,*" he'd whine.

Tracking was fraught but efficient. At the end of eighteen days we had all the songs down. I was exultant. I had envisioned our grooves rendered with a sort of New Wave tightness, and here it was. From then on, my job was to keep everybody from wrecking it.

I failed. And I'm a hapless archivist; were I better at it, I would have made sure I walked out of the Power Station on day eighteen with a tape in my hand. I could've put it in a drawer for years, and then released the director's cut.

We mixed the album at Sony Studios, far on the West Side of Manhattan, next door to a hulking, windowless building topped with satellite dishes that served to house machinery for the phone company. Behind the studio was a room that Mariah Carey had furnished when she was mixing there. Couches deep as queen beds, tasseled pillows, gold-filigreed wallpaper. The band lurked in there, getting high, as I sat next to Saul at the console.

Saul was a gossip. He was a *compulsive* gossip; sometimes the candor made me uneasy, and I tried to change the subject, but he was relentless. He told stories about record company presidents' mob ties, which label president had been excoriated by his Japanese corporate suzerains for the raggedy waywardness of his wife, which singer had a meth habit, which radio executive liked to get high on coke at his country house and shoot a pistol at imaginary rabbits, which singer fucked every guitar player she ever worked with—thus, any producer who wanted to finish a record with her had to keep her from fucking the guitar player until tracking was done—which R&B superstars had begged their labels, to the point of tears, to let them step outside racial and musical boundaries and make a rock record or a country record, story upon story of singers who were abject idiots, and, uncomfortably, stories about black artists whom he'd call, *"So* smart. So *smart."*

I thought he was taking me into his confidence. He wasn't. I bumped into the drummer from Sugar Ray a year later, and he asked, "Is it true your bass player once _____?"

We did a song for a sound track during a break in mixing. I had us work with a producer guy who had done some fantastic lo-fi recordings with some outlandish indie bands; I wanted that scratchy sound. "Who is this guy? You didn't ask us," the band guys barked, about a month after his hiring was confirmed.

Contrary to my scheme, the producer guy was taking this opportunity to use a major label budget to up his game and leave his lo-fi rep behind. He booked five days at an expensive studio to record one song. I told him we needed one day, and he laughed me off.

The assistant engineer on the session was a wild ass-kisser. "I can't believe I'm working with *Soul Coughing!"* he kept saying. "You are the *most incredible* band I've ever worked with. You sound *incredible!"*

We did the sound-track song in a day. Like I told the guy. Then, as I was packing up to split, I heard the band playing one of the tunes we had already recorded with Saul.

What's going on? I asked, my heart rate speeding up.

"I just want to *play*," said the bass player. "For the first time in months, I just want to *play*."

I got in the vocal booth, queasy, and we did a take. My bandmates were whoohooing. "Oh my God, *that's* the take, that's the *take!*" said the assistant engineer. "I can't *believe* how good that sounded."

The band started talking shit about Saul Mongolia; we never wanted to work with that guy! Fuck that guy! He doesn't know shit about this band! They talked about how Saul made them *change* things, like beats, like phrasing, how he asked for things to be done over and over again. "That's fucked up!" said the assistant engineer. They had this conversation as I stood there. They didn't look at me.

Soon the lo-fi guy was out, and the assistant engineer was producing the sessions.

We went about rerecording half the songs we'd already done with Saul. Saul was already on edge, because the sampler player—goaded by his wife, the receipt-obsessed former accountant, who made him sleep on the couch when she suspected him of wasting money—had called him up and screamed at him, and I mean *screamed*, for booking a little project studio to try out some sonic stuff without asking the sampler player first. His wife had screamed at him, in turn, about the money. Then Saul discovered that the band was rerecording half the album at a different studio with a different guy. Saul was obliged to show up and watch as the assistant engineer, who was after all an *assistant* and thus no maestro, enthuse, "This is the *best* record I've ever worked on!"

We hired a guy named Henry as an art director for the album. I was sleeping with his officemate, a rosy-cheeked, plump girl who smelled like rosewater and Kool-Aid; we got high and fucked, after hours, on the floor of her cubicle in the grey-carpeted corridors of the record company, Souls of Mischief crackling the woofers on her office stereo.

Henry had a personality like Eeyore. I think he was closeted and had a crush on me; he would call me, complain for an hour that no one at the record company understood his pristine vision, that they were diluting his art merely to *promote bands*. I'd try to get off the phone and he'd *wait-wait-wait* me into staying on for a moment, again and again; the litany of his complaints lasted for hours.

He put me in a lime-green seersucker suit and clown makeup, and had me photographed offering a bouquet of glass roses to the camera. Most of the photos were group shots of the band, taken in a suite at a honeymoon resort in the Poconos; there was a round bed and a heart-shaped tub that Henry filled with pink and white balloons. The sampler player took mescaline, was wandering off, bumping into walls, and staring fascinatedly at his hands. Sometimes he'd walk up to a piece of furniture and lick it. The makeup artist cajoled his tripping self into the makeup chair; the stylist cajoled him into one of the sleek, matching outfits Henry chose; Henry and the photographer cajoled him into the shots. He argued vociferously with Henry about socks; he refused to wear them on principle.

Weeks later, when we saw the proofs of the pictures, the sampler player became convinced that Henry was plotting to put my clown picture on the cover—as if Henry and I, in cahoots, could make the CD cover a picture of me under their noses—though, to be honest, I wouldn't have complained. Henry denied it, but the sampler player called him a liar, repeatedly, and pressed him and pressed him until Henry quit in tears.

(Incidentally, the photographer wrote a video treatment for us: set at a house in Duchess County, the band played Frisbee in tall grass, drank iced tea, sat around a picnic table staring into space: inside, a teenage couple had graphic sex, detailed scrupulously in the treatment. Alas, this was when videos were meant to be on television, not online.)

Saul Mongolia was working at Columbia back when we met yelling Johnny. Apparently Johnny actually thought we were shit and didn't want to sign us. He told Saul, "They're not *stars!*"

Saul related this to me during mixing, vengefully, dropping an insult that wouldn't bloom until later. It burst in my head when I was home, mourning the record, and it broke my heart.

It mystifies me now that he'd want to give *me* a slap across the face, but I guess he just saw me as part of the despicable herd.

In the morning, the sampler player lectured me on being uppity, that it was selfish to have those clown pictures taken without my bandmates in them.

You're not a *star!* I yelled at him.

The wife of the label president, the guy who wanted to build the turbine-powered cave-house, was installed in Henry's place; she put together a stupefyingly ugly mishmash of the photos. The cover image was the top half of the bass player's face. My bandmates approved it. Disgusted, defeated—thinking it right that the hideousness of the whole process be visible right there on the CD cover—I approved it, too.

We toured Europe. In Barcelona, I lay sleepless all night, obsessing about the horrible record cover; it could never be erased. This awful art was permanently lodged in my history. The window was open; I heard the chatter and joy of the Spanish carousers out in the street. I gritted my teeth and obsessed until it was dawn, and time to fly to Portugal.

I was a ball of anxiety and rage. If I had to be near the bass player, not on stage, I didn't hide my repulsion. I treated the drummer like an idiot. I was sadistically condescending to the sampler player. I would have spells when I'd lie awake all night hating them. I railed to friends about how horrible the band was; when I got started, I wouldn't stop, just going on and on, barking about what chronic fuckups they were, not noticing how weary my friends became.

(That's exactly how my mom's rage worked, and how I responded to her. The realization devastated me.)

Gus called my rage-self "Fat Doughty." Because when it gripped me, it was as if I blimped out to three times my size.

I got a chest cold on a European tour, and thought this would be a good excuse to quit smoking. The withdrawal turned me into a monster. The bass player said something bratty, and I screamed GO EAT SOMETHING! four inches from his face. Onstage in Italy, a song was skipped, and I took it as a slight; I threw my guitar down, started screaming, kicked the stage door open and ran into the street, yelling curses.

We played on a prestigious French talk show called *Nulle Part Ailleurs*. I fucked up a guitar part, and thought it was because my bandmates had sabotaged me musically. (Honestly, maybe they had.) I knew I couldn't blow up in the middle of a TV show, but it had so seized me that I was actually shaking. I started cursing; I couldn't stop cursing. I tried to keep it under my breath, but some words I would just bark, involuntarily. The French record company people were staring at me incredulously.

We stopped for a day off in a sun-soaked town by the sea. I was walking down a cobblestone alley, flowers on the balconies, pretty women strolling, and I was filled with hate. I kept thinking, *Look where you are, don't you see where you are? Stop the hate, stop it, stop it.* But I couldn't.

My bandmates were talking about making a video. I had spent a month exchanging e-mails with the video person at the record company. But, utterly disregarding the work I'd done, they had suddenly landed on some half-baked idea. I filled with so much rage that I shut down. I could barely speak. I had to control my movements severely. I felt that if I were to let a little bit of the rage out, my body would explode. We went around to radio stations all day, and at each of them I sat in the corner looking like a chimp shot with a tranquilizer dart. The record company guy ushering us around made desperate, forced jokes to the radio people to draw attention away from the singer's bizarre comatoseness.

"It's scary when you yell," said Stanley Ray. "But it's scarier when you're *quiet*."

In the midst of recording an album, we went to meet with the head of the art department at Warner Bros.; she was going to show us the portfolios of photographers and graphic designers. In the car on the way over, the sampler player said, in a noble tone, "Whenever we visit the record company, I realize that their jobs depend on *us*."

Us? How about I break up this fucking band and you'll see what the fuck *us* means? But I didn't say anything. Again: trying to keep the rage from busting me apart. We went into the art director's office, she passed around the books, I sat there shaking, scowling, unable to get it together to be the slightest bit cordial, professional. "Is there anything . . . wrong?" she asked.

I mumbled an answer that maybe wasn't composed of actual words.

Stanley Ray took me to a club called Fez—in the lounge was a portrait of Oum Kalthoum in a gilt frame—in a basement on

Lafayette Street so deep that the subway overpowered the music when it rumbled under the stage. A band called The Magnetic Fields was playing: never heard of them. Also, this guy Elliott Smith. Never heard of him, either.

The show changed my life. I mean, it *actually* changed my life.

The Magnetic Fields's singer, Stephin Merritt, was sort of troll-like, with a low, croaking voice. The songs were transcendent and the lyrics cuttingly shrewd. I'd say it was an arch take on the best '80s pop, but imbued with huge, tragic heart—but, though apt, that description can't capture the ineffable wondrousness of the songs. He kept giving the sound guy a death stare during the show for something messed up in the monitors.

Elliott Smith was a solo acoustic guy—as I used to be—with a wavering voice; gripping, stringent songs that seemed to *unspool,* lyrics radiating passion and desperation.

There was a blizzard the next day. I walked to Avenue A in a spooky, blank world. There were no cars. I walked in the middle of the white street. The racket of Manhattan was gone. Other-worldly. I heard my boots crunching in the snow, the wind. I went to a tiny record store, picked up an Elliott Smith CD and a Magnetic Fields CD.

It was just a few months after the nightmare of the second album: January 1996. It was time to do something where I only had to rely on myself. I took some songs that my bandmates had rejected—too normal—and wrote some new ones. I named it before I made it: *Skittish.*

There was a producer named Kramer who had made albums by two bands that I loved, Low and Galaxie 500. The spare music floated in a billow of reverb.

So I would abandon the Soul Coughing sound entirely.

Kramer's studio was in an extravagant New Jersey suburb. He had bought a house once owned by a disco drummer of some renown who lost his fortune to a crack habit. There was a studio the size of half a gymnasium, bedecked in shag carpet—floor, walls, and ceiling—with concentric sun patterns set off in slightly beige-er shag.

We cut nearly twenty songs in a single day, just acoustic guitar and voice, me sitting in the darkness of the vast carpeted chamber. Kramer was invisible almost the entire time, seated below the control room window, smoking joints. An assistant did the work. Kramer's one solid contribution was to disallow me from doing a second take on an electric guitar overdub. Yet it sounded *exactly* like I wanted it to sound. It was unmistakably a Kramer record. It was more than the reverb—which was achieved with big echo plates running down the sides of his garage—there was an eerie plaintiveness to the music. It wasn't the assistant: he was a new guy. Kramer put some other parts on after I left, but mostly it's just as it was laid down that day.

I walked with a tape. Later, I tried to get the master tape from him, and he equivocated weirdly. It turned out that Kramer only owned two reels of tape, erasing and rerecording on them, for every record, over and over again.

Stanley Ray was irritated when I played *Skittish* for him. He'd spent a lot of energy keeping us from breaking up. He certainly wasn't going to help me get Warner Bros. to put the record out.

I make inexplicable decisions to get with a certain kind of woman. A short woman, a Latina, an Asian woman, an artist, a non-artist, a woman above twenty-nine but below thirty-three; it's less than a fetish, more like an arbitrary criterion. Maybe my unconscious mind wants to limit my possibilities, and keep me lonely. Lonely is safer. I decided that what I wanted was an English girl: the accent.

I did a vocal on a song by a techno band from Manchester (do you call it a band when all the music making is done in the studio, and live, it's three guys standing behind machines, watching data turn into music, like Laverne and Shirley watching the bottles on the quality control line?). They flew me to Britain to shoot a video.

The set was an abandoned airstrip. The German lady directing the video made me chase a truck, until I was wheezing, lip-synch in front of flame jets, and lie on the cold, wet asphalt. All the band had to do was stand in a triangular formation in their mod jogging suits, looking past the camera, regally.

They had a potbellied guy named Rufus with them, who didn't dress groovily and had an unfashionable mustache. "Do you want some pyooaah?" Huh? "Some pyooaah, mate." Oh, *pure*. Pure what?

"Whizz, mate, pure whizz." Rufus held up a bag of white powder. I didn't know what "whizz" was, but I sniffed some anyway. It was something other than cocaine—probably speed? My displeasure at lying on an airstrip in the drizzle dispelled.

There was a girl cast as the girl in the video. I wasn't that attracted to her. She was, in fact, the German lady's pinch-hitter for the girl role—the model who was originally cast dropped out, and this woman was somebody who worked in a production company the German director was affiliated with. She was a half-Chinese girl with an extremely snooty-sounding English accent, incongruously named Françoise. Her friends called her by the last syllable of that name: Swaz.

How do you say that name when making love to her? Well, it's sexier than the phlegmy charms of Breggggggkkkkkggggggggya.

We were taken to a trailer, where a gay guy with an Afro and circular glasses wielding blush and eye shadow had transformed Swaz into a glamour icon. Her sudden transformation into a beauty was disquieting.

In the makeup chair, I said, They want me made up to look like a dead man.

"Really?!"

No, I said, not really.

He got sullen.

We were seated in the cab of the truck I had chased, for shots in which I lip-synched while Swaz pretended to drive. They shot one angle, then another from the side, then one from the front, then a close-up. Then the German lady said, "And now it is time you and Swaz vill have a snog."

We were startled. Did they tell us beforehand that the job description included making out with a stranger? Cameras rolled.

I leaned in and gave her a real kiss. My lips brushed hers, and I budged in closer. Her mouth yielded. A long, soulful, all-enveloping kiss.

In the car back to London we talked about poetry, and then we met the next day; she came over to my hotel room and took a shower with the bathroom door open. I watched her soap herself up, scrub herself off.

At some point in the six hours we hung out, it was decided that I was going to abandon New York and come live with her in London.

I went back to Brooklyn. She called me, blind drunk, when I was throwing my stuff into boxes, and slurred over and over, "Are you going to save me? Are you going to save me?" Unnerving. I told her to stop, she kept repeating it, I pleaded with her, Stop, please stop, but she kept saying, "Are you going to save me? Are you going to save me?"

I boxed up my life and went anyway.

Swaz and I would get high and say words back and forth to each other.

Swear, I said.

"Swah," she responded.

There, I said.

"Thah," she responded.

We went to see a refurbished version of *Star Wars*. I learned that the English put sugar on their popcorn, and they ran a parade of arty commercials before the previews.

The movie started. "Is Han Solo Luke's brother?" Swaz asked. "Or was it—Obi Wan Kenobi is Luke's uncle? . . ."

No, I said. Darth Vader is Luke's father.

"DARTH VADER IS LUKE'S FATHER?!" cried Swaz in the middle of the theater.

I was a terrible boyfriend. I'd get home from tour and not want to do anything but lie on the couch—of which Swaz had two, called the Major Couch and the Minor Couch. I sat on the Major Couch, smoked weed, and ate the Cumberland bangers that Swaz cooked for me.

Swaz was a terrible performance poet. There's a certain kind of would-be artist who chooses poetry because of its materials: to make a film, you need a bunch of people, a camera, lights, a script; to write a song, you need a guitar or a piano, and you need to learn how to play; to write a poem, you need a piece of paper and half an hour. Swaz's performance involved undulating while she intoned in a ridiculous sexy-fairy voice. In poetry, she found a way to vend her sexiness.

She performed around London, sometimes just a few blocks from our place. I could've gone and been good and clapped and kissed her. But I never went. Lousy, lousy boyfriend.

Since then, she's become a kind of quasi-academic. She gives performance poetry workshops all over Britain, and the world: Bogotá, Sarajevo, Dublin. Vending your sexiness works in any medium.

At that time in Britain, it had become near impossible to find good drugs, unless it was cocaine. Swaz had the country's last decent Ecstasy connection, a bug-eyed, chubby guy named Alfonso who seemed totally hapless and sometimes wore a bolo tie over a Hawaiian shirt.

I was in a club, sitting on the floor, rolling my jaw around and obsessively feeling my skull. A guy came up, shouting over the music.

"Whadeegetyapah," he said.

Ha ha, what? Ha ha.

"Where did you get your pill," he repeated.

Alfonso!

"What? Who?"

This guy named Alfonso. Ha ha ha.

"Where is he?"

He's, ummm, I don't know, he lives . . .

"Did you get it here?"

No, no, we called him. My eyes crossed and uncrossed.

"You don't give a fuck, do you, you daft cunt?"

Ha ha ha.

"You fucking twat, you don't even know where the fuck you are, do you?"

Ha ha ha. Eyes rolling and rolling.

(I don't do E anymore. I'll hang out with you when you're on E. But if you start rubbing your face and telling me how amazing your face feels, I *will* make fun of you.)

Alfonso called, sounding coked up and disturbed. He said he wanted to be an artist, he wanted to design CD covers; you make CDs, can I design your CD cover?

Um, Alfonso, why don't you bring some art over next time?

"Can I come over right now?"

Ah, no, right now we're . . . um, we're . . .

"I want to make a positive change in my life," Alfonso said. You could hear his heart pounding in his throat.

Swaz told me that she heard voices. She had sudden, bug-eyed outbursts: she'd burst into tears and shriek at me. She had an evil streak. She'd say something innocuous that would devastate, and she pretended she wasn't trying to hurt me.

I'd go back to North America to play shows, mostly in brown, cold cities on flat terrain; at the end I'd fly from Columbus or Cedar Rapids back to London. I would be exhausted by the weeks on the road with the band that hated me. I smoked lots of weed and barely wanted to move off the Major Couch. Swaz mocked me cruelly for being crippled. She was a versatile mocker.

We went out to clubs, taking Alfonso's pills. We heard all the great jungle DJs of London, a scene in full flower. We dropped the pills, the high came up, and I desperately tried to get away from

Swaz. I was frightened when my druggy eyes looked into hers.
She reached out and pulled me to her face. She kissed me. She'd
been dutifully swigging water, as a cautious E-taker is supposed
to: the inside of her mouth was cold.

I fled, and went around asking for sips of peoples' drinks,
greeting everybody with ostentatious fake love, being the most
annoying person on Ecstasy you could imagine. Particularly considering how unapologetically E'd-up I was, when everybody else
in the place was probably on adulterated cocaine.

When I got back to Swaz's, and the high was coming off, I
hated myself for the idiotic, chemical affection.

She poured me a glass of Scotch to ease the internal clatter. I refused, but she was persistent. I drank.

It tasted like adulthood. *This is really nice,* I thought. The jitters
smoothed.

I thought: *As coffee is a vehicle to help me transport from the sleeping
state to the waking state, maybe alcohol is something to carry me from
waking back to sleep again.*

I flew to East Lansing for two weeks' opening shows for Dave
Matthews.

I put one of Alfonso's pills on my amp during sound check at
the Boston Garden. Halfway through the set, between songs, I
stepped back to the amp and gulped. I wanted to be coming up as
soon as the show was over.

We played to a crowd that had mostly not shown up yet. There
were pockets of people in the chairs on the arena's floor—people
who paid big bucks for the good seats—who mostly drank their
beer, looking bored. The people in the cheap sections were more

likely to show up for the opening act: after the tunes, we'd hear a muted roar from the back of the hall.

I began to feel the glow. We clambered down the stairs and into the strange middle ground behind the stage, with big road cases gathered together like cattle, cables running from the stage to generators somewhere, Dave Matthews's techs in states of distraction. By the monitors there was a tiny TV screen hooked up to a camera, currently showing an empty drummer's stool. The guy's kit was so huge, jungled with cymbals, chimes, tom-toms, that they needed the TV screen to communicate.

There was one lonely guy sitting at a computer. His job was to feed lyrics into the teleprompter. I thought: *Who does this guy drink with when he gets on the tour bus at night?*

Our dressing room was a visiting-team locker room. There were empty massage tables and stationary bikes; the lockers had been covered with white sheets. A guy from Warner Bros. stood by the sandwich platter. He had horn-rimmed glasses and an aw-shucks, kid from the cul-de-sac, Encyclopedia Brown demeanor. The high ratcheted up and I started to think he realized I was oozing into another state of being. He seemed weirdly menacing. He engaged me in some good-show-excited-for-New-York-tomorrow? chat; my eyes must've been ping-pong balls.

I got more googly-eyed as he chatted; I hopped up on one of the stationary bikes and started pedaling. Idly, then furiously. I stopped pedaling, and the force of the exertion shot an intense blast of drugs—when you're on E, and you move intensely, then stop, you feel like you've ignited. This is why E goes so perfectly with dancing. My body shook in pleasure and disorientation. Encyclopedia Brown was still talking. I dismounted and walked off midsentence.

Dave Matthews took the stage to grand hurrahs. I walked out of the barricades and into the crowd, looked up at the people in the stands, the spotlights tracing over them. The whole place seemed to be breathing in unison.

I was grabbed by a girl in a hippie dress and pulled into the seats. "Dance with us!"

Are you on E? I asked idiotically.

"No! We're drunk!" she said. My bones were noodles.

I felt like a vice-presidential candidate. I walked the rings of the stadium, slapping hands with fans here or there who recognized me. I was by myself, on drugs, grinningly holding up the all-access pass on a lanyard around my neck to security as they stepped up to block my way. They parted resentfully. This is what I wanted to do with my life. Be outrageously high, be absolutely alone except for the random high fives and yelped *You're awesome*'s.

Our bus was parked with a dozen other buses in a concrete chamber beneath the stadium. One weirdness of an arena tour is that you go to sleep on the bus at night as it heads to the next show, and then wake up inside a hockey stadium, in a giant grey room—some of them big as a double football field—lit with yellow fluorescence, neither in daytime nor night, in the loud thrumming of all the buses' generators. Once you had your coffee in you, you had to clamber all over the arena searching for an exit to see what kind of day it was.

Our bus was rented from a company that painted the same murals on all their buses—a beach scene, in a purple sunset, with gentle waves, driftwood, and a beached rowboat—with subtle variations of the elements in the picture, like a puzzle in *Highlights* magazine. There were several buses from the company on this tour. After one night, early on, when I looked in panic from bus to muraled bus, not knowing which one was mine, I memorized an aggregation of seagulls to know which one to get into.

As the bus pulled out of the arena that night, I was in the back lounge of the bus. The E began to wear off, and in grief I gulped another. I came up as the sun came up. Not knowing what else to do, I took off all my clothes. I lay on the banquette, savoring the ever-diminishing buzz. Each time I felt it subside a level, I would get up and manically improvise weird calisthenics, causing a rush. Each rush less satisfying than the one before it.

In New York, we played Madison Square Garden. I had one E left. Dave brought me onstage to do something with the band—I improvised an onomatopoetic melody: frighteningly manic, scary fake joy. I danced circles around Dave—literally. I'm guessing now that every member of the band was staring at me with bayonets in their eyes, this freak who had seized their stage. I was oblivious. I introduced each of them in detail—though I couldn't remember some of their last names—by their star sign and their affinity for hiking or swimming. The audience—fucking sold-out Madison Square Garden—looked like a sea of love lapping at the stage.

The second night I smoked weed: the jam was more contemplative. I scorned myself for wasting that one E on the drive out of Boston. Luke had come to the show, and I took him on my customary perambulation. We stopped on one of the upper levels to watch the music a little. There was a fifteen-year-old hippie girl dancing. She turned around and saw me. Her eyes lit up. I realized that I was wearing the same clothes I had worn onstage with Dave, and having essentially been in the Dave Matthews Band, I was a celebrity. I playfully shushed her: don't reveal my secret identity. She screamed. In seconds I was dogpiled by fifteen-year-old girls. Like a Monkee. Luke yanked me to safety.

After a year of cold London rain, my heart was sick; I wanted to be in the sunshine. Gus was from Pensacola, so I went there to rejuvenate. He put me up with a guy named Nick, one of his henchmen. (Gus had dudes in Pensacola he called henchmen: Henchman Nick, Henchman Tim, Henchman Ramel.) So I went down to the Florida Panhandle to dry my soggy soul in Nick's spare bedroom.

It's said that Pensacola isn't really Florida, but rather the part of Alabama that they put in Florida. The houses around the near-deserted downtown were battered shotgun shacks. Nick's small house was under a giant pink overpass; the cars on I-10 whooshed towards Jacksonville or Mobile. I had mailed myself eight different varieties of weed on the Amsterdam stop of the European tour right before I moved there, so I had this little rainbow of marijuana—yellow-haired buds next to purplish ones next to ones with a sheen of silver crystals. I got stoned and sat on the porch writing songs, as the freight train rumbled past on tracks thirty yards from the house.

(A couple of years later, Nick briefly worked for Soul Coughing on tour, tuning instruments poorly. He remarked about one tune, "I remember that one—you wrote it on my porch!" My bandmates glared disgustedly.)

Nick's name wasn't really Nick. He had picked up some girl by pretending he was an English guy named Nick, and the lie snowballed. For years, he had to use the accent around her. Nick was a devoted cigarette smoker, merrily acknowledging the deadliness. This was when I was still smoking; hanging out with Nick was celebrating tar.

(I smoked three packs a day. Ridiculous. It was like a job. I woke up, and began the work of the first pack. It was a repetitive, manly task, like getting up early every day to chop down pine trees.)

Nick owned Sluggo's, the punk rock bar in Pensacola. It was on Palafox Street, which was the main drag until the malls came along. Most of the storefronts were empty, except for a knick-knack shop run as a vanity project for a navy officer's wife, and a uniform store. Sluggo's didn't draw a sailor crowd; the sailors went to a bar done up as an ersatz New Orleans house with a wrought-iron balcony. Pensacola was a born-again stronghold; occasionally at the fake New Orleans there'd be demonstrations against moral turpitude. They held up signs with pictures of Hell and Bible citations. The protesters stayed politely across the street from the bar, obeying city ordinances. When 8 PM came around, they put down their signs and dispersed.

Sluggo's was threadbare, dirty-carpeted, furnished with ratty couches, festooned with band stickers. Nick's sound engineer and factotum was a guy who'd dropped out of the air force and drifted to Sluggo's. His name was Ryan, but he went by the rapper-inspired handle Ry Moe Dee. The club survived on the local alternative community, which was oddly substantial, and the happenstance that when touring acts had a gig in Tampa, and then a gig in Birmingham or New Orleans, they needed someplace to play in between. You'd see British bands, feted in the hyperbolic U.K. music publications, bewildered to be playing this dingy joint in front of five people on a Tuesday night.

A San Francisco queer-punk band played. The bass player pulled out a floppy dildo and waved it around between songs, talking about how he hadn't gotten laid, and thus it had gotten much usage on the tour. The audience squealed in delighted shock. I bumped into him after the show. He did a double take; he was a Soul Coughing fan. "What are *you* doing here?!"

Nick also had a rave bar around the corner called Bedlam, where in the early evenings a fat guy on Ecstasy would flop around, shirtless, on the empty dance floor, his folds jiggling in the mirrored walls. There was this weird thing where half the people in Pensacola called Sluggo's "Sluggo," and Bedlam "Bedlam's."

A guy named Kent lived in Nick's garage. He was known around town because he'd done an airbrush portrait of David Lee Roth on a t-shirt and had given it to him backstage at a Van Halen show; D.L.R. actually wore it, with the sleeves cut off, in the video for "Jump." Kent was quiet and strange, and was supposedly involved in twelve-step programs, which creeped me out. There was a picture of him tacked to the wall in Sluggo's—among other pictures of the friends of the bar—twice his current size, bloated and red. He left a copy of Caroline Knapp's *Drinking: A Love Story* lying around, and I read it one afternoon, doing bong hits between chapters.

I met a lot of girls in Pensacola. Slept with some. None of them smoked weed, and were thus unsuitable for repeat visits. How many beautiful women did I blow off because they didn't get high?

We did a package tour sponsored by a clothing company; they set up a little concourse of booths in the back with snowboarding gear on display, and complementary energy drinks. The booths were run by a crew of post-collegiate kids who were so excited to be traveling in a tour bus with a bunch of rock bands they could've shit themselves. Every night was a party on their bus; they'd entice off-duty strippers to come aboard and get drunk with them, then their alpha, the pack leader—so selected for his huge cock—would get one to suck him off while the fratty rabble applauded.

Naturally the bands used the concourse kids' bus as the party salon, keeping the riffraff off their own buses. There I touched a set of fake tits for the first time.

Off-duty stripper: "I just got them!"

Me, taking them in my hands: They're so FAKE!

I ended up in an irritating threesome with her and one of the concourse kids, a guy with a pharaoh's beard and gigantic raver pants. He ate her out while I kissed her, and she made out with me, dully. Then we switched. I was better at eating her pussy than the other guy; she kissed him passionately, thrilled.

The headlining band had a reputation of self-righteous sobriety. The strongest item on their rider was a package of Pixy Stix, which they would rip open, downing the baby-blue powder in one gulp, while laughing at us as we stumbled, wasted, from our dressing room.

Their singer was this veteran of half-assed alternative rock bands who had finally hit pay dirt, sinking hit after hit. Casual conversation with him usually involved radio-industry-ese, phrases like "It got great phones," and words like *spins* and *adds*. There was almost always an ultra-hot girl waiting for him by the side of the stage. I figured out his racket; for their encore, the roadies would troll the crowd, taking girls by the hand to the stage and then lifting them up on it, along with a few token boys. The crowd laughed and jumped around to the song, and then, as they were filing off the stage, the singer would grab his selected girl by the wrist, just as she walked behind the speakers and out of the audience's view.

I thoroughly player-hated the guy. Plus, what good is trumpeting your pious sobriety if you're just going to be addicted to something else?

The other act on the bill was the rapper Redman. I met him when I opened the door to the back lounge of the concourse kids' bus and happened upon his ass as he was fucking a plump girl who still had her shirt on. Rock bands were required to maintain a dour decorum-of-authenticity, but Redman's bus was wrapped with a gigantic ad for his album. His record company hired street-teamers; as he played, they stood out in the crowd with placards, waving them up and down.

He had two hype men, twins whom they called "the twins"— they interjected "yeah" and "uh-huh" into microphones while Redman rapped the verses—a DJ, and a white guy who was selling mushrooms. The entire party tripped for most of the tour. Mushroom-fed Redman felt indestructible—he took a fake swing at a security guard at a show in Idaho; his fist swooshed inches from the guy's face. Then Redman just wandered away.

At a show in Montana, Redman was busted for weed; one of the tour managers talked the constables out of taking him in. On a tour with fifty, maybe sixty techs and musicians and decadent energy-drink purveyors, most of whom carried some kind of contraband, the *one guy* who gets busted is *the black guy.*

Redman liked a song of ours, and one night just showed up on-stage with a mic, singing the chorus. The next night he came on and did the chorus and the little chant section after the chorus. The next night, he added a freestyle. By the time he left the tour, he would come on and do two freestyle verses, two choruses, and a throw-your-hands-in-the-air chant; we'd end the song with the simulated death of Redman in a hail of sonic gunfire.

He left because he got a better offer. Rock agents would've scrupulously turned down the money because they'd committed to the lower-paying tour, but hip-hop agents were more cutthroat. He was replaced by the Black Eyed Peas—then unknowns—who were supergeeky and wanted every member of every other band they could round up to join them for a big jam at the end of their set. I'd say, "Sure," and then would find someplace else to be when the time rolled around. *These guys are going nowhere,* I thought.

The buses traveled as a caravan. One night, at 3 AM, all the buses stopped for an hour. We found out that the concourse bus had seen a car flip over, tumbling into a ditch. One of the concourse kids was trained as an EMT, and he ran out onto the median and held the head of the driver up, keeping his broken neck aligned.

Apparently he cracked corny jokes for twenty minutes until the ambulance arrived, to keep the guy from going into shock. "He'll probably never walk again," said the kid, "but it was a good night."

I was supereffusive with the EMT kid, called him a superhero. The next night, and every night for the remainder of the tour, he would come into our dressing room—uninvited—drink our beer, grin cheesy grins, and make schmoozy, repetitive small talk about the night he saved a life.

We played New York on the tour's last night. I met a cute blonde girl from the hedge-fund belt of Connecticut and brought her back to my apartment. I crushed Ecstasy pills, cut the powder into lines, and we sniffed them up.

I put Marvin Gaye on. "Why are we listening to this *old* music," the girl said. "Do you have any Sublime?"

I kept sniffing the lines, and she, nervously, kept sniffing them alongside me, trying to keep up. As we were fucking, I noticed she was frowning. I came, and she ran to the bathroom, where she lay on the cool floor moaning.

What do I do if this girl dies? I thought.

No compassion.

"I'll be OK," she kept saying.

I went up on my roof, naked, freaked out on the E, feeling radiant under the New York sky, which had been turned green by the city's ambient light.

When we went to Los Angeles to make our third record, I had more or less given up. In Pensacola, I'd taken recordings of the drummer, made in rehearsal, loaded them into a sampler, looped them, and wrote songs to them. In the studio, I laid the loops down as a scratch track, recorded my vocal over it, and then went back to the Magic Hotel, a place of dingy apartments around a pool—there were porn shoots in the suite next to mine—next door to the magicians' clubhouse, the Magic Castle. The rest of the band came up with parts and recorded them to the track while I was gone. I mostly didn't care.

I was beset with migraines, almost daily. In the midst of recording, I'd see a spot in my vision, shaped and colored like a diamond, shimmering. It gave me a psychedelic blind spot—I'd look at my hands and see fingers missing, look at myself in the mirror and the left side of my face would be blank. Over an hour or so, the diamond spot would grow, I would get blinder, eventually the whole world would look strobe lit. Then the pain and nausea came on. I spent much of the sessions lying in my dark room in the Magic Hotel, trying not to focus on the horrendous throb in my temples, popping Valiums and Ambiens. Occasionally getting up for dry heaves.

An L.A. friend took me to the Formosa, a shabby Hollywood bar left over from a '40s heyday as a star magnet. She introduced me to a gorgeous friend; we went out for drinks, then parked her Nissan in front of the Magic Hotel and made out. The next time we were meant to go out, I had a migraine. I called her with regrets. Then the next time: the same. The third time our plans were preempted by a migraine, I didn't even call her. I was too embarrassed. She came to the Magic Hotel and called my room; I unplugged the phone. She left a bewildered message, called the next day, called the next.

I was walking down Hollywood Boulevard, which I did every day to the studio, just to confound conventional Los Angeles behavior. I was stopped on the corner, waiting for the light, and a powder-blue pickup truck with three Mexican guys came screeching to a halt directly in front of me. "Hey, clown! Clown! You fucking clown! Ha ha, fuck you, you fucking clown!"

I turned around and saw a guy in a clown suit standing there looking embarrassed.

Stanley Ray didn't *believe in* my migraines. "They're not that bad. It's just an excuse for you to get out of the studio," he said.

We went out to see a band we both adored, after the session. When I walked into the club, I saw that the head of the opening act's singer was missing. It had been blanked out in my brain by an oncoming migraine. I told Stanley Ray.

"Well, we're already here, don't even *think* I'm going to drive you home," he said, indignantly.

I waited for an hour in front of the club for a taxi, the diamond spot in my eyes slowly growing.

Stanley Ray and I went to a comedy show at Largo, on Fairfax, every Monday night when we were in Los Angeles making the record. Patton Oswalt, David Cross, Paul F. Tompkins, Sarah Silverman, Todd Barry, all these amazing comedians playing this small room. The then-unknown Jack Black's Tenacious D would debut at that show, alas, the week after I left California.

Stanley Ray and I got stoned before the show in the car. We were both at the point where getting high barely got us high: we just got paranoid and groggy. "Why do we do this?" said Stanley Ray. "It doesn't make anything better. Isn't that what addiction is, when you keep getting high, but it doesn't do anything, and you don't want to, but can't stop?"

What? I said. That's *ludicrous*.

Amusingly, Saul Mongolia was appointed the head of A&R. I met him at his office—Warner Bros. Records was in a big wooden building that looked like a ski lodge from 1974—and spat bitterly about how terrible the tracks were, that I didn't give a fuck. I expected him to sympathize. But now his job was to make sure the acts on his label recorded something the radio guys at the label could use.

"You're still going for a *single*, aren't you?" he asked, disconcerted.

Um, yeah, I said, realizing on the spot that I had to lie.

We had a break. I went back to Pensacola with the understanding that I had to write a single. I got high, took Valium to soothe the paranoia, wrote guitar parts, wrote melodies, ordered Papa John's twice a day. Our manager kept calling and asking if I was writing.

I was tortured, freaked out, convinced that the jig was up, that Saul Mongolia would crumple us up and throw us out if I didn't come up with the goods. As I was grinding through chord progression after chord progression, I wondered what my bandmates were doing at exactly the same time.

I wrote a couple of good ones, one of which had the chorus "I don't need to walk around in circles." I was talking about the endless stupid cycle of life in the band. The first verse referenced, obliquely, the Winchester Mystery House, where the widow of a rifle magnate, convinced that the ghosts of those killed by her husband's guns were coming for her, built endless rooms and extensions on her mansion—she kept having them built until the day she died—staircases going nowhere, superfluous corridors, all to disorient the evil spirits. "When you were languishing in rooms I built to foul you in," went the first line of the song.

It would remind radio programmers of Sugar Ray's "Fly," and Sublime's "What I Got," giant hits that, hilariously, were both produced by Saul Mongolia. "Circles" was the biggest radio song Soul Coughing ever had.

It was 1998. I moved back to New York. I looked at places in Brooklyn, but realized that I couldn't get drugs delivered out there. So I got a place I couldn't afford on Rivington Street in Manhattan.

Luke, now living on Avenue B, had a roommate with a great drug delivery dude: the tackle box man. His tackle box had compartments of every drug you could want: Vicodin, cocaine, Ecstasy, Quaaludes (Quaaludes! In 1998!), weed, those skinny, four-dose sticks of Xanax—everything but heroin (because heroin is *bad,* right? I mean, you're OK being fucked out of your mind on five different drugs every night of your life as long as you're not on *heroin*). Alas, the tackle box man had a very specific clientele and didn't like the looks of me. So I went to Luke's house whenever I needed something that my own drug delivery guys wouldn't get.

(Luke and I had the same favorite scene in *The Godfather:* the one in which the singer Johnny Fontane—whom the Godfather sprang from a contract by having the severed horse head put in the bed of his studio boss—is asked by Al Pacino to repay the favor: appear at his casino in Las Vegas. The look on Johnny Fontane's face says he realizes it's bad for his career, but Johnny says, "Sure, Mike. I'll do anything for my godfather, you know that." He says it without resentment: he's loyal, selflessly obedient. *Duty, Honor, Country:* the West Point motto. We absorbed it.)

I returned to the studio with "Circles" and was spiteful; as we mixed the album, my bandmates increasingly contemptuous of me, I was vindictive; I struggled to get the artwork done and was despondent.

In the album photos, I wore a hat. The graphic designer used a miniature silhouette of me in an upper corner of the back cover as a graphics detail; the bass player called him up and told him to shave the hat off the graphic, lest somebody examining the back cover with a magnifying glass—who remembered I was the hat guy in the inside photo—would recognize me.

My bandmates told me they wanted the credits to simply be our names, not identifying the instruments we played. Meaning, nobody would look at the CD and know which name was the singer's.

Now I was in a constant state of shivering rage.

Stanley Ray brought us up to a meeting at the record company offices in Rockefeller Center. Our manager was there.

"Before we continue with this, Doughty," said the manager, "we want to be clear that you want to be a part of this."

"Things are really good, and you don't care, it's like you *want* to be a problem," said Stanley Ray. "You can't be unhappy. *I'm* the one who's allowed to be unhappy." He actually said this.

"Don't be stupid, G," said the drummer, "you don't know how good you have it. We don't want to hear you complain anymore."

The other two band guys glared at me with their arms crossed.

I stood up, wobbling. Tears were coming on. I couldn't break down in front of these hateful people. I stumbled towards the door. Stanley Ray followed me. "You can't leave," he said, urgently, kind of bug-eyed.

I went to the bathroom, got in a stall, and let the sobs out. It was a marble bathroom; the sobs pinged off the marble at outrageous volume. I heard somebody come in. I didn't want, like, the new guy in the marketing department, or whoever it was, to hear me. So I pulled the sob in, and gulped it down, and my eyes went dead. I sat through the rest of the meeting, waxen, lifeless.

So here I was in this universe where I was the problem; I was the devil's asshole at the center of Hell. Stanley Ray, the manager, Encyclopedia Brown, even the roadies, were, like, What the fuck is wrong with Doughty? Why can't Doughty just get it together? Wouldn't everything be fine if Doughty just chilled the fuck out?

None of these guys considered that, maybe, if I called it a day, maybe they'd be out of a job. It didn't occur to me, either.

After that meeting, they got me to a shrink. I went up to one of those doorman buildings on the Upper West Side with shrinks in every nook on the first five floors. If you go to a certain part of the Bowery, around Delancey Street, every other building has a lighting store; there's a part of Hell's Kitchen that's all wholesale gardening supplies; there's an area on Broadway around Twentieth Street filled with stores selling hair for weaves. As there is the lamp district, the flower district, and the wig district, so there is the shrink district.

I mentioned casually, within the first fifteen minutes, that I smoked weed: not problematically, I just needed it to make music and have sex.

"Oh," she said. "There's twelve-step meetings down on St. Mark's Place. You might be interested in what goes on there."

What? What the *fuck*? Is this what shrinks do, just immediately assume anybody into drugs is an addict? Recommend the corny self-help jive without the slightest understanding of your nuances?

I kept showing up for therapy, even as I was becoming ever more disconnected to my life. She'd ask me what was going on, and I'd say, Nothing. Oh, wait, tomorrow I'm flying out to go on tour for a couple months.

"Tomorrow?! Where are you going?!"

I don't know.

"You don't know?"

No, I'm getting picked up at one, and then I'm flying to— um—Arizona? I think.

"Where do you go after Arizona?"

I don't know.

"You really don't know?"

No.

I was waking up in the morning, trying to figure out where to get coffee; I'd lie in bed until the late afternoon, unable to decide.

I forgot how to take out the trash. A city of trash grew around the wastebasket, empty bags of Chinese delivery food that I used as supplemental garbage receptacles. They surrounded the trash can, five bags deep.

How do people do this? I thought. *How do people take out the garbage?*

My shrink got out of her chair and sat on the floor. "I'm a bag of Chinese food," she said. "What am I trying to tell you?"

I laughed. She persisted.

"Talk to me, I'm the Chinese food, what am I saying?"

They sent me to the shrink because they figured that, naturally, she'd go, How can this guy not realize what a fantastic band he's in? Why would he ruin everybody's fun? Let's cheer him up and set him right.

She did nothing of the sort. She was leading me to realize that I could, when the moment was right, leave the band, get out of this freakish, abusive relationship.

When I first saw the shrink, I demanded antidepressants. My shrink sent me to this guy uptown whom I loathed, but he gave me drugs. I even duped him into prescribing some Xanax. The antidepressants worked, but I lost the ability to have orgasms. It was worth the trade: for a good long moment, the crushing depression slightly eased. I could function, with the raging shake downgraded to a quieter ticking.

I got a gig writing a pseudonymous column called *Dirty Sanchez* for the *New York Press*. It was a venting of the ugly things I'd learned about the music business, an expression of self-hatred, of how cheated I felt that, in attaining my dream of rock stardom, I ended up in this horrible band of torturers and cockroaches. Mostly, though, I did it because I needed the money. Despite our putative success—playing to 2,000 people a night, selling hundreds of thousands of CDs—when I moved back to New York I wasn't making enough money to get by in Manhattan.

It was a good time to be a satirist. The music world had gone goofy and bizarre: this was the golden era of the boy bands. I went to Times Square for an NSYNC appearance on MTV's *Total Request Live,* amazed by the sound of the girls screaming. One girl would start screaming on some high-pitched note, then another would up it to a higher note, then another higher, and all the screaming girls gravitated to the same note, while some ultra-screamer in the bunch found a note even higher than that, to waver above the din. The most inspired avant-garde oratorio I ever heard.

I exulted over the triumph of choreographed fluff over angsty, earnest alternative rock. The diminishing rock stars whined about the death of realness; I always felt trivialized or ignored by them, so I dashed off column after column reveling in their self-pity.

The *New York Press* was started in 1988 by a guy who wrote a column called *Mugger;* in menacing '80s New York, this was audacious, but in clean, peppy '90s New York—where screaming teenage girls could gather safely in a Disney-renovated Times Square—it was an anachronism. He was a mean-spirited Republican from Long Island who grew up a Red Sox fan—to grow up a Red Sox fan on Long Island bespeaks a long career of calculated assholery. The editor was John Strausbaugh, who wrote about UFOs, maverick artists, angelically insane fringe-theorists, defiantly weird old-guard downtowners, blackface minstrelsy, and the emergence of Elvis-ism as a legitimate faith. He wrote a spellbinding allegory of alien abduction as the experience of a trout, caught, then thrown back into the lake. He coached me in the delicate art of interviewing the insane before I went out to Crown Heights to interview an old man who wrote a book listing the 223 ways to tell whether someone is possessed by demons. Strausbaugh was the heart of the thing. The joy of it was the friction between him and the incongruous Republican-ness, but most people identified the paper simply with *Mugger*'s gleeful repugnance.

"The *New York Press?* I don't read that, who does?" said Peter Mack, sniffily. He'd grown up to own a company making video games.

I write this column called *Dirty Sanchez*, I said.

"YOU'RE DIRTY SANCHEZ?!" he yelped.

We had released our third album; our shows had gotten bigger, and our video was now on MTV. There was a modicum of actual fame in my life. But every Monday I had to shut the curtains in my hotel room, type up the column and e-mail it.

We had a day off in Santa Barbara. Everybody else went to the beach; I sat in a room banging out the column. It was only 800 words, and all I had to do was look up some piece of music news online—usually just grabbing it off MTV.com—and riff on it bilefully. An hour's work? Two hours? There was a bag of weed sitting at the edge of the desk. I told myself I wasn't going to smoke until I had finished the column, but, of course I smoked, and then I was lingering, stoned, half-lidded, over the keys, trying to get a sentence together. An hour or so after that, I told myself I wouldn't smoke again until I'd finished the column, but I did. It took me nine hours.

Every week: I'm not gonna smoke today, I'm gonna finish the column and then I'll get high. But every Monday I ended up with a pipe in my mouth, and the excruciating struggle to write.

I got a video camera and became obsessed with it. I started making this endless, aimless movie on tour; I'd record something for three seconds, then cut to the next arbitrary, oddly beautiful thing: a tour of randomness.

I was in Amsterdam, and I spent the day videotaping Dutch snippets, then took a break to get stoned. I went to a coffee shop called GOA, where I flirted with the bespectacled bartendress. As is de rigueur for arty Americans in Europe, I tried to bond with her by ridiculing Americans. I smoked some weed—purple-threaded, sparkly-crystal-dusted—and fell into paranoia, and then I was unable to speak to the cute bartendress anymore.

There was a guy sitting alone in the corner of the coffee shop with a bong. He looked to me like an American who had come to Amsterdam on vacation to get high for a week or two. He took bong hits and lolled back in his chair. A Portishead record was playing, and every time a chorus soared, he pumped his fist in the air, oblivious to those around him, anguished joy on his face.

I went videotaping in the red light district. All the whores sit on stools, behind glass doors, in gaudy pink light. You knock on the glass to see what the price is, and the whores age fifteen years immediately upon opening the door. I was shooting the empty windows, making an elegiac reel of empty stools sitting in pink-lit doorways, meaning the whore was in the back with a client.

I wandered the endless alleys, door after door. You could select a woman of any possible combination of attributes—a plump red-head? A skinny Latina? A tattooed black woman? How weird to think that, if I wanted to buy sex, I'd have to *decide on my type*. It was like the Strand bookstore in New York, where the shelves are so numerous that you shouldn't go if you're looking for something *specifically*, but rather in the hope you'll stumble on something unexpectedly. Otherwise, you'd be cursed to wander the aisles forever.

So I kept videotaping the empty glass booths. "Hey!" I heard a voice behind me. I turned to find a gigantic black woman glaring at me.

"Are you *crazy?*" she said.

I blinked. Then I said: Yes. I am crazy.

"Give me camera," she said through gritted teeth.

No, no, I'm not shooting people, just the doorways—no *people.*
"*Give me camera.*"

No, please, look, I said, flipping the viewscreen around. I played the footage back. Empty doorway after empty doorway.

See? I said. No people.

She laughed a forced laugh. "Huh!" she said. "Maybe you want to take picture of some of this now, right?" She squeezed her tits together with a vicious look on her face.

Sure, I said, and raised the camera.

She glared confusedly. Then she spun around and marched away.

I was walking around Chicago, taking minuscule videos of architectural details, when I dropped the camera. It burst. Wire guts boiled out of it.

I took it to my guitar tech, J.D., back at the hotel. We sniffed iffy yellow cocaine and drank the minibar as he tinkered with it. It ended up deader than before, the metal skeleton and transistors exposed.

"What is *that?*" the sampler player asked when he saw it.

"That's the yellow coke," J.D. said.

J.D. hooked us up with better cocaine; he knew a guy who knew the guy that was allegedly Metallica's coke hookup. "He said *ask for the '80s stuff!*" J.D. reported gleefully.

I stayed up all night sniffing it after a gig in Texas. Each of my bandmates peeled away, one by one, until it was just me sitting there, packing my face with cocaine. I made myself stop as the sun came up, and took an aching walk around the lake. I went to the airport shaking slightly, in growling pain, as the coke worked its way out.

"I can't believe you made it all day without doing more," said an astonished J.D. I was adamant about controlling my use. I was like a fist held so tight, for so long, that the arm jacks up and goes numb.

Somebody J.D. knew brought some heroin from Los Angeles. Black tar, which came wrapped in a blue party balloon. He took a pen and removed the ink cartridge, so the pen was just a plastic tube. He put the dark nugget on a piece of foil and held a flame under it as I sucked up the fumes with the pen-straw.

"*Git it! Git it!*" J.D. enthused as I chased the plume of smoke around the foil.

Then I turned to the coke. Very stupid. I should've done the coke all night and then used the dope to come down. But J.D. was so proud of his heroin—he went into loving, racist detail telling how one buys dope in Los Angeles—"A *taco* comes and spits it right out of his mouth!" he said—that I couldn't deny his parental delight.

Again, the four of us sat there, taking turns on the coke. Out the window, by the pool, a woman was going down on a fratty-looking guy. He came, his body jolting. She sucked down his come maniacally until she was hurting him: he pushed her head away. Then she lay back in the lawn chair, and he went down on her.

I got out my new video camera and started taping. I held my breath as I taped, thinking that outside and three stories down they could hear me breathing.

His head bobbed up and down between her legs ineptly. He would work up momentum; she arched in the chair; you could see her twitch, getting close to the plateau before coming; then his stamina seized up, he lost control of his head and slowed down involuntarily.

Behind me—again—each of my bandmates stood up, at intervals, and left the room. I stayed up for hours, the tape rolling—he almost gets her off, he falters, he dives in again—sniffing the cocaine, holding up the camera until my wrists shook.

I got a number for a dentist from some friend of my manager's. She ticked off a list of all the band guys who had gone to him. "He's great with the gas," she said.

Indeed he was. I lay back on the dentists' chair, he strapped the little pig-nose gas-purveyor onto my face, and cranked the nitrous. He put a radio Walkman on me, tuned to a classic rock station; as the gas came on, I realized I wanted to listen to Hot 97 instead. My thumb twitched on the tuner-knob. The music became less and less recognizable as the gas was taking over; it turned the music to abstract mush.

What kind of music is this? I thought. *Is it classical music? Salsa?* I was intellectually thrilled that the drugs had erased genre lines, suddenly I was free of prejudice, listening to music just as it was—at last, I could *hear!*

The dentist snatched the headphones off me, giggling. "You're listening to static," he said. I had maxed the volume; the white noise blasted so loudly that he and the hygienist could hear it over the drill.

He had a sort of sniveling mien. Maybe his eagerness to give you all the gas you could want came from a need for those who passed beneath his drill to like him. He gave me a prescription for fifty Percocets.

I gulped three or four pills and logged on to AOL instant messenger. I had set the privacy settings so anybody could see I was online; the moment I was signed in, it went *ding ding ding,* as a dozen chat windows filled the screen. There were scary chatters who typed, in all caps, "IS THIS THE SINGER OF SOUL CAUGHING?" I ignored an all-caps guy and he went berserk. "FUCK U I HATE UR BAND U THINK UR SO GRAT U SUCK UR BAND SUX."

Someone would type, "Hello, I saw you in my friend list but I don't remember who you are? . . ." I knew this was a cutesy set up, that I was supposed to say, It's me, Soul Coughing guy, and they'd go "No way, what a coincidence!" and I'd go, No, really, it's me!

Nice try, I typed back, then hit the block button.

I wasn't capable of going somewhere to meet actual people, so my social world was this series of random instant messenger windows. I couldn't keep track of who was who and which window was which, so I was tossing out disjointed communications at random. I smoked a bowl, took more Percocet, and typed through the night.

At some point I went to bed; when I came to, I found the laptop was still open. The top window said:

They: "i luv ur band :)"

Me: Uwabt u ciykde gi tge8u stib=re abd tgeb u;d byt nysekgf a e3kuidiys 370n 9 rd9rr33.

They: "ru ok?"

Me: Yteah if ciyrse ium pl. ehjsy yfp upi yjoml. o, kidy fine.

They: "hello?"

Me: nothing

They: "hey doughty ru ok? hello?"

Stanley Ray's mother was ill. He seemed tranquil. "When my mom dies, I don't want anybody to call me," he said. "I don't want anybody to make a big deal about it at all."

A week after she passed, he was too angry to look me in the eye. "I can't *believe* you didn't call after my mom died, that's *really fucked up*, you don't care about *anybody*, there's something really *wrong* with you," he said.

I met a sensationally gorgeous girl in Dallas, on a radio show. She had wandered backstage without intending to; the security let her through because she was so beautiful they figured she must belong with the rock stars. She said she was going down to Jamaica on vacation in a week, did I want to go? Pretty good for a first date. I said yes.

I stayed at a rundown hotel down the beach, but I bribed a uniformed guy with a nightstick to gain my way into her all-inclusive resort, drank the watered-down beer they offered, and tried to get her high. She refused the joint, so I smoked the whole thing, and wastedly tried to make out with her as we floated in the placid water. She rebuffed me, but I kept coming on. When you invite somebody down to a tropical island for a vacation with you, you must know you're going to fuck them, but this girl had worked out, in her mind, some accelerated, but quite proper, version of a three-dates-before-sex schedule.

That same day, I had her naked in her room, and I asked her to go down on me. She leaped up, yelling, told me she barely knew me, and get out.

There was a guy who worked at my hotel—in no clearly defined position—named Eustace. He had a fishing boat bobbing out in the water by the hotel painted with the name THE AMAZING EUSTACE. He sold me some coke, and some weed, and some stuff he called opium, but which was black tar heroin. I asked him for some aluminum foil so I could smoke it, but he had no idea what I was talking about, so I rolled it up into a joint, which will do you little good with black tar heroin. I smoked it anyway, crestfallen, because there was no way I was going to wait until I could get to a store and get some foil.

I did coke until the morning, then passed out, woke up near dusk, and bought some more coke from Eustace. I was chatting with him in my room, tapping out a pile of powder, when the door opened and the Texas girl came in. She was penitent; she smiled sweetly at me. She sat on the bed. I offered her a line, and she refused, so I sat there sniffing coke as Eustace made polite conversation with her. Finally, half an hour later, she got up to leave. She paused before walking out the door, but I didn't follow her. It wasn't that her earlier rejection had so humiliated me; it was that I had a pile of cocaine and what I wanted to do was sit there in my room all night and sniff cocaine.

"Why did you let her leave?!" asked Eustace, shocked.

I was there for a week, doing coke, smoking weed, occasionally going down to the beach and drinking, but never going into the water. I may as well have been in St. Louis.

One night I couldn't find Eustace; I went out to the beach looking for drugs. This haggard guy behind a palm tree hissed, "Coke! Coke!" He whipped out a bag and named a price. I was wasted, trying to look at the bag and maybe negotiate, but he hissed, "Quick! Now! The cops are coming! I can hear them!" I gave him the dough, he disappeared in the trees, and I found myself holding a baggie of laundry detergent.

The next day I saw Eustace and recounted the tale jovially, thinking I'd get a laugh out of him, but he turned to me, fuming, "Why didn't you come to me?! I have to feed me pickney!"

Years later I came back, sober. I went to a twelve-step meeting; it was in a church across the street from that hotel.

We flew to Portugal to play a festival, second on the bill after the Pretenders. I was certain we were hot shit, because the last gig we'd played in Oporto was sheer adoration, the audience banging on the stage, calling for encore after encore.

Instead, we played for an indifferent crowd. In the front, at the barricades, an affronted woman waved her fists. "PLAY MUSIC!" she yelled, indignantly, during the songs. "PLAY MUSIC!"

I stayed up all night afterwards, because I was catching a flight to Frankfurt, then a flight to Bangkok, and then a flight to Cambodia. Having been everywhere in North America and Western Europe, I wanted to go someplace weird.

There was a night's layover in Bangkok. I stayed at a Days Inn by the airport. I videotaped the clock radio in the room—the numbers blinking, the DJ speaking the intoxicating tumble of the Thai language.

I spent one night in Bangkok before a holiday in Cambodia.

I landed in Phnom Penh in sunshine that was not so much blazing as boring: boring in the other sense, as in, it bored through your eyes and into your skull. I carried a sheaf of teletyped papers with the rainbow logo of a tour company; I was scared to wander through Cambodia unguided, and in any case, wanted to be drunk or high most of the time, and was thus in need of someone to drag me around.

We deplaned into a square building that looked like a library in Kansas. I was met by a slight, effeminate Khmer guy from the tour agency. He wore a white shirt over a Cambodian *krama*—a wide, multicolored scarf—wrapped around his waist like a skirt, and plastic sandals. He was immediately suspicious of me.

I had a couple of beers in the hotel buffet room, staffed by sternly obsequious waiters dressed like UN translators. I went up to my room and opened the curtains; I looked out over the Mekong River, away from the city, onto an endless marsh. As if Phnom Penh, the chaos behind us, wasn't there at all. There was a *Sheraton Phnom Penh* message pad on the desk. I videotaped it. Over the bed hung a painting of topless women with plump, conical '60s tits, bathing in a pool by the temples of Angkor.

I was given a lugubrious tour of the National Museum. Every four steps we would stop in front of a statuette for a long recitation of dates and kings' names. I wanted to be out in the broad dirt lot between the museum and the riverbank, where kids zoomed around in dust clouds, kicking soccer balls made of wicker, in the wild weirdness, the bike-rickshaws and mopeds, some with families of five clinging on: Dad at the helm, Mom in the back, two toddlers sandwiched between them, and a baby perched on the handlebars.

To my great relief, the guide to the Silver Palace had gone missing. The guy who'd picked me up at the airport was somberly apologetic. The king still resides in a cordoned-off portion of the Silver Palace—at that time, King Sihanouk, a French-speaking, jazz-saxophone-playing cosmopolitan who presided over his country's atrocious poverty and, before selling out his subjects to the murderous Khmer Rouge, directed epic movies depicting a suave, glam Cambodia of beauty queens and sports cars.

My guide told me that he used to be a ballet dancer. He asked me if I planned to do any shopping. I told him, just for the sake of conversation, I might possibly look for some jewelry. He lit into a hysterical whisper: "What do you want to buy?! Rubies?! Silver?!"

He showed me Tuol Sleng, the junior high school that had been used as a torture house by the Khmer Rouge. Mug shots of people about to be murdered, a map of Cambodia made from the skulls of the tortured, metal bed frames onto which the tortured were bound. I walked out of the gates and back into the drowsy suburban neighborhood.

I was devastated, I couldn't figure out if I was fighting back tears or if the very ability to cry had been sucked out of my head. I told the ballet dancer that I couldn't go to the planned next stop, the Killing Fields.

He said, "Do you feel pity for my people?"

Somehow I heard this as: Do you, the privileged white colonist, look down upon us, the unwashed, in our primitive distress?

I barked, No!

Freaked him out.

It haunts me, the memory of misunderstandingly yelling at him; makes me wince.

I got the ballet dancer to take me to a market to buy some weed before returning. We walked into a covered market and right up to a stall where a guy scooped awful yellow stalks of marijuana into a plastic bag. The guy in the next stall was selling fortified wine—bottles, boxes, and two-gallon-sized oil cans with greased-up, flexing bodybuilders on their labels, analogizing the alcohol content.

In the car, the ballet dancer asked me what I was going to do with the weed—cook with it? No, I was going to smoke it. He giggled kind of psychotically. "Why you smoke that?! That for *old man!*"

I flew to Siem Reap, where the temples of Angkor are. A guy who looked like a Khmer frat boy drove me to a nondescript hotel. The lobby was lousy with glum Italian tourists.

I went to the market and bought a pipe with a ceramic bowl shaped like a skull, a poster of a benevolent King Sihanouk looking off into the distance, and the de rigueur tourist item, a t-shirt with a Jolly Roger and loud script in Khmer and English: DANGER!! BEWARE MINES!!

There was a pharmacy across the street, about the size of a closet, with barely enough room for a counter and glass shelves lined with medicine. I didn't want to sully the pipe yet—I had to get it through customs back into America—and I had no idea where one would buy rolling papers in northwestern Cambodia. They didn't have rolling papers, but behind the glass shelves was a box of twelve generic Valium. Somehow I had the gumption to casually ask for the Valium. She plopped it on the counter and I paid a couple bucks for it. Preposterous luck.

I popped a couple of them, and drank some beer. The frat boy met me in the lobby and drove through the woods, to Angkor. We saw a temple called Ta Prohm, which had been left unattended for so long that the jungle was taking it back. Muscular trees had broken through the walls, and massive roots, like bridge cables, grappled with the carved stones, gripping them, an excruciatingly slow act of violence.

There was a kid, maybe a seven-year-old, trailing us.

"Hello!" he cried.

Hi, I said, smiling.

"SAME TO YOU!" he yelped, and ran away.

He came back and tried to sell me postcards. I didn't want to appear rude to a seven-year-old Khmer—these were, after all, *his* temples—I flipped through them.

"Look!" he said. "Look!"

He was pointing at two stone lions flanking a staircase.

"Lion!" he said in an urgent whisper. "Lion. Lion."

The frat boy led me slowly across a frieze that illustrated a creation myth called "The Churning of the Ocean of Milk." He assiduously described every tiny bas-relief of characters and plot points. My benzodiazepine buzz was wisping away.

The frat boy paused before an image of a man in a tree.

"Who is this?" he asked.

I don't know.

"This is *thee* Buddha. He is in *tree*. See? What is this?"

A pack of elephants?

"Elephant! Elephant are hit the tree. They try to knock thee Buddha from thee *tree*. But no! They can't do it! Because of thee *perfection* of thee *Buddha*."

He made a shrill, joyous cry. "Noooo! They can't do it! Because of thee *perfection of thee Buddha!*"

I sat with the glum Italians in the hotel bar. There was a large, strange band on Khmer TV—stringed instruments both plucked and bowed, and animal skin drums. They all wore military fatigues. Two singers, man and woman, stood amid them. The band struck up a hypnotic racket, each instrument veering away from each other out of time and tune, like avant-garde jazz taking a wild detour through folk music. They stopped abruptly and one singer stepped forward and caterwauled a long, jumbled melody line, also utterly liberated from the tempo. Then the man stopped singing, the band played another cacophony of elongated riffs, then stopped, then the woman stepped forward and sang. The music was mystifying.

In my room, I videotaped a tube of Ta Prohm toothpaste, and a wild Bollywood dance spectacle on TV. Men danced the cabbage patch and threw paint on each other.

The boring light ceded to a conjuration of pink and orange. I looked out the window and saw Khmers zipping around on their mopeds, pack animals, magical chaos. I didn't want to see the temples, I wanted to sit on a bed and watch bizarre, exotic life through a window and on a screen. Not to be in it, but to long to be in it.

The waiter at breakfast tried to set up an appointment to practice his English. Heavy-headed, I assented and then flaked. The next day, he was genuinely confused as to why I didn't make it. I skipped breakfast the day after.

I went to the tiny pharmacy to clean them out. I piled box upon box of Valium onto the floor, then noticed—more preposterous luck!—boxes of codeine. I started flipping those out of the case as well.

I heard a French-accented voice behind me. "What are you looking for?" I turned around and saw a manly, unshaven guy in mirrored shades. I said something half-assed and dismissive.

"Maybe I can help you find what you're looking for," he said.

I snarled, kept rummaging. He shrugged and went away.

Maybe he was trying to help me in the way I wanted to be helped. Who knows what that guy knew how to get—heroin? opium? Here we were in the immediate vicinity of the Golden Triangle. There were a number of basic drug-addict skills that I never got together.

The frat boy took me on a tour of a floating village: barges and boats tied together in the Tonle Sap Lake, with houses and stores on them. It's populated by ethnic Vietnamese; they're a minority in Cambodia, regarded with suspicion and contempt.

Our boat was steered by a Khmer kid, maybe thirteen, in worn jeans, with a heart-shaped American flag patch sewn on the ass pocket. We cruised slowly through the weird scene. Rowboats loaded up with goods—plasticware, cookware, canisters of condensed milk, fruit, inflatable toys—eased past us. Naked kids jumped gleefully into the water from the railing of a houseboat as we passed, shouting to me. The frat boy laboriously cut open a durian fruit with a pocketknife, and we ate the soft, stinking flesh. We floated up to a barge where plastic picnic chairs were gathered around under a canopy.

The proprietor produced beer from a cooler. Then the entertainment began. There was a monkey chained to a rail. A beer was cracked open and handed to the monkey, who grabbed it with both hands and feet, rolled onto his back, and gulped it frantically. The proprietor brought another cooler and set it down, opened it up, reached in and removed a huge snake. He swung the hissing monster at the terrorized, drunk monkey. The monkey shrieked. Everybody on the barge laughed. I faked a laugh because I didn't want to seem unappreciative.

The snake was taken away, and the monkey crouched there, unnerved, his eyes shifting around wildly. The proprietor plucked a cat from under a table and brought it towards the monkey. The cat mewled and struggled. He brought the cat down to the monkey and held it down. The monkey drunkenly grabbed the cat's flanks humped its back. The cat wrestled out of his grip and shot away.

The proprietor came over with another cat, a grey one. This one wasn't struggling so much. It seemed resigned. The monkey took the grey cat by the ears and humped its skull.

"OHHHH!" squealed the frat boy. "HE IS SUCH A NAUGHTY MONKEY!"

They gave the monkey another beer. He drank with greedy relief.

I was back in New York, and out of Cambodian codeine.

A girl with an unsingable name sent me an e-mail out of the blue, saying she was on a high school field hockey team with the assistant of a woman who worked at a music magazine, and that she loved my music. Her name was a melodious string of vowels. Just looking at the e-mail, I decided that a girl with that name must be beautiful.

She came to a gig at Irving Plaza. She was a funny Valentine, with a long, strange nose disfigured by plastic surgery received when she was teenage and still growing, and blue eyes so pale they were translucent. She was shit-faced, but she walked steadily, with folded arms.

We met a week later at a Moroccan-themed bar. We sat in an alcove, downing gin and tonics and Vicodins that I had gotten from the gas-happy dentist. Her mom was from Kiev: I made her say ridiculous things in Ukrainian to me. We made out messily. I don't remember if she came home with me.

She worked at a jealously regarded web company—this being the height of the cash-shitting internet boom—that would one day crash and dwindle to nothing, along with all the other jealously regarded web companies. I met her there to take her to dinner. She was glassy-eyed. She didn't eat. I should have asked for a bump of her dope right there.

I had been in the band for seven years, and I had given up. I didn't know yet that I could beat the stuff that was killing my heart. I listened to Stanley Ray, who shook me to my core with masterful strikes of passive-aggression when I made feeble efforts to convince him that I could leave—because I couldn't just walk away from the band, I needed someone to *tell me it was OK* to do so. I believed the dudes in my band, who did all they could to keep me insecure. I believed my manager, who commissioned on gross, of course, and thus would make more money if we stayed together.

So I woke up one morning in 1999, and there were a few bags of dope left over from the night before. I said to myself: There's no way off this despairing march. My promise to myself to keep the heroin use somewhat in control, because I wanted to protect my artistic faculties, had become laughable. Why? I was going to get high first thing this morning, and the next, and the next. I'll stumble along, show up when they tell me to, sing when it's time to sing. I'd eke out a mediocre existence. The very worst thing that could happen, death, seemed outlandish, but, were it to come, maybe wouldn't actually be the worst thing at all.

When my flight back from Cambodia landed, I immediately convinced the girl with the unsingable name to call her heroin guy. We went back to my tiny place on Rivington Street, cut lines on a CD, and sniffed them. We lay in bed all night, listened to Sam Cooke and the Soul Stirrers, and felt that spreading ease. "Must Jesus bear this cross alone?" they sang. "There's a cross for everyone. I know there's a cross for me."

She bumbled out of bed in stark white morning light—I didn't have curtains—and off to the lavish loft of that internet concern. She took a bag of dope. She told me later that she liked to do little bumps in the bathroom during the day, using a pen cap as a spoon.

I put on my t-shirt with the skull and crossbones and the admonishment to watch for land mines, and set up my video camera on its tripod. I then sniffed a line, and smoked some weed from the ceramic-skull pipe. The tape rolled as I nodded out in a chair.

One morning we woke up together, and were junkies, and she was in love with me. The first month of our three-sided love affair—me, heroin, and the girl with the unsingable name—was beautiful.

We kept listening to the Soul Stirrers. Redemptive songs: Jesus, the woman at the well, touching the hem of his garment, the river

Jordan. In delirium, I began to think of myself as a Christian. Of course, I thought, anybody who says they believe in god is lying; but to profess a belief in god, to go through the motions, to be among other people who knew you knew that they knew that it was all a sham: there was redemptive power in this. I wrote "Help me, Jesus" on a Post-It and put it up over my stove.

I sniffed some dope before going to sleep, though I didn't need any more to pass out—"You're going to build up a tolerance," the unsingable girl chided—but I wanted that soothing tingle as I drifted off. The moment before oblivion was the best part of life. The girl with the unsingable name had these tiny hairs on the back of her neck; I would spoon her, brush my lips back and forth across them, smell her smell, raise chill-bumps on her flesh. We stopped having sex—our intimacy was transmitted through the heroin and the hairs on her neck.

I came to the conclusion that the unsingable girl wasn't good enough—partially because what person who could love me could be good enough? I resented her, devalued everything about her, felt sorry for myself, refused to think of her as my girlfriend. What am I doing with this awful girl?

We went out drinking; I bumped into some friends. I left the girl with the unsingable name in the corner as I flirted shamelessly with a friend of mine's girlfriend. At one point I drunkenly reached out and pinched her nipple. My friend stood by trying to stop himself from punching my lights out. I shrugged at the girl with the unsingable name, and she followed me home.

She called me from work and said, "You don't care about me. You think I'm lo-fi. You're going to dump me."

I would say, Why would you think that? No, no.

I beeped the guy at five. "This is Greg. Send me a numeric page. Do not leave a message. Send a numeric page, a numeric page, a NUMERIC PAGE."

The buzzer rang—glorious buzzer, the drugs were here!—and he came up the stairs, looking like one of those polished, mellow neo-soul stars in his buttery-soft leather jacket. I came bounding down two flights to meet him. What a nice customer, I wanted him to think, he doesn't even make me come up all five flights. What a good egg.

(Years later, clean, when I had Thai food delivered, I'd hear the buzzer, and my heart would involuntarily leap.)

He palmed me two bundles of dope. A bundle is ten bags, tiny glassine envelopes bound with a rubber band. For years I remembered, fantasized, about what those two bundles felt like, cupped in my hand: two little ruffles tied in rubber bands.

Greg liked having a minor rock star as a client. Sometimes he'd call back and say he had no plans to drive into Manhattan, then say, well, maybe he would, if he did, he'd call me. He always came. Once he gave me two bonus bags of a new brand called Krack-House! to test. You hear warnings to take new brands slow, as they might be unexpectedly pure and kill you, but I sniffed them right up, never thinking that I could be so lucky. I mean, lucky to get fabulously pure heroin, not to die. Well, perhaps, on some level I was dimly aware of, lucky to die.

The drugs worked less and less well. I became more and more of an asshole. The unsingable girl yelled at me, "You don't get *high*, you just get *fucked up!*"

She would go home to the Bronx and detox for the weekend, and I would stay home and detox, too. We reconvened a few days later and got high again, but it was never as satisfying as the first month.

Detoxing became routine. After a weekend without heroin, just weed and liquor, I could get a bundle and sniff it for a couple of days, and get high the way I used to, though soon I'd be back to maintenance using again. The gap closed: a weekend's detox made a day being high; then I could be high for the time it took to sniff just a bundle. Then I'd detox for five days, sniff a bag, and be high for just a blissful fifteen minutes.

It was worth it to me. That's all I had for delight in my life: my body stopped making any chemical that would make me feel good. Nothing was funny or pleasurable unless it was inside the window between detox and the re-onset of maintenance. I plotted longer detoxes: maybe if I stayed off it for two months, I could get high for a weekend? Six months of a grey, miserable slog through existence in exchange for a good week?

There was an episode of *Behind the Music* about the Red Hot Chili Peppers. Their guitar player was a dope fiend, and the show used some footage from a Dutch documentary depicting him as a bug-eyed, imbalanced wreck, mumbling about how heroin allowed him to keep a connection "to beauty." His skin was yellow and grey. He was barely coherent.

The unsingable girl and I had both just detoxed when we saw it.

"Wow, doesn't that make you jealous?" she asked, longingly.

Oh, good lord, yes, I said.

There was an episode of *The Sopranos* in which the Jersey gangsters go to Naples to finesse a smuggling connection. The youngest one, Chris, a junkie, sees needle marks on one of the Italian en-forcers' arms, and they spend the whole trip nodding out in a hotel room with the drapes closed.

Chris keeps talking about going to see Mount Aetna. "I'm gonna go see that fucking volcano," he says. He doesn't. He flakes on sumptuous dinners, saying he's got a stomach bug. He's a teetering cadaver by the time he lands back in Newark, where he hurriedly buys his girlfriend gifts in the duty-free shop; the older gangsters make fun of him for not going to the famous luxury stores of Naples.

Message: Chris has chosen a piteous, destructive stasis over what could be a fascinating life. But I watched him with tremendous envy.

The unsingable girl pitied me obsequiously, wailing that I couldn't stop.

We're both junkies, I said.

She gasped. "We're not *junkies!*"

She had a list of ex-boyfriends who quickly became more pronounced dope fiends than she was, and she would rail against the terrible things they were doing with their lives.

My lungs weakened. I had so little breath that I would routinely have a panicked, choking fight for air just by standing up from a chair too quickly. I like to leap up and pace whenever I get a good idea. So creativity was hazardous.

I couldn't stand all the way upright; I shuffled, half bent. It took me ten minutes to cross my tiny apartment, piss, and return to bed. It took half an hour to go down the stairs of my building—I walked backwards, gripping the rail, as if I were descending an Alp.

I never connected this with the $300 worth of dope I was sniffing daily. I was twenty-nine, and I thought, Well, twenty-nine, you know, getting older, the body starts shutting down.

Seriously, I thought this.

There was a Jennifer Lopez video that was on all the time—synopsis: Jennifer Lopez, a carefree girl from the Bronx, goes and picks up her paycheck at the beauty parlor, then gets on the train and heads out on the town with her friends, laughing. The video bewildered me. I knew, just from passive pop-culture consumption, that she was one year older than me. How's she able to do this? To *function?*

It was about four blocks to the bank machine. Every day I beeped Greg, and then headed for the stairs. Thirty minutes down. Then one block down Ludlow Street, which was transitioning from a discount market—Hasidic Jewish guys in their black hats and quasi-nineteenth-century garb selling knockoff leather goods—to a groovy-people playground. I felt invisible on the street. Maybe life was moving around me so much faster than I was that I was invisible.

Most likely, though, people were just averting their gaze from this guy who was clearly dying. I didn't look like a dope fiend, more like a cancer patient.

It took me three lights to cross Delancey, a wide street leading to the Williamsburg Bridge, looming grey in the distance. One *Walk* and I started across the westbound lanes. When I was halfway across, *Don't Walk* started flashing. Drivers would wait, rolling their eyes—gruff white commuters, thuggy dudes in decked-out Mazdas, delivery vans, Jersey-plated cars filled with girls in sequined outfits, en route to parties—as I finally got to the traffic island. Some time spent wheezing on the traffic island, my heart racing. Then I started crossing the eastbound lanes. It took me ninety minutes, sometimes two hours, to the ATM and back.

Puking became so normal that I stopped kneeling. The only thing in my fridge would be a dozen corn-syrup-loaded green or pink simulated-fruit drinks. I'd get ridiculously thirsty, so devoid of nutrients, and down one in a gulp. Five minutes later, I'd walk into the bathroom, stand by the toilet, aim, and puke the entire drink, still the same color it was in the bottle.

The radiators in my apartment broke down, but I didn't want to get the landlord in there—my garbage can was piled past the brim with empty heroin bags, I'd sometimes take a handful, ball them up, put them in my mouth, suck on them—so, utterly sick, I lay in bed with layer upon layer of clothes on, under the blankets, my breath steaming in the air of my own bedroom.

Greg was primarily a coke dealer: he offered heroin as a comedown option. I think being a coke dealer entitled him to feel a little superiority. This was undermined, perhaps, by watching me die.

I had a month's abstinence from heroin. A friend—secretly a junkie for years whom I always did coke with, but never did dope with—maybe a drug variation of that O. Henry Christmas story about the watch chain and the comb—called me up, looking for dope for *a friend*. I beeped Greg.

"Hey man, where've you been?"

I, uh, I said, making up a lie, I've been in *California*.

I loaded a lot into that compact lie, and he got it. "That's *good*, man, that's *good*," he said. But when I asked him to come into Manhattan, he said, "Uh, there's nothing really going on with that right now."

No?

"No."

Are you sure?

"Yeah."

It's bad news when your dealer cuts you off because he doesn't like watching you die. I didn't really get it.

In New York, heroin traditionally comes in a tiny glassine envelope with a brand name stamped on top, to identify differences in quality between dealers. I can barely remember the brand names I had: there was one called Ruff Ryders, after the rap label. There was an empty—naturally—bag I found on the C train with the silhouettes of Civil War soldiers firing their rifles and the brand Glory. There was a legendary bag in the early '90s called Tango and Cash—after a Stallone movie—that was laced with fentanyl and killed a bunch of dope fiends. The dope bag made the cover of the *New York Post*. Once, after I was clean, I bought a basket at IKEA, looked down into it and thought, hmmm, that tag's about the size of a bag of dope, thinking nothing of it until months later, when I reached in it and came out with a bag called Timberland. (I flushed the bag— actually, more truthfully, I ripped it open and lovingly sprinkled the powder into the water, then flushed the bag itself—then called clean friends for reassurance. They all told me I had done the right thing; my friend the rock legend said, in a merry tone, "Ah, what a waste.")

There was a single brand—other than the sample Krack-House! bags—that Greg brought, and I can't remember what it was. There wasn't a logo, it was just the brand, in a simple font, stamped on the bag. My house was filled with hundreds of these discarded bags, ripped open, the contents sucked out. Strewn on the floor, all over the table where I sniffed the dope, stuffed in those bags of leftover takeout Chinese. The name's just out of reach in my mind. Baffling.

Before the heroin binge began, I had gotten a new doctor, the fiancée of a photographer friend from the Knitting Factory days. She liked drugs. Freud's *The Cocaine Papers* was on her bookshelf; she had appeared on TV, advocating the decriminalization of Ecstasy for clinical purposes. The first thing she did was switch me to another antidepressant, and I could have orgasms again.

Now, much later, to help me detox, she prescribed a sizable quantity of oxycodone and wrote out cessation plans neatly on legal paper. First day, five pills every two hours; second day, two every three hours; and so on for a week until you were gently delivered from your cravings. What I did was spend three days detoxing, and then gulp them all down on Tuesday. Then I would despair that somehow her detox program hadn't worked.

I was indignant that the antidepressants had stopped working, too. I went to her and whined, and she prescribed me more. Still no dice. As I sniffed bag after bag, then licked the sniffing plate, then put the bags in my mouth and sucked on them for residue.

It was New Year's 1999. We all thought, merrily, that when the clock turned to 2000, money would disintegrate in the banks, airplanes would fall out of the sky, the power would go off forever. I had detoxed a week earlier. The Cocaine Papers doc had prescribed Naltrexone to me, which is what they call an "opioid receptor antagonist"; you can use all the dope you want, and you won't get high.

The unsingable girl came with the only champagne she could find in a convenience store near the Spuyten Duyvil Metro-North stop; it was Whoopi Goldberg–brand champagne. It came in a shrink-wrapped box: two plastic champagne flutes, and a bottle with Whoopi's signature on the label.

I snarled at her all night. She kept trying to be nice, to have a good New Year's. But I was intractable. Finally, she said, "Fuck it, I give up." She pushed me towards the bathroom, where she had been sniffing dope off a random book—a coffee-table book depicting buses in Hong Kong—all night.

I sniffed some, but the Naltrexone worked, and I didn't get high. Alas.

One day she called and said, "It's my birthday. You forgot my birthday. You don't want me anymore. You're going to break up with me."

I said, You know what? You're right. I'm breaking up with you, right now.

"What?!" she said.

By the end of that month I wanted her back. I needed to nuzzle the back of her neck and smell her shoulders. So I went uptown and met her at a decrepit sports bar, and we got drunk.

I tried to kiss her and she pulled away. "You broke up with me on my birthday," she said.

That was your birthday? I said.

It turned out that on her birthday, on the very day I dumped her, she went out to a bar, saw a band, and made out with the guitar player. They moved in together by the end of the weekend.

"When you broke up with me, I was stunned," said the unsingable girl. "It came out of nowhere."

I never asked her to come back to me again, but I was obsessed. I had disdained her, but now she had become perfect. When I got clean, the longing became more acute, partially because she was still out there in the world getting high, like my drug life had just gone on after I left it.

After I was clean, I started writing songs again: they were all about her. I didn't realize, as I wrote them, that they were in fact lost-love songs addressed to heroin. When I met her, I realized that her beautiful, strange name would make an excellent song title. I tried and tried, but there was something maddening and elusive about it—the accent was on the wrong syllable for the melody, or the sequence of vowels was a clumsy fit on the bar. Every song I wrote for a year was either a song about her, or a song that began as a song about her. In each song there's some three-syllable point, usually a descending three-note thing of a certain scansion, where her name was. One began with the lyric, "That girl that brought me low." (As if it were me, not her, who got the boot!) Another was built around the name Madeline, a stand-in name. Another was called "Unsingable Name."

Stanley Ray called me, speaking in a grave whisper. "Don't think I don't know *exactly* what you're doing," he said.

Uh-huh, I said. Gotta go.

That was the last time I spoke to him. Soon after that, he lost his job at Warner Bros.; a new president took charge of the label and sent him a few CDs that he, as an A&R guy, was to review. Stanley Ray found this insulting and fucked-up, refused to surrender his punk rock vainglory, and was fired.

I heard years later that he would rage about what an ingrate I was, how I had once been rad but was now an asshole, didn't even call him when I was in L.A., that I'd used him and dropped him.

I was still showing up for therapy. It was the only thing I had to do other than write *Sanchez*, which provided my drug budget.

I didn't realize how my appearance was changing; I was hollowing, greying out. I became aware that the doormen in my shrink's office building were alert to me as I waited at the elevators; soon they would stop me and ask where I was going. I was affronted.

I sat in the high-back chair across from her; I nodded out midsentence. I awoke to find her smiling at me. "There are twelvestep meetings down on St. Mark's Place," she said.

What?! I said. Are you *listening* to me?!

I figured the messed-up state of my lungs was asthma. I never had asthma before—even when I was smoking three packs a day. *Why me?* I kept thinking. I still didn't connect it to the daily two bundles of heroin.

I went to a peculiarly foul-mooded physician recommended by the Cocaine Papers doc. I told him, cheerfully, that I was addicted to heroin. He gave me an inhaler, showed me how it worked— hold it to your mouth, pump the top, and a little *psssht!* of mist goes down your throat. He barked at me never to do more than two pumps at a time, never more than twice a day.

If he told me that my problem wasn't asthma, but that I was overdosing almost daily, I didn't hear it.

It helped, a little, when my lungs would seize up on the long trek to the bank machine. I ignored the two-pumps rule; nearly collapsed on the traffic island, I'd *pump-pssht!-pump-pssht!-pump-pssht!-pump-pssht!* the mist until I could almost stand upright.

The sampler player came over to pick up something. I sat in a chair, shriveled, all bones, while he rolled a joint of my weed. We smoked. I offered to tap out a line for him.

"I have things to do. I can't do *heroin*," he said, with a disdainful chuckle.

He called me later and asked me if my heroin guy could get some coke for him, and if so, could I give the guy a call?

I overdosed at Thanksgiving dinner. My parents and my brother and the family of one of my dad's colleagues were there. Everyone said grace, and I pushed the cranberry sauce around the plate. I went into the bathroom, sniffed some dope, came back to the table, and my lungs started to close up. I pumped at the inhaler desperately, but to no avail. My brother drove me to the hospital. As I sat in the car, gagging, my dad looked at me from the doorway, unsettled, having no idea what was happening.

In the emergency room in Cornwall, I told them, genially, that I was a heroin addict. They strapped a mask to my face that emitted a spooky mist.

The last Soul Coughing show was at the Bowery Ballroom in 1999. It was a benefit for an illustrator at the *New York Press* who sent a prank e-mail in the guise of a more famous cartoonist, who sued.

I sniffed some dope before heading to sound check, got two cheeseburgers at McDonald's en route, threw them up the moment I got to the dressing room. Sniffed some more before we went onstage.

In the second song, I felt my lungs spasming. My brother was stage-side, watching the show. Nearly unable to speak, I motioned him over to me, gasped that I needed my inhaler; it was in the dressing room, in my jacket. I leaned against the proscenium, struggling to breathe. Ages seemed to pass; the audience stared at me shocked and confused; I was trembling, unable to stand. The band vamped on the same groove; my brother came back with the inhaler, and I pumped the mist furiously. I finished the show, which, because it was a benefit with a bunch of bands playing, was mercifully abbreviated.

This guy kept e-mailing me about some festival in Antwerp called *Die Nachten,* Flemish for "the nights." He wanted me to read poetry. The first time I read the e-mail I was high, and said sure, and after that I couldn't get rid of him. Once he showed up backstage in Rotterdam—I walked into the dressing room, and he was just sitting there, which was infuriating.

Eventually he succeeded in confirming me. I was set up on a tiny tour that included a show in Amsterdam and *Die Nachten.*

I brought a couple bags of dope on the plane, sniffed them in the bathroom, and passed out in Premium Economy on Virgin Atlantic. When I landed in London to connect, I drank a beer at the first bar I came to in the airport; I puffed miserably along my way, barely able to walk. I took an insanely expensive ride all the way across town to London City Airport. I slumped in a black cab on a bright, beautiful day, through London traffic.

I was met in Antwerp by an English tour manager named Pete, an aging Yorkshire rock guy, very meek, who saw his job as making sure the band got where they needed to go, taking utterly no responsibility for anything after that. He'd done a bunch of Soul Coughing tours; once I walked onstage to find that my guitar wasn't out there, and I ran backstage, scrambling among the road cases of all the other bands' guitars looking for mine, and Pete just stood there, shrugging. The one thing he was diligent about was letting you know whether or not breakfast was free at the hotel. He wrote it on the slip of paper your hotel key came in, told you verbally as you got your bags, and left a note under your door at night. This despite the fact that everybody slept through breakfast unless something was wrong.

A consequence of his not giving a fuck was that he was really pleasant to be around.

I got to the Antwerp hotel and into bed, wheezing, body aching. I opened the minibar and drank everything in it, probably spending every dime I'd make on the tour. My phone rang, and I woke in a panic; it was pleasant Pete telling me that the promoters wanted to take me out for dinner that night. I said, call me back in three hours, and he did, and I said, can you call me back in two hours? Pete informed me that it was 7:30 and if I wanted to go they'd be showing up in fifteen minutes. I didn't. I spent another fitful twelve hours in bed, sleeping and then not sleeping, dreading the time I'd have to go to the theater, and then it came, and I packed my shivering body off to work.

The show, in a plush national theater, was barely attended. Between acts a booming disembodied voice, raspy and menacing, spoke in unfathomable Flemish. Apparently the voice was telling jokes; people were laughing. I went onstage looking like death, and when it came time to speak and sing, my voice took miserable dives on the high notes, squeaked through the lower ones. When the disembodied voice started talking as I left the stage, the people laughing, I was sure it was at the travesty of my performance.

Somehow Pete got me to Amsterdam, and I played a packed room, barely able to sing. They yelled, "Tune your guitar! Tune your guitar!"

Luke came over the first night of a detox. He walked in, drunk, and I handed him a Valium. My shrink called. You have to go, I told him. "No no," he answered, very amiably, "I'm just gonna hang out." He walked into my bedroom, picked up a guitar and played loudly. I hung up the phone and told him to leave.

"No, it's cool, I'm just gonna hang out," he said.

Somehow I ended up punching him in the face—the only time I've ever punched anybody in the face. I then came at him, absurdly, with an umbrella, and he whipped out some weird martial arts move he learned in the seventh grade, and knocked me onto my back. A farcical, slow-drunken-motion fight.

I shoved him out my door. He banged on it to be let back in. "You're a fool!" he kept yelling. "You're a fool!"

I actually called the cops on him, saying a guy was menacing me at my door. I immediately realized what a stupid idea that was, and didn't answer the buzzer when the cops rang. Luke descended the stairs drunkenly, calling out, "You're a fool, you're a fool, you're a fool."

That was my last detox from heroin. I cadged painkillers from people occasionally, but mostly I just drank. I figured that 1 PM was a respectable hour for a rock star to have a drink with his lunch. I was waking up at noon.

The sampler player wanted me to record a bunch of cover songs for some website. I e-mailed him that it was a stupid idea. He e-mailed me back, saying that I'd make a little money, and there was no other way imaginable that I'd make money playing solo. I wrote him back that he should go fuck himself.

My phone rang. "Doughty, I'm sick of your nastiness—I QUIT." Click.

This guy who ran a studio in Greenpoint, a friend of my bandmates', got robbed. I heard through a friend that they'd had lunch with him and told him they'd do a benefit. Apparently the sampler player was back in the band. The guy from Greenpoint called—not my bandmates—and told me about the proposed benefit. He spoke with a pleading tone.

Our manager called me. I learned later that he was calling to fire us. I launched into babble: I can't do this anymore, the sampler player was in and then out and then in again, they planned this show and didn't even want to call me.

This was a convenient for the manager, queasy about firing a man at his lowest. "If you want to quit," he said, "now would be a good time."

I called the drummer and told him I was quitting. "That's OK, you can go make a solo record, and then in a year we'll tour."

No. I'm *breaking up the band.*

"That's cool, you can do that there acoustic thing and we'll make another record next year."

I yelled, I'M LEAVING THE BAND.

"Yo, G," he said, "you're making a *mistake.*"

Somebody told me that he had a hard couple of years after the band split. Nobody else would put up with "Yo, G, it's the same beat."

I called the bass player's voice mail and left a message saying I was out. Next, I called the sampler player. He was upstairs putting the kid to bed, his wife said. Have him call me back, I told her.

I got an e-mail from the sampler player an hour later. He said: "The bass player called right after you did and said you were quitting. I didn't call you back because I don't want to talk unless it's important."

The next day, I made the rounds, calling people to tell them before they heard it elsewhere. I pretended it was courtesy, but I was really just overjoyed to relay the news. At last. At last. At last.

I called Luke. He was cagey, said he had to go. It turned out that the bass player and the drummer were sitting in his living room, talking about what a selfish asshole I was; they were waiting for the tackle box man.

We pulled into Pittsburgh in a white Buick. When I got up to the hotel room, I opened two minibar bottles of Jack Daniel's and poured them into a glass. I brought the glass to my face and was instantly repelled by the smell. Piss. Somebody drank the whiskey, then pissed it back into the tiny bottles.

The next day, I was wearing the DANGER!! BEWARE MINES!! t-shirt from Cambodia and suddenly realized it was way too tight. My jeans and coat, too. I realized that I'd been downing booze and drunkenly ordering mashed potatoes for months. When that angry physician who gave me the inhaler gave me a checkup in the fall, he weighed me at 135 pounds. My dope-fiend fighting weight. Skeletal. The Cambodia t-shirt rippled off me like a flag in the wind. When I weighed myself months later, I weighed 220. Assuming I was up around that weight that day in Pittsburgh, I'd gained eighty-five pounds in five months.

I was on my first solo tour in North America, with a tour manager driving me from town to town. I got drunk before the shows—onstage, I felt like I was playing the songs with a three-foot barrier of liquid between me and the world—and got drunker afterwards.

I felt so elatedly relieved that I'd finally cut the band loose, but everywhere I went, people talked to me as if someone had died. I saw my gigs as a triumphant emergence, they saw a postmortem.

One morning, driving out of Toronto, I realized my body was shaking. Having been a dope fiend, it was instantly recognizable: withdrawal. I went to a gas station looking for beer. No beer. We drove a couple hours to the border, where I bought an extra-large bottle of Jack Daniel's at the duty-free.

For the rest of the tour I stayed as close to the drunk/not-drunk line as possible, the border between functional and shit-faced. I pissed the bed every night. I flipped the mattress before the maid came, and if we were staying somewhere for more than one night, I would throw a bottle of water on the bed, like the maid might mistake piss for spilled Evian.

As we drove to Cleveland, I said, "I think I'm an alcoholic."

"Oh yeah, you're an alcoholic!" the tour manager said. I expected a reaction of surprised concern. "You drank that entire bottle of Jack in four days!"

That was actually two bottles ago.

I played a basement club that night, at one of the universities: the college pub, in a student life center. A blackboard advertised that night's student-spirit activities: "Beer, Wings, and M. Doughty."

I awoke in piss. Then I ordered a pizza from room service. Thirty minutes later, there was a knock on the door. I stumbled up to open it and found a gay white guy in a vest and bow tie, standing next to a tiny black girl in pigtails, maybe eight years old. She held the pizza box.

"It's Take Our Daughters to Work Day," the gay guy said. "Do you mind if she delivers your pizza?"

The girl gingerly carried the pizza box to the desk to the gay guy's encouragements. "Okay, honey, put the pizza on the desk—okay, now take the bill to the guest—make sure he has the pen, honey—okay, now open up the bill, the guest has to sign it, honey."

I flew to Minneapolis the next day. I had gotten into the routine of drinking red wine before brushing my teeth, but I forgot to take the bottle from the club the night before. No whiskey either. I got into the airport shuttle, where a chatty guy with golf clubs pestered me incessantly with mild chatter, What's the guitar for? Do you know how to play it? Wow, have I ever heard of you? No, never heard of you, but I'm not up on the music scene these days, heh-heh.

I thought, *Please just let me vibrate to death.*

I connected in Chicago, desperate for alcohol. I tried to buy a bottle of Jack Daniel's at the duty-free shop. The cashier asked for my boarding pass.

"This isn't an international ticket, sir," she said.

Oh, of course, no no, I'm flying domestically, but here's the thing, I will *pay duty.* I'll pay it!

She looked at me with withering disdain.

I blundered around the terminal looking for a bar. I finally found one, just opening at 11 AM. I ordered a double whiskey, but found I was shaking too hard to lift it without spilling. I dipped to it, like a cat lapping at a saucer.

The bartender looked at me with withering disdain.

On the plane, I got a few of those tiny liquor bottles. The shakes subsided. Liberty. Peace.

There was a girl in Minneapolis whom I had slept with a couple of times. She worked at a liquor store across the street from the

Marriott. She had some crystal on her, did I want to get a little speedy?

I was in no shape to play the gig, and maybe it would've helped, but I refused the speed. My weird parameters.

I played the 7th Street Entry, a tiny room affixed to the First Avenue club, where the old band had done multiple-night stands, 1,500 people per gig. The Entry was half full. Har Mar Superstar opened—he was just a local Minnesota guy at the time. I sat in the basement dressing room watching him prepare his boom box, hanging out in the underwear he performed in. I resented him for being new.

During the show a grinning kid up front, loving the show, jubilantly cried out the name of my old bass player. Pumping his fists, *"Whoohoo!"*

The liquor store girl and I went back to the Marriott and fucked. She produced her tiny bag of speed and tapped it out onto the table. I sniffed a line. It felt amazing. Naturally. *Hey!* I thought. *Perhaps I should spend some time with this particular drug before cashing in my chips.*

I tossed back a glass of whiskey, and immediately threw it up onto the liquor store girl.

The next day, I was driven to Wisconsin by a girl somebody at the club knew; I sat in the shotgun seat pouring whiskey into a Coke can, so the cops wouldn't see me drinking it openly. I passed out, then I came to, and then I passed out again.

Years before, I had dated a woman named Molly Escalator—a performance poet with a hilarious fuck-you aspect to her writing; she didn't speak in that kind of boring poet's singsong but sounded like a melodic comedian. She had this love poem that started:

Get away from me!
I mean, come here.
No, wait, that's too close.

We met at a gig when Soul Coughing was just a local band. She had been sober for years. She told me stories of her salad days as a runaway in the old, weird New York; shooting dope on the Lower East Side as a teenage punk rocker, weaning herself off heroin on her mom's farm in Delaware, facilitated by shooting up horse tranquilizer with gigantic veterinary needles. By the time we were dating she figured out that I had a major weed appetite. Which she tolerated.

On New Year's Eve, I heard about this disagreeable guy who had bought a shit-ton of cocaine and was throwing a party. He let people have his cocaine so they'd hang out with him. But, alas, I was just stopping by. Molly had lent out her tiny East Village studio apartment to her twin brothers, and therefore had to stay the night at my place in Brooklyn.

So I packed my face with this guy's cocaine, fast as I could get it in. Then I went to Molly's, sweating like a monster, looking so freaked out that I concocted a lie about getting accosted on the subway. Molly and I went to a boring party that most people had already left, and I kissed her, and then dove into a long babble about Wow, Molly Escalator, you're really special, and I just want to tell you . . .

"How much cocaine did you do?" she asked. She could taste it in my kiss.

On tour, I went to sleep in a motel in Akron, Ohio, on a warm evening, listening to soft rain; when I woke up, it had turned into a violent snowstorm, and I got an e-mail from Molly saying she'd left me for a famous artist from the rooms.

The rooms were twelve-step meetings. They're shorthanded as "the rooms," or "the program," or "the fellowship," among other things. I find calling the rooms "the program" to have a Huxleyan vibe, and "the fellowship" sounds to me like something involving a skull-faced man screaming about Jesus. So I'll go with "the rooms."

(I'm going to walk a line between talking about my experiences in the rooms, and not violating other peoples' anonymity. Twelve-step programs are not called, for instance, Narcotics Talk About It in Your Book, or Alcoholics Reveal Themselves Publicly, but it would be disingenuous to pretend I'm not riding a line by talking about it. The danger is that you're going to read this book and think that I'm speaking some kind of party line. I wouldn't be anybody's spokesperson, it's unlikely anybody would want me to be their spokesperson, and there *is no party line,* truly, definitively, absolutely none.)

(More likely, you might think: fuck this guy, if I ever was interested in twelve-step programs, I'm not anymore, because those rooms are chock full of self-righteous Mike Doughtys. That's not the case. There is variety in the people, just as there is anywhere else in life—you can find people who reflect your experience, or people who reflect something completely unlike your experience. I found freaky intellectuals who cultivated their insanity, whom I wanted to be like.)

(Here's the other thing: like I said, I might get fucked up again.)

When Molly talked about the rooms, my mind's ear heard a prison door clanging shut. There was something sort of alluring around the edges when she'd talk about a meeting she'd just been to—a sense of peace and grooviness, like the meeting had done some sort of magic—but mostly I saw it as a weird cult.

It exasperated me, for utterly no reason. She told me how she'd met a famous ex-junkie singer at some event, and later he knocked on her hotel room door and said, "Want to go get some soup?" Soup! What's romantic and reprobate about *soup?*

After Molly dumped me, I moped around, listening to the Teddy Riley remix of Mary J. Blige's "Changes I've Been Going Through" over and over. Tiresomely, she kept calling. "You *have to* be my friend," she said. Like fuck I have to, I replied.

Molly kept showing up now and then, and she'd always have something new going on: she had fallen in love with Bach's *Goldberg Variations,* so she'd learned to play piano; she read all these mystery novels, so she started corresponding with the authors; she'd gotten interested in horse racing and was writing a book about it.

I was the rock star, I was the one with the things going on and the awesomeness. What business did she have with an interesting life?

In fact, what I was doing was getting high alone in a room, getting high in the back of a bus, getting high as I lay in bed.

I sat in a hotel in Madison, Wisconsin, shaking because I hadn't had my morning drink yet, and I typed her an e-mail. I told her that I went through a bad heroin binge, and it nearly killed me, and now I have to be drunk all day. On some essential level, I could accept being a drug addict, but I can't accept being a drunk. Can you please take me to one of those meetings of yours?

That's why she kept that line open all those years.

I woke up on the third of May 2000, looking at a half-full glass of Jack Daniel's. I had passed out before the task was through. Somehow I managed to pour it out into the sink.

The tour manager drove me home, shaking, stuffing myself with chalupas. The trip took a day and a half; when I got home, there was beer in my fridge but I didn't touch it. There was dusty weed on my bedside table, glued to a sticky layer of NyQuil. A half bottle was my longtime nightcap of choice.

I sat across from Molly at Kate's Vegetarian Joint on Avenue B. She was staring at me curiously across my plate of tofu Buffalo wings. She was about to take me to my first meeting.

(The unisex bathroom at Kate's Joint had two amazing pieces of graffiti: *Yaphet Kotto Fucking Crazy.* Which meant—Yaphet Kotto is fucking crazy? Or an echelon of crazy, like, "Man, that shit isn't just crazy, that's like *Yaphet Kotto fucking crazy.*" And in silver pen: *"Robot" is a Czech word. It means "worker."* Next to it, sardonically: *Did you learn that at NYU?* Next to that, in shaky script: *no Larry told me.*)

So, I asked Molly, why should I stay clean if I go to these meetings? Can't I just go between binges?

She made a wistful face. "That's what I was going to do," she said, sincerely.

It disarmed me. I had grey skin, dead eyes, and anybody with half a mind would've slapped me. But Molly had loved drugs; she just knew they had stopped working, would never work again, and she didn't want to die.

I had a bottle of Valium in my pocket; I had hustled a prescription from the Cocaine Papers doc earlier that day.

You see movies and think that a twelve-step meeting involves somebody holding a clipboard. There was no clipboard. A guy who used to be a wasted drug fuckup read something at the beginning, another guy who used to be a wasted drug fuckup told the tale of his addiction, and then a roomful of former wasted drug fuckups spoke, each in turn—nobody interrupting anybody—about where they were at, or what happened to them, or where they wanted to be, about their lives both with and without getting fucked up.

Every variety of person was there. One guy talked about living in a shelter. Another guy talked about owning a business, but feeling trapped by it. A woman I recognized as a goth icon sat in the back row, knitting. She raised her hand and spoke of anguish over a crackhead ex.

There were heroin people, coke people, meth people, weed people, prescription-painkiller people, liquor people, beer people. Most of them, actually, a mixture of the whole list, serially or simultaneously.

The atmosphere was reverent, but not pious; it was both ritual and intimate. Whenever something borderline corny went down—the phrase "we share our experience, strength, and hope," a reference to god, the room saying, en masse, "Thanks for sharing," when somebody had finished talking—Molly turned to me and rolled her eyes sympathetically. But actually I felt an incredible warmth.

"Now's the part where we all hug and pray," she whispered into my ear, half sarcastically, as the meeting came to a close. "I should've mentioned that."

Everybody stood up in a big circle and put their arms around each other. "Let's have a moment of silence," said the guy who'd told his addiction story, "for the addict still sick and suffering, inside and outside of these rooms." And then everybody said the serenity prayer. I half knew it. And it made sense to me.

I typed the serenity prayer here, but then I deleted it: you've read that prayer thousands of times. I beg you to see it like this:

you want to get high. You know that it's going to kill you, or humiliate you, or drive you to desperation, that you're not really going to get *high* at all, but every part of yourself wants to. You want to get out from under it, and you've tried, but you don't have it in you to do it alone. You're willing to take a half step towards something big and weird, something that you don't even know you believe in, hoping that it, or they, or she, will help.

I met a guy named Leon, who knew the moment he looked at me that this was my first meeting. He gave me his number and a meeting list, and told me to call him the next day. I went to a diner and sat in the window, amazed to feel hopeful. I found another meeting to go to, late night, far on the West Side.

There was a deranged man in headphones dancing obliviously in the middle of the room; somebody shooed him away. Homeless guys slept in the back. There were two glamorous women, dazzlingly made up, in dresses and heels. Two men spoke: the first talked about how he had spent his life fantasizing about having a farm to grow his own weed and mushrooms, but then, bafflingly to him, had become a crack addict. The second guy had recently been homeless and had worked as a gravedigger before his life went haywire. His story went like this: "I went back to the shed and had a couple of belts. Then I went back to digging the grave. Then I went back to the shed, and had a couple of belts. Then I went back to digging the grave. Then I went back to the shed . . . "

Back at my apartment, I put the beer in front of my neighbor's door and went to the roof. I pitched the bottle of Valium; it arced upward, barely missed the streetlight on its way down, and exploded dramatically in the intersection, whereupon it was run over by a taxi.

It was the fifth of May—Cinco de Mayo. The day the Mexicans defeated the French. In the years to follow, I would think of Cinco de Mayo as my day of surrender. The beer industry celebrates the anniversary every year with commercials about boozing up on Mexican beaches.

That night in Pittsburgh when I almost drank the bottles of piss, I had gone drunkenly online and bought a ticket to Laos, adjacent to the Golden Triangle: you know, the place where they make the heroin.

In the reading they did at the top of the first meeting I'd ever gone to, there was a part that went something like, "If you're new, we suggest you make ninety meetings in ninety days—if that sounds like too much, make a meeting a day and the ninety will take care of itself." My addled mind didn't hear that as, *Go to a meeting every day for three months*—I heard it as if you could do ten meetings a day for nine days and you're set. I'll make forty-five meetings this month, I thought, go to Laos, then come back and do the latter half.

I told Leon the plan. He did not tell me it was insanely dumb. Instead, he took me to his apartment on Duane Street, rummaged around, found a photocopied guide to meetings all over the world, and copied out for me a phone number in the Laotian capital, Vientiane.

If the rooms were about people shaking a finger in my face, telling me what I must and must not do, maybe I wouldn't have stayed clean. I know some people who were told rigidly what to do, but that wasn't my experience. The people I met must've been experienced in defiance—what addict isn't? I was chock-full of terrible ideas. Nobody told me they were terrible. Somehow they disarmed me, and I dropped them.

Two days clean, I had this weird show to do; a symposium on New York musical history, thrown by the *New York Press*. A bunch of éminences grises were to do onstage interviews, and then a few locals would play.

I called Leon in a panic. How did I do this, in a bar, not drinking? He told me that somebody he knew was one of the guests. Who? He said the name of a rock legend, the singer of a band that more or less invented both punk and glam rock at the same time in the '70s. Wait. *Who?* Really?

I went to a meeting in the West Village, on Perry Street, a clubhouse that held meetings around the clock. It was an undecorated storefront surrounded by spendy bistros. The interior was painted pink. The guy who spoke was an actor; he'd just played a drunken hobo on a cop show. "It's amazing what the Russians can do with a potato," was one of his lines, delivered while gazing admiringly at a vodka bottle.

I walked all the way across town, past NYU, through SoHo, through Chinatown, to the Bowery Ballroom. My editor, Strausbaugh, was out front, taking a joint passed by one of the music writers, a delicate white kid in rapper drag, coordinated yellow Wu Wear billowing around his tiny body. Strausbaugh called out my name, but I kept my eyes to the pavement and asked where the rock legend was. Why—you know him? Huh? How? He hadn't shown up yet.

When the rock legend arrived, I stumbled up and told him who sent me. He reached into his pocket and pulled out a piece of fax paper; on it was a few lines from a Sufi poem:

> *Look to this day, for it is life!*
> *The very life of life*

The paper had gotten stuck in the fax machine; the remaining lines were distended like phantoms, illegible.

Somebody snapped a picture. It was in the paper the next week, with other photos of the event: the rock legend, handing me a poem, the very moment I met him.

His interview was hilarious. A story about being thrown in jail in Memphis. "I was dressed like Liza Minnelli at the time." A story about stalking Janis Joplin, stealing a Pepsi can she drank from at the Pink Teacup, which he used as an ashtray; how he obsessed over her like gay guys stereotypically obsess over Judy Garland. A story about standing next to Jim Morrison in Max's Kansas City: Morrison drank a bottle of Jack Daniel's in three guzzles and said, "Takes the edge off the acid." A story about being up for three days doing coke with David Bowie—"He was giving me the stink-eye!"—and discovering that his nose had bled all over his face and soaked his shirt. A story about tripping so severely at Altamont that he didn't know anything weird went down. A story about seeing Led Zeppelin play at the Central Park Zoo—"I thought they were a joke!" (surely he's the last of the late-'70s hipsters to have regarded Led Zeppelin as a crass enterprise)—and his distaste for the Beatles—"You'd get beaten up if you listened to that in my neighborhood."

The interviews went long, and the two acts that stuck around—me and a neo-hair-metal band in pink leather—played to ten people. The singer from Spacehog was there with Liv Tyler, as well as a renowned '70s groupie who walked around the Bowery Ballroom shoving her fantastic tits into rock dudes' backs, then smirking salaciously when they turned around. I made snide jokes at Ms. Tyler and the Spacehog guy, because I was an envious, sneering, bitter fuck.

I went to the bar afterwards for a Coke. They gave me a huge glass with the straw's wrapper curled gaily above the lip, like a flag, declaring, *This man isn't drinking, there's something wrong with him.* I met a redheaded girl whom I had seen in the crowd lip-synching my songs. She pretended she'd never heard my music before, gave me her number, asked if I wanted to come out to Bay Ridge next week and watch the series finale of *Beverly Hills 90210?* It just so happens I used to write a *90210*-summation-blog called *Peach Pit Babylon,* I told her, pretending like she didn't know this, and she pretended to be surprised. She left, and I met another girl who said she'd flown in from Denver, and would I like to take her back to my apartment and fuck her? Yes. We went to my place, a fetid disaster of a drunk's burrow; she pushed me onto the bare mattress and rode me. I'm going to come, I said, within a minute. "Don't look at my tits, and just breathe through it," she said.

I came instantly.

Something lingered after she split. Guilt? Loneliness? Embarrassment? I couldn't tell. I was used to crushing that stuff with something. Without mitigating substances, sex involved feelings.

(I saw a parody of *Mad Men* on *Sesame Street:* Muppets in suits, in a conference room, enacted emotions: "We're *mad!* We're *mad* men! Now we're *glad*—glad men! Now we're *sad* men!" I needed this; I had a toddler's emotional-identification skills.)

The next day I went to the Upper West Side. I wandered into the meeting late, blundering my way through rows of people. I sat down in the first empty plastic chair I found. A guy sat next to me, eating an unripe banana and drinking bodega coffee. I didn't see his face.

"How you doing?" he asked. I turned. The rock legend.

I feel like shit, I said, too caught-off-guard to lie.

"That's *gooooood,*" he said. His smile glowing.

After the meeting, I followed him around like a puppy as he received people; he was like the mayor. I stood there feeling dumb and ugly.

He took me to the park and told me, in his fantastically gravelly Staten Island accent, the twelve-step creation myth. Grinning, he spoke of revered figures in twelve-step history as "drunks" and "degenerates." He told of his own drunken miseries. How could alcoholism, a behavior, be a disease? I asked him, and he told me the old parable of the jaywalker: guy's really into jaywalking, his friends are all like, ha ha funny, then he gets hit, they figure he's done, he does it again, this time gets both legs broke, the friends are like, whoa that's weird, and then he does it again and they're bewildered, and he does it again, and they abandon him, and he does it again, and he does it again.

"You can wear life like a loose garment," the rock legend said. He was plainly serene.

I wanted what he had. I called him every day. He pontificated. I bleated complaints.

"I got two words for you," he said. "Books."

He buried me under a pile of them, spiritual tomes on every level of user-friendliness. Alan Watts, Thomas Merton, *Autobiography of a Yogi,* the Upanishads, Jorge Luis Borges's poem "Everything and Nothing," a loopy, ass-pocket-sized book called *Metaphysical Meditations,* a slim, wry volume called *How to Be an Adult.*

He told me that I could have an idea of something bigger than myself without narrowing into a set dogma, that I could hold entirely contradictory ideas about god—an iteration of what George Carlin mockingly called "the invisible man that lives in the sky," some of the quasi-Buddhist quasi-Hindu stuff, some cluster of weirder notions—simultaneously, and in fact, not really understand what it was I believed in, and that this addled, playful version of god-consciousness could be genuinely *useful*.

"If we had true knowledge of the cosmos, our skulls would burst," he said. "You're like a flea contemplating the Empire State Building."

He lived in a weird time warp in regard to the New York City subway system. There's a certain brand of lifetime New Yorker who refers to the 4, 5, 6 trains as the IRT and the B, D, F as the BMT, after their names when the subways were operated by independent companies. He was beyond even that. I invited him somewhere. "What train?" he asked. The F. "No way I'm taking that! The broken wicker chairs, the straps banging against the windows . . ." Um, that's the way the F train was *in the early '70s*.

He quoted Saint Francis and Casey Stengel. He was given to non sequiturs.

"Do you ever see some degenerate passed out in a doorway and think, 'I could do that'?"

"I shot dope when I was sixteen. My mom thought I was sick and made me chamomile tea."

We were sitting at a picnic table in the park, in midwinter, eating sandwiches. Suddenly he said, "Did I ever tell you about the time I made Buddy Hackett cry?"

You never heard anybody's last name in the rooms, so there was nickname upon nickname: Larry T., Larry C., Larry G., Quaalude Wayne, Howdy Wayne, Jersey Dave, Miracle Dave, What's-Cookin' Dave, Weepy Rita, Dave the Magic Man, Bill the Wizard,

X-man, Todd the Painter, Pool-hall Ria, Big Anthony, Hardcore Tommy, Stick-and-Stay Scott, Mikey Bagels, Scottish Craig, Ian the Goat-Sacrificer, Rocker Mike, Ed the Buddha, Nine-Year Bobby, Five-Year Bobby, and Fucking Chris, who would say, "I hate it when they call me Fucking Chris, I don't want to curse, I'm not going to fucking curse anymore."

(I know three people named Barclay in the rooms. Two men, one woman. *Three people* named *Barclay.*)

There was this one guy, a gangly, sinewy guy, maybe my age, who came to meetings on a blazing chrome bike with handlebars so high he dangled from it, like a medieval prisoner. He wore a silver helmet with a row of Germanic spikes lined front to back. He had about a year clean. It seemed incredible to me that somebody could put down drugs for a year. If a guy like this can be clean, I thought, a guy who won't surrender the things that make him weird, I can do it, too.

There was this kind, sagacious Jamaican guy named Wayne. He grew up in the projects, the only black kid there who was into rock music. He got beat up by the kids in the projects for wearing a The Who Long Live Rock jacket, and beat up by the white kids at the school he was bused to for being black. He had sometimes bought drugs at a Harlem record store called Da Hardest Hard. (Hardest *heart?* "No, *hard.*") I thought of his old self as Theoretical Wayne. Theoretical Wayne carried multiple knives, robbed crackheads, smoked angel dust, lived on cinnamon buns—they came in a package of two, so he'd eat one, throw the other one to the rats in the alley, whom he thought of as friends—and Nutrament, had a mom who dealt weed—her house on Long Island was once subject to a drive-by shooting. Somehow Theoretical Wayne, the dust-smoking knife-fighter, had turned into Compassionate Wayne, a guy who rode out on a motorcycle to South Dakota every summer to visit a Lakota Sioux tribe that had adopted him.

Barely a few months clean, he was asked what he wanted from recovery. "To stop the noise in my head," he said.

One thing I kept hearing in the rooms was, "If you don't use, you won't get high." But I got high all the time. I got really into getting up early in the morning to watch the light come on. I'd walk to get coffee and be stopped in my tracks when I saw the Manhattan Bridge against a pink sky, framed by tenements.

As a teenager, I scoffed at the TV stars in pastel sweaters, on the cover of *People* magazine, I'm-off-the-drugs-and-high-on-life! But here I was. Off the drugs and high on life.

I was awakening to what was around me, and in doing so, realized I'd had no idea just how shut off I was. One evening I had the TV on, and the weatherman said, "It was unseasonably cool today." Yes it was! It was unseasonably cool. *I was there!*

I was desperately trying to figure out how to pray. I felt lucky that I'd had that romance with Sam Cooke's gospel records—my flimsy link to the universe of faith.

I saw an episode of *The Simpsons* in which Homer is shanghaied into missionary duty in the South Pacific. "But I don't even believe in Jebus!" he says. As the plane takes off, he's told that there's no alcohol on the island. "SAVE ME JEBUS!!" he screams.

I was leaving a meeting, feeling utterly out of focus and purposeless, and I walked around a corner and found a liquor store. I looked past the towering god-bottle of champagne, the absinthe posters with devils on them, the gallons of Georgi vodka, and found the bottle of Jack Daniel's. Stared at it.

Save me, Jebus! I said. I laughed.

Thus began my spiritual awakening.

Every morning I poured out a stream-of-consciousness prayer into my notebook: please help me, what am I doing, help me, be with me, and on and on for pages and pages. It looks crazy when I read it back. But it was scraping the ugly veneer off myself like scratching a lottery ticket with a coin to see the number.

I felt that the Cosmos was communicating to me through my lucky number: twenty-seven. As a kid, I picked twenty-seven because I felt I ought to have a lucky number, and it was the one that sounded best when spoken and was the most interesting to me, graphically. That first year clean, I saw it on license plates, on bus-stop placards, on receipts. When I was dwelling on a depressing fantasy of relapse, or feeling hopeless, twenty-seven would appear. I was reading a guide-book for Southeast Asia, and I came to a passage that was something like, "If you want to try opium, and you're in X town, go to N restaurant and look for one of the desperate-looking guys in grimy clothes, and . . ." Suddenly Snoop Dogg walked onto my TV, across the set of MTV's *Total Request Live* with a giant twenty-seven on his jersey. I took them as messages from the Almighty that I should feel bolstered and backed by forces beyond my comprehension.

(I did a poetry reading with a guy wearing the very same jersey and tried to bond with him over the significance of twenty-seven. "Yeah, Eddie George—best running back in the NFL," he said, hesitantly.)

I started feeling connected to everything. Looking back on how earnestly I believed in the benevolent number-spirits, I wonder just how insane I was. I wish I had an ounce of that irrationality today. My irrationality took care of me.

Still, I fantasized about fleeing. I'd run home after meetings—I had the urgent business of isolating to attend to—and get online,

dial up travel sites, look up fares. I set up itineraries to Tashkent
or Caracas or Kolkata, luxurious travel and accommodations, fantasized about going to those places and just getting high. To lie
back on a plush bed in a mysterious faraway city, and just be high.
When I came to the page where you type your credit card information in, I clicked on "cancel."

My spiritual guide Homer was succeeded by John Coltrane. I
first heard his music on WBGO the day I moved to New York in
1989; when the chant of "a love supreme, a love supreme, a love
supreme," came in, I realized that I might find an entrance into
jazz, which had never interested me. I read the liner notes to
A Love Supreme:

> During the year 1957, I experienced by the grace of God, a spiri-
> tual awakening which was to lead me to a richer, fuller, more pro-
> ductive life. At that time, in gratitude, I humbly asked to be given
> the means and privilege to make others happy through music.

There happen to be some twelve-step codes in there: "grace of
God," "spiritual awakening," "gratitude," "humbly asked." Phrases
used not just in the recovery books, but *in the actual twelve steps*. I
have no idea if Coltrane was a twelve-step dude, but I clung to it.

I listened to, and got lost in, *Transition, Sun Ship, Afro Blue Impressions, New Thing at Newport, Kulu Sé Mama, One Down One Up*.
Coltrane is beyond classification: he's beyond jazz, he's a spiritual
force. He kept pushing, until his death in 1967, getting wilder,
scarier, more powerful, more hallucinatory, more transcendent
with each recording.

I saw a video of a performance he did with Eric Dolphy: first
Dolphy solos, and it's amazing; the man was a giant for sure. Then

Coltrane comes in and explodes the music with the power of the ecstatic. Next to Coltrane, even a giant is *just playing the saxophone.*

Before the late '50s, Coltrane was a fair-to-middling sort of workaday jazz guy. Roughly around his cited date of 1957, he got inspired. I was used to the *People* magazine pieces about artists getting clean and becoming blandly cheerful paragons of lite rock. Like I said, no idea if Coltrane really had a twelve-step thing going on or not, but with him in mind, I became determined to be clean and chase art.

I'm on a cocktail of pills for bipolar disorder. Briefly, when I was newly sober, I got on an antidepressant, and it helped, but I was conflicted about leaning on a drug. I thought of the old canard "Better living through chemistry" and thought that I wanted to be able to say, "I've achieved better chemistry through living."

I couldn't. I felt like an aircraft carrier was on my chest.

After much anguish and second-guessing, I went to a psychiatrist—meaning he had an M.D. and could prescribe drugs. He was a rabbinically bearded guy with a Texan accent. It took a year and a half for him to dial in a working combo—he put me on two pills, increased the dosage of one, removed another, replaced it, decreased the dosage on one, et cetera. Now I feel pretty sturdy. The drugs are a huge part of that, but so is talk therapy, the rooms, friends both of the rooms and not, songwriting, eating the occasional vegetable, moving around in sunlight. Sometimes I'm disappointed that I need a pill, but I can accept that there's an element of my whole thing—not, by any means, the whole shebang—that's a physical part of my body.

Personally, I think the appellation "bipolar" is a shuck. It's a trendy diagnosis; it doesn't even mean you oscillate between two poles anymore. That's not uncommon—for instance, "borderline personality disorder" is still a valid diagnosis, despite that nobody considers the disorder to be on the border of anything anymore. I don't have those insane lows and highs now. My attacks of anger and resentment—lying awake all night, unable to stop my mind from swiping at phantoms—are my mania.

Actually, I find the term "maniac" to be more accurate. And fun.

Whatever it is, I can't dispute that the rabbinically bearded guy from Texas has dialed me in. The cocktail of meds has wrought amazing relief. There aren't any notable side effects, sexual, soporific, or otherwise. Though I sometimes feel naggingly inauthentic. As if it were cowardly to need medical help.

Leon, who had maybe fifteen years clean when I met him, relapsed. He had a cold and started using Robitussin for it, and in time he was drinking the equivalent of a six-pack a day of it. He did a circuit of different pharmacies on different days, buying only a single bottle at each stop. (If I were into cough medicine, I'd go to the same place every day and be matter-of-fact about it, a way of saying, If this was a real problem, I'd be trying to hide it.) I was sitting next to Leon at a meeting and all of a sudden he said, "Is it ridiculously hot in here or is it just me?"

It was just him. I didn't think anything of it. Maybe he had too many layers on.

At some point he realized what was happening. Those who scoff at the concept of addiction as a disease, I have no comprehensive argument to present, but please note that he was drinking *six big bottles of* Robitussin *daily without realizing something weird was going on.*

I chased a princess around the rooms. She was a Slavic girl of noble birth, her swank family displaced by a revolution. I had no purpose, and when I saw her, I thought she might as well be it. She was thirtyish, like me; Hockney-pool-eyed, citrine-yellow-haired, ever so slightly weathered. I had fantasies of being with a thirtyish woman like this. It seemed proper. At the time when I had twenty days or so, she was approaching a couple of months.

I went to this one meeting uptown, near a studio where they shot soap operas. It was peppered with TV-handsome alcoholics, with that sheen of blazing health common to people who've been in recovery for a couple of years. The meeting was once populated with movie stars: it was some kind of agreed-upon movie star hang. The movie stars drifted away, leaving the B list. Eventually, the soap stars would move on, too. Years later, one would occasionally see a baffled movie star walking in, looking for his tribe.

The drama of my every day was whether or not the princess would be there. I never spoke to her; sometimes I'd be standing adjacent to a conversation between her and a mutual friend. She spoke of a glamorous life of beaches in France and jet-setting. I hoped one day she'd talk about the politics of her homeland, that I could maybe jump in and show off my brain.

I heard rumors about her—that she was a sort of concubine to a certain husky-jawed movie star, renowned for his prodigious drug intake, that she kept drifting back to him. That her strange cross-addiction was sucking off strange men, that she'd find some man in public and take him around the corner, moments after meeting him. I lamented never finding a way to be caught alone with her near a bathroom, but realized that I would've fallen in love with her the moment I was in her mouth.

I felt a little lowly around her, because she was a few weeks ahead of me, but that changed. I had two months, and then she relapsed, and the next time I saw her, she had five days. I had four months, she had four days. I had six months, and she had two weeks. I had ten months, and she had eight days. I saw her picture in a restaurant review: she sat at a table with other glamorous types, a drink in front of her. I saw her again: I had two years, she had a month. On it went, until I didn't see her around anymore.

The first time I spoke at a meeting was that soap-opera-star one. I was up in front of everybody behind a table, rambling about whatever, and I got to when I was pissing the bed every night. I started talking about the etiquette of pissing the bed in a hotel; flipping the mattress, balling up the sheets and throwing them in a corner yourself, so the maid wouldn't have to deal with your piss. And just when I was realized that I might regret talking about my history of pissing the bed, I looked out and saw this beautiful woman, smiling at me. She was older, and had silver hair, and an elegantly lined face, and she was looking at me directly in the eyes and beaming.

I'm full-bore bat-shit crazy with regards to Soul Coughing. If somebody says they love Soul Coughing, I hear *fuck you*. Somebody yells out for a Soul Coughing song during a show, it means *fuck you*. If I play a Soul Coughing song, and somebody whoops— just one guy—I hear *fuck you*. People e-mail my own lyrics at me— "Let the man go through!" or "You are listening!"—oddly often (how weird is that, to blurt somebody's own lyric at them?), and I type back, "Don't put that on me, I'm not that guy anymore, that guy's dead."

If somebody comes up and says, I've been listening to you since 1996, it means *I had a definitive youthful drug experience to an old CD, and now you'll never escape that band that you loathe, and you are forever incomplete without those three hateful faces.*

When somebody hears your voice for the first time—particularly if they discover the record in school, or at some developmental juncture—they stake out a little place in their minds for you. Your work can get more sophisticated, truer, closer to your ideal, but you'll never get out of that place. No song you make can get to them: it will fail to turn them twenty again.

There are six or seven Soul Coughing tunes that I like, mostly ones that sound more like my solo records. On those songs, my bandmates' surliness and contempt makes way for keenly felt accompaniment, contrapuntal profundity. Honestly, I don't truly love more than six or seven Jay-Z, or Regina Spektor, or AC/DC songs—I'm a song guy, not an album guy—but I'd tell you, without hesitation, that I adore those artists. Again: full-bore bat-shit crazy.

There are a few others that I'm proud of as songs. I dislike the recordings, but, when I play them by myself, I feel what I meant. Unless they provoke whoops of approval, in which case I'll immediately hate them. My insane-slash-conniving bandmates convinced some deep part of me that I'm not the songwriter. Songs I picked out alone in my room, for which I wrote the chord progression, the melody, the lyrics, the rhythm: not mine. The band's. Not mine, not mine, not mine.

The rest of the Soul Coughing tunes sound dreadful to me. Geeky, weighted down with a waka-waka Vaudeville thing, diseased with *terminal uniqueness,* pompous, crammed with ostentatious parts that barely acknowledge the songs, that fight to push the voice into the background, fight every other instrument because each guy's convinced his part's the most important. The really great instrumental parts are weakened, transformed from fantastic hooks to stumblers in a jumble. There's often a refusal to play something that would just make a listener *feel good,* because what's unique about that? Instead, those parts are self-consciously obscure, fake sounding, insincere.

(Did I like the recordings when we made them? Two answers of equal weight, the first being *yes and no,* the second, *I don't remember.* I remember loving tracks in this way that seems manic, injected with denial—I remember loving tracks that, now, should I hear them in a bar, nearly provoke me to jump over the bartender and bang my fist on the sound system's off button, I remember loving some tracks when I was high, I remember loving some tracks in a way that seems genuine in retrospect but baffles me now.)

We were a relatively successful cult band, but I think that, had my bandmates chosen to let me be a bandleader, we could've been Led Zeppelin. How do you tell that to someone who loves an album? Yes, you love it, so fiercely, but in my mind I hear something *so much better,* and thus reject this thing you love. All the people that wrote us off as geeks—I will never reach them to say: there was something great here, but we failed to let you hear it.

Being strapped to ancient work would be stultifying to any artist, in any medium. It took rigorous effort to get out from under it. I played Soul Coughing songs on my first solo tour, but fewer on the next tour; even fewer on the next. Now I don't play any. I busted my heart fighting a crowd that wanted old stuff. The people who came back came for the new songs.

When people yell out song names, I repeat them:

Madeline!

Madeline, yes, a few songs from now.

Disseminated!

Disseminated, nope, don't play Soul Coughing tunes.

Only Answer!

Only Answer, not tonight.

40 Grand!

40 Grand, maybe later, it's on the bubble.

I do this because a reviewer in Austin once wrote that the crowd was incessantly shouting for old stuff; I wearily, vainly tried to push new songs. But that crowd wasn't shouting for old stuff. I don't know if the writer didn't hear the requests for solo tunes, or if he ignored what actually went down, but in any case, the better story was, "Bitter man fights his past." So I say titles aloud, to make damned sure that nobody can write that story again.

Each batch of songs I write feels realer than the last batch. But the bulk of the public, the ones who *aren't* coming to my shows, don't bother to investigate. Who leaves a famous band and gets *better*?

(Somebody I know was at a marketing meeting where they were kvetching about nobody buying Elvis Costello records, despite Elvis being on a creative hot streak. "It's because people have enough Elvis Costello records," she said. They hated her.)

The critics didn't stampede to my shows, either, and sometimes when they write about me, they won't hear, can't hear, what I'm doing now. Some of them think I've downgraded: where once the music had experimental elements, now it's a guy with a guitar, as there are thousands of guys with guitars. If I had no past, maybe they'd hear the music as what it is.

(I make exactly the kind of songs I love. So when I listen to them, I dig the hell out of them. When they're new, I'll listen to them on headphones on the subway and love everything about them, in a manner disconnected from my pride and narcissism. Just as songs I love. This being the case, of course I feel like I'm genuinely an unrecognized champion. Maybe I'm as good as I think I am; maybe it's purely myopia.)

(I met M. Ward at a benefit. He professed to be a Soul Coughing fan. He asked me, "So what are you doing now? Writing plays?"

I was crushed. He's a solo-acoustic guy like me. I feel myself to be an artist of his echelon.)

When I do an interview and the writer apologizes for not knowing anything about Soul Coughing other than "Circles," I thank her or him exuberantly.

There is a Soul Coughing fan reading this whose heart I've just broken, who picked up the memoir of the guy from a band he loves, and it turns out I hate what brought him to this book in the first place. Some Soul Coughing fan is going to read this and come to a show to implore me to love what he loves, to *sell* me on it. How can you hate this? It's *yours*.

All I can do is my work, work, work; give everything my best: write songs that I love and believe in, play shows, try to dial into that energy, whatever it is, to let it seize me. My bitterness demolishes me, wakes me at 5 AM and won't let me fall back asleep, drives me to waste hours fighting ghosts in my head. But, in my struggle to stay with the music, I've lucked into people who are *with me*.

Every song seems to be somebody's favorite song. The audience seems to be hearing the nuances and the deeper aspects of the tunes. I struggle to ignore whatever my narcissism tells me I should resent—for instance, that I began my solo work just as the big record labels hit icebergs and began to sink, and, being that I know how to write a decent hook, maybe, were it 1997, I'd have a hit or two on the radio, a big one or a small one, but certainly a song or two with enough presence that M. Ward might not think I had dropped out of music entirely. Because if there's just fifty-five people listening to the music I make, and I'm eating food and sleeping in a bed—and making music I love and believe in—I have a fantastic life.

I'm so grateful for these listeners. Maybe that's you: I'm grateful for you.

I was playing in Vancouver in 2000, only four months after the band's death, three months after I'd drunk my last drink. I was alone at the mic with an acoustic guitar. Some guy shouted, "Do you miss the other guys?"

No, I said. Do you?

"Yes," he said, from somewhere in the crowd.

Ooooooh, the crowd went.

I peered out, but he didn't reveal himself.

You should go get your money back, I said. They're not hiding behind the curtain. They're not coming out later.

I almost pulled out my wallet to offer a ten-dollar bill right out of my pocket.

There was much unkindness on the internet. "Doughty's gonna end up with a gun in his mouth when he figures out the solo career isn't going the way he thought he would," somebody said.

"Fuck Doughty selling out," said another. "I miss the old Doughty, who ate E's like candy!"

I played a show in New Orleans. I was selling CDs off the front of the stage afterwards. A woman came up, grabbed my hand, held it to her breast.

"You have to get back together with your friends," she said.

My *friends,* I said. Bewildering—but, of course someone who loves a band thinks it must be a roving party of merry compatriots.

I tried to sound gentle, though I felt punched in the gut. That's not gonna happen, I said.

"But how are you going to play *'Casiotone Nation'?"* she said shrilly, as if the fact it was her favorite song meant it was an integral spoke in the universe, and she was helping me—poor, misguided man—to understand my true mission.

How am I gonna play 'Casiotone Nation'? I'M NOT. I yelled in her face.

The look of shock on her face suggested she felt screamed at by someone she had tried to helpfully, compassionately steer in the right direction.

I was shaking as I packed my guitar, wrapped up my cables. Tipsy guy walked up.

"That was my girlfriend. She's a dancer, she wants the beat, that's all," he said.

Uh-huh, I said, wanting to get the hell out of there, go somewhere to be alone.

"That was the most honest show I've ever seen," he rhapsodized. "Every note you played was like magical blar blar blar et cetera et cetera."

I have to go, I mumbled, and hotfooted towards the door.

He was suddenly furious. "BUT I'M NOT DONE COMPLIMENTING YOU," he barked after me.

Fandom is often not altruism. Effusive praise, in these cases, isn't meant to make you feel good, but to get something out of you. He wanted me to provide him with, appreciatively, dutifully, a gratifying encounter. So, in lionizing me, he felt he was extracting from me an unquestionable obligation.

I did a gig at a college. The next day, I plodded near-blindly around the campus, in a quest for espresso that got more daunting by the minute.

I was barely looking up from the sidewalk, lurching among students carrying books who careened, in all directions, around me.

A kid walked up in front of me and just stopped there, blocking my way. He was beaming. He started to speak.

I stopped him. "Hey, hi, uh, I can't really talk right now, I have to . . . go do . . . uh . . . see you later . . . " I hastened clumsily away.

Months later, I searched my name. This is a terrible thing to do to yourself if you're lonely and hoping for munificent admiration as a balm for loneliness. You will always, always, always find something horrible. If your mind works similarly to mine, one spiteful sting will ring truer than ten pages of accolades.

I found a review of the show at that college. The gig was described shruggingly, by a student who, later in that issue, wrote an editorial about hockey. In the comments beneath the article, there was one that said, "I bumped into M. Doughty near the humanities building and he was an asshole, I'M GOING TO THROW AWAY ALL HIS ALBUMS AND I'M NEVER GOING TO GO TO HIS SHOWS AND I'M NOT GOING TO GIVE HIM ANY MONEY."

(Some affronted fans threaten to withhold their cash. Do they feel their relationship to music and musicians is, on the most essential level, as a consumer?)

Saul Mongolia dropped me from Warner Bros., telling my lawyer that it was because I was going bald.

(He would go on to gain a measure of infamy for being the guy who dropped Wilco from Warner Bros. when they turned in *Yankee Hotel Foxtrot;* he told them there wasn't a single on it. Wilco found a new label, and the record sold more than 500,000 copies.)

I got a new manager, this very short and stout, expansively convivial guy. He was married to a gorgeous, redheaded fashionista who towered over him. She dressed him flamboyantly, gave him a lavender faux-hawk and dressed him in linen shirts with complicated floral embroidery. This squat, bespectacled Jewish guy from Long Island, dolled up in *L'Uomo Vogue* clothes.

It turned out he was clean, too, for a dozen years. I don't know of anybody else who would take on a newly clean, shaky addict who'd just been kicked off his record label. I wanted to go out and play solo shows; he actually took me out for *driving lessons.*

I got a rental car, put the guitar in the trunk, printed up cheap copies of that acoustic album *Skittish* that I made with Kramer, and played wherever they'd have me. I drove 9,000 miles, by myself, on the first tour. After the show I sat on the front of the stage with the cardboard boxes of CDs and sold them for $15.

Skittish had somehow gotten out on the internet; some people knew the songs. For the most part, the audiences were disappointed; they knew Soul Coughing, they wanted Soul Coughing, and here was the extreme opposite: one guy with an acoustic guitar—a fucking *balladeer?* Some of them were genuinely indignant. Angry. But in the front row, there were cute girls in thick black glasses lip-synching the *Skittish* songs.

The next tour, the audience was smaller: the Soul Coughing fans were abandoning me. I was still selling *Skittish* in a plain white sleeve, no label to publicize me. From there, an audience for my acoustic thing was built.

I played the Great American Music Hall in San Francisco—the same place where Jeff Buckley and I had sniffed heroin in the basement. The bass player from that renowned queer-punk band whom I had met at Sluggo's in Pensacola was managing the place. He asked me, with an implied wink, whether I *needed anything.* I laughed. No, no. I'm fine with the Diet Pepsi in the dressing room cooler.

Years later, I bumped into him in the rooms in Brooklyn.

I tried to jump back into songwriting and wrote terrible, trite songs. That was because my receptors were charred, disabled by the drugs' assault on my brain and my heart, and because for the last couple of years of the band, I had just given up on trying to write a great song, knowing that I was in a band that didn't care.

The rock legend exhorted me to pray. The idea spooked me too much. But I started writing prayers in my journal—maybe not prayers, but scrawled entreaties, please let me get through this day, please help me to not throb to death, please, please, please. Hours and hours, pages and pages.

I started praying to god, then praying sarcastically to god, then to my certainty that I couldn't trick myself into belief, then to a blurred spiritual notion, and then back to a god that I fully believed in again. In a loop.

(I want to note that I really dislike capitalizing "god." It's more like saying "music" or "light" than, for example, "Doreen" or "Uzbekistan." But my copy editor is telling me that conventional usage dictates "God," not "god," and typing "god" calls attention to itself, implies a more complicated philosophical point than I'm capable of making, and makes it seem like I'm one of those people who wants to be e.e. cummings when he grows up.)

One day, without me noticing it, the ability to get something new out of the guitar, out of my voice, came back. I went into those notebooks and pulled phrases and sentences and thoughts out. They became lyrics. Some songs were addressed to god, and I changed them to address the unsingable girl. Some songs were addressed—wistfully or angrily—to drugs themselves.

There were songs in which I was speaking to a beautiful woman, listing all the reasons she'd be better off not loving me. I didn't mean to be arch, or sardonic. This was just how I felt. The songs just fell out that way.

The new crowd grew from curious to fanatical. I'd start songs—
new songs, songs that weren't on albums yet—and within two seconds they'd recognize it and whoop. ("No offense intended," said
an amazed acquaintance, "but to me, your songs are kind of sim-
ilar." None taken. The guy was right. Happily, the four songs I
repeatedly write are my favorite four songs, and, seemingly, some
audience members', too.) People asked me to sign their arms and
then had the signature tattooed. I did a live recording; people yell
out the *between-song jokes* at me.

I got stalkers. There was a woman who wrote me long e-mails
to the fan-mail address on my website as if I had always been her
boyfriend: I can't wait until you come home, we'll go to _____ for
dinner, go play cards at _____'s house, we'll make love by the fireplace. There was a girl who got my phone number and would
leave interminable messages, sometimes professing love, sometimes screaming at me for something imaginary I'd done to her
brother. There was a girl I saw by the back door of a club in Philly.
She was standing with a bunch of other fans, who were getting
stuff signed. Do you want me to sign something? I asked. She
stared at me, stunned. What is it? "Don't you remember all those
e-mails you wrote me?" What? No—what did I say in them? "All
kinds of wonderful things," she said. As is my pattern with crazy
people, I thought it must be me: I wondered if I really had sent
her e-mails and had forgotten about it. There were two stalkers
from Maryland: one was a gorgeous nineteen-year-old with an unnerving look in her eye who looked like a *Playboy* model circa
1963. She showed up at gigs hundreds of miles away and then said
she had nowhere to stay, could she stay with me? There's a mountain of a blonde woman who drives a dump truck in Baltimore.
She's got my signature and the art from my first solo record tattooed on her massively flabby right arm. She writes e-mails asking

if I want to meet for lunch, then, when I don't respond, pleads: "I don't understand, what have I done, why don't you want to be friends with me?" She offers to buy me expensive gifts. She would hug me after the shows, her body twice the size of mine, and squeeze the air out of me. I had to struggle to get loose. She drives long distances, too, and stands in the center of the front row, never looking at me but glowering at the floor, lost in some distressing reverie.

I played a gig in Rochester with this miniature Scottish singer-songwriter. He entered the dressing room and said, in a Scots burr, "We'll get along fine if ye'll drrrrink with me!"

Uh, actually I don't.

"Oh, then do ye smoke weed?"

Nope.

He looked kind of scared. "Are ye in the prrrogram?"

We drove to Philly together the next day. He spent the whole drive making unsolicited excuses. "I trrrried cocaine once and I didn't like it. I don't drrrrink before shows, I don't drrrink as much as my frrriends. I didn't smoke any weed at all last Febrrruary. I've never done herrroin, I don't . . . "

The litany was ceaseless.

I asked if usually he got stoned on long drives. Yes. I pulled into a Shell station; he walked behind it and got high. We talked about other means of getting fucked up as we drove. What's your favorite drug? Opium. Opium? Was it a squishy black lump? Yes. Did you smoke it off a piece of tinfoil? Yes.

It's *very* unlikely that's opium—it's probably black tar heroin.

He was appalled. But haven't you ever taken Vicodin? Percocet? That's the *same shit.* I mean *literally* the same. In your brain, it's exactly the same chemical—it's morphine. It's like saying "Well, I like gin, of course, but I'd *never* drink whiskey."

On September 10, 2001, heavy clouds were over New York. I walked over to my manager's office to pick up a box of CDs to sell at my gig that night in Massachusetts. My last view of the World Trade Center was directly down West Broadway; clouds gathered at the midpoint, obscuring the tops of the towers.

I had come up with a new chord progression, and I was messing with melodies in my head as I drove. I pulled into Northampton in the rain. I stood outside in the drizzle before the show; there was a church across the street with people standing around a back door, smoking and drinking coffee from paper cups. Clearly, a twelve-step meeting.

I was opening the shows with a Soul Coughing song, the first line of which was:

> *A man*
> *Drives a plane*
> *Into the*
> *Chrysler building*

So sick of that song, I thought. Need an excuse to stop playing it.

I fell asleep to thunder, and woke up to a brilliant day. Green leaves scraped the motel window. I turned on the TV. Ann Curry was interviewing Tracey Ullman on the *Today* show.

I had been clean a little more than a year, and I was still doing the thing where I woke up early every morning to watch the day come on, in love with light. I kept myself company with the TV, so I was accustomed to the rhythms of the *Today* show; it starts at

7 AM with hard news; the news goes until 8, when the cookbook authors show up. It was just past 7:30; that Tracey Ullman was being interviewed so early meant it was an uncommonly slow news day. Tracey Ullman, in fact, had draped her legs over the arms of her chair and batted at Ann Curry's questions breezily. It was such a slow news day that even Tracey Ullman couldn't plug herself in earnest.

I like news, not celebrity corn. I switched it off, mildly bummed. Reproachfully, I told myself the old Chinese curse: May you live in interesting times.

I got Starbucks; the sky was wholly blue, in a cloudless condition that happens after strong storms called "severe clear." I drove south listening to the BBC. They said a small plane—a one-passenger plane, like a Piper Cub or something—had crashed into the World Trade Center. "Foul play is suspected," said the Brit reading the news.

My brother called and left a message. Two planes had hit the World Trade Center, could I see them from my place? My living room window had a direct view of the towers. The Brit hadn't said anything about a second plane. *Two planes, ridiculous,* I thought. *Rumors are so weird.*

The Brit acknowledged the second plane. "Foul play is suspected," he said again.

The BBC sputtered and faded. I hit the seek button and landed on Howard Stern. The first tower fell. Then Howard's signal sputtered away, and I switched to a station that had just put a feed from a local TV station on. The anchor's vantage was exactly that of Howard Stern: sitting in a studio, looking at a monitor.

A friend called. She had a gig at the fashion shows in Bryant Park that week: her job was to scratch the bottoms of the models' shoes with scissors, so they didn't slip on the runway. She said the White House had been bombed.

The second tower fell. It became clear that if I drove back to New York, they wouldn't let me in. So I drove over the Newburgh-Beacon Bridge on I-84, turned around, drove back. Howard came back on. Howard was howling. I turned again, the local anchor came back, just trying to fill up the air with authoritative anchor-ese, but clearly halfway into a freakout. He faded; back to Stern howling.

I wanted to call my parents. The cell-phone lines were jammed up, so I stopped at a Dunkin' Donuts and tremblingly asked if I could use the phone: I lived near the towers and wanted to call my family, I said. "It's a local call, right?" said the Dunkin' Donuts guy.

Apparently my mom, a guidance counselor, spent the day making sure none of the kids used the attacks as an excuse to skip class.

I got through to a friend who'd just gotten out of a rehab in Connecticut and was living in a small apartment near the hospital, working at a record store—she blew the mind of the record store manager, having a résumé with heavy music management companies on it but applying for a job stocking the racks in this tiny shop. I picked her up, and we immediately went to Starbucks, which had a sign in the window that said CLOSED DUE TO THE NATIONAL EMERGENCY.

We ate pizza, then hoagies, then Mexican food. Every indulgent thing we did, we joked, "It's for the war effort!"

I actually *saw* the collapses, for the first time, on a small TV in a gas-station convenience store. Before that, having no idea what it looked like when massive buildings came down—or how long 110 stories actually was, measured in city blocks—I wondered if they'd fallen on my building.

I slept at her place for a few days, then drove back to the city. I was somewhat surprised to find that Avis charged me a penalty for the extra rental time.

Every lamppost, every door, nearly every flat surface, was covered with MISSING flyers: photocopied images of a smiling relative at a BBQ or a graduation. Hundreds of them, rippling in store windows, coming loose from their Scotch tape and floating gently to the street. As if these people had wandered out of the towers just before they'd fallen and were wandering around Manhattan in states of half sleep.

There were papers strewn on my roof, memorandums and printed e-mails and other business-type communications. They had fluttered out of the towers and were collecting on every roof within a half mile.

I knew that the unsingable girl worked serving drinks at a private club down by where the towers were. It was up in an office building, a place for alcoholic day traders who came to drink all day and watch the numbers ticking past on the monitors above the bar. I wondered if she'd been caught up in it. I finished that new chord progression as a song about her. "Call me back when the war is over," went one line. "Call me back when your boyfriend's gone."

I went to a meeting. I buttonholed a guy and started to babble the tale of my September 11th, but his face went slack, and it was clear that the notion of hearing yet another's person story made him weary. I met a kid with a pair of drumsticks in his pocket who'd just gotten out of a detox center on Long Island; he caught the last train into Penn Station and was wandering around in that newly clean shaky state, looking for a meeting, when he saw the towers come down. He's still clean.

We, the addicts, were lucky to have the meetings. We had someplace to talk. We had people to be with. We had a tenuous defense against an overwhelming urge to blot it out—it seemed like everyone in the city was getting wasted. I heard a guy talk about how, upon realizing New York was under attack, he bolted from work, resolving to immediately smoke some crack—if he was going to die, what the hell, right? He'd been clean for years; he had no idea where to cop. He found a homeless dude and offered him $20 if he'd lead him to a spot. The homeless dude talked him out of it.

After a meeting, a friend and I—the friend from the fashion show—bought miniature flags on the street. Conspicuous patriotism was mostly unfamiliar to the Lower East Side of Manhattan. We kept holding our flags up to each other and saying "America" in bad redneck accents. Uh-murr-kuh. Uh-murr-kuh. Uh-murr-kuh.

I did get back to Southeast Asia when I had a year clean. I got to the last page on the travel site and clicked "purchase" instead of "cancel."

I was alone in Phnom Penh. All I did was go to the riverside, eat Khmer pizza, read, journal, drink coffee. Normalcy was somehow easier, transposed on an exotic city.

I went to an English-speaking meeting in an internet café on a shabby lane. I walked up to a bearded white guy. "Are you a friend of Bill's?" A code for somebody in the rooms.

He looked surprised. "I *am* Bill," he said.

I got on the back of a moto-cab.

"So," the driver said, "you like *girl?*"

No thanks.

"Ohhhh," he said, "you like *boy.*"

I'm afraid not.

"You like *dreenk?*"

No.

"You like *smoke opium?*"

No, no.

"You like *shoot gun?*"

I paused.

Yeah! Yeah, I can do that!

He drove me to a place at the city's edge. There were some Brits hanging out, drinking beer and shooting every pistol on offer. For $20, the proprietor handed me an AK-47, and I unloaded the whole clip on an archery target. He tried to show me how to aim, but I was content just to feel the metal shuddering against my shoulder.

This was a little after the 2000 election, when the Supreme Court awarded the presidency to George W. Bush. He hadn't been inaugurated yet.

The moto driver was gassing up. I bought him a Pepsi.

"So," he said. "George Bush is president now?"

No, next month, he'll be president.

"My friend say that when George Bush is president, Al Gore leave?"

Yeah, that's right.

"But now he is second?"

He's the vice president.

"Second?"

Yes.

"He is *second*," said the driver, "and he just *leave?*"

I went to Ethiopia in August 2004.

I saw an Olsen twin deplaning as I sat in the departure lounge. She was tiny, and wore chic, frayed clothes, and big sunglasses; she was flanked by matronly handlers. The airport newsstand was wallpapered with new issues of *In Touch* magazine that happened to have an Olsen twin on the cover, and the headline, "Is She Out Of Control?"

People sat in the lounge reading that issue. I think I was the only one who saw her.

Addis Ababa, the Ethiopian capital, is sprawling, dusty, chaotic; there are big neighborhoods of tin and mud shanties next to high-rises; haughty urbanites in Western suits-and-ties passing guys in shawls, with head wraps and walking staffs. Children yelped *"Faranji! Faranji!"*—Amharic for "foreigner," actually a mangled version of the word "French"—at me. Donkeys and goats jostled with taxis on the streets; a guy in an Eminem t-shirt herded sheep. Amharic music was everywhere, a warped-sounding, cheesily orchestrated, careening, fascinating sound, in stuttered waltz-time.

There was an Ethiopian Airlines billboard over Meskel Square— a vast intersection of multilane roads, without traffic lights, with minibuses and old Soviet Lada sedans battling for lane changes and turns—that advertised "Stockholm: Savour the Old World Charm." This, in Ethiopia, where the skeleton of one of the world's most ancient hominids—called Lucy by the anthropologists who dug her up—was found.

I went to a cathedral, where the throne of Haile Selassie was strewn with plastic coffee cups. There was a ferocious hailstorm. The roof sounded like it was being assailed with gunfire.

Singing came through a loudspeaker at a church by the hotel all night. Ululating melodies unspooled as I lay trying to sleep. I got out of bed and turned on Ethiopian national television, which was broadcasting the Brendan Fraser vehicle *Blast from the Past*. It cut inexplicably to Olympic footage for fifteen minutes, then back to where we left off in the Brendan Fraser movie.

In the morning, there were rhythmic chants in the hotel gardens. From my balcony, I saw no less than five wedding parties: brides in Western-style white, bridesmaids in matching pastel prom dresses, relatives singing and chanting, stepping in circles. Pictures were taken: a trio of Japanese tourists with cameras and fanny packs were pulled into a shot by a fountain.

They sang their way to the limousines. The bride got in. The party danced its way around the limousine a few times, circling, switching direction. Then the limo pulled away, to cheers and applause, and the wedding party dispersed to waiting minibuses. Then another minibus would pull in and a new wedding party would disembark.

An Ethiopian guy sidled up. He told me it was the rainy season—the lucky time to get married—and that the wedding parties were chanting, "Teff, teff!"—a grain that's the primary ingredient in *injera*, the spongy-bread staple of the Ethiopian diet.

The guy invited me to a party up the hill from the hotel. We walked to a concrete house, where we sat alone in a room with white couches and a coffee table. A stream of college-age girls filed in, each shaking my hand as they passed. They filled the couches, sitting on the arms of the furniture.

"We will show you traditional Ethiopian dancing." They turned on a boom box and danced uninspiredly, arrhythmically. They grabbed my arms, trying pull me up to dance with them. Four bottles of honey wine were plopped on the table. "Drink some with us!" I'm sorry, I don't drink alcohol. "There's no alcohol in this!" I sniffed. Lies.

There was a Bob Marley poster. Something about the presence of a Bob Marley poster made me certain I was being scammed. But I wanted to be polite. I ordered a Coke.

A lab-coated waitress brought a bill on a silver plate: 453 Ethiopian birr. That's $50. My overpriced dinner at the hotel cost 50 birr. I stood up, making a show of outrage. I wasn't angry, but I thought it was the only thing that would get me out of there. I pulled a 10-birr note out and threw it on the silver plate. That's for my Coke. I'm leaving.

A stout, older guy with a mean look came in. "Is there a problem here?" The problem is I'm not paying you 453 birr.

"Don't worry, that's Ethiopian, not U.S. dollars!" one of the girls chirped. "Don't worry!"

I strode out. One of the girls followed me, looking genuinely baffled. The lab-coated waitress followed, too, pointing to the figure on the bill and holding up the 10-birr note like she didn't understand.

I realized I'd left my umbrella on the white couch; I turned, probably quite foolishly, and walked back in. One of the girls handed me the umbrella, her left hand supporting her right elbow as she handed it to me—the polite way to hand something to somebody in Ethiopia.

(453 birr, $50, I thought, days later. I've spent more money on a shirt I ended up never wearing; what difference would it have made if I had just cheerfully let them bilk me?)

An Ethiopian band and dancers played in the hotel restaurant: a drummer, a guy playing a one-stringed fiddle, and two guys playing these lute-looking, guitar-sounding instruments called *krars*.

The tone of the bass *krar* sounded for all the world like the bass on the Jackson 5's "I Want You Back."

They were out of tune; after every song there was a long, only partially successful tuning pause. Then they played. Fantastic. Potent, fevered jams, the energy intensifying. They switched between waltz time and four-on-the-floor in the middle of tunes, suddenly switching the beat's accent. The transitions felt like loop-the-loops.

Two white tourists picked tentatively at their *shiro* and *injera*; stoic waitresses in bow ties, with nameplates reading "TRAINEE No. 35" or "TRAINEE No. 8" solemnly took their empty glasses away.

I wanted to hear more. I got into a taxi and told the guy I was looking to hear some Ethiopian music; he took me to a dim bar where a guy in a suit crooned into a wireless mic in front of a guy playing a Yamaha keyboard, with drum machine and automated bass line.

I told the cab driver that I wanted to hear some more traditional music: he took me to a place called the Concorde Hotel. I walked into the bar—the uniformed security guards saluted me formally—to see a band and dancers, finishing up a tune to much applause.

I went the bathroom. When I returned, the band was gone, the dancers were gone, R. Kelly's "Step in the Name of Love" was playing, and the bar was filled with whores.

One of the whores cornered me on a bar stool and asked me to buy her a drink. Yeah, OK, why not. Mistake. She stood guard over me for the next half hour, giving churlish looks to the other whores, lest they intrude.

I think I was drugged. I was drinking a bottled water. My heartbeat accelerated; I started to feel shaky. I recognized the feeling: the Donald. The Donald is a feeling you get when you take Ecstasy, when the drug is coming on, but before the euphoric effects: an anxious, panicky feeling.

Once, at a Dutch festival, a tech named Steak Sauce (an English guy nicknamed for his condiment of choice) had these E's with imprints of Donald Duck's face on them. I downed a pill, waited a while, started feeling agitated.

Swaz called, and I described my state of being. She said, "Is it the Donald?" Yes, the *Donald!* Describes this feeling *exactly*. But she just meant Steak Sauce's E's with the Donald Ducks on them.

So I was freaking out. I hadn't been on any drug for just shy of five years. I almost hired a whore in a Kangol newsboy's cap to give me a back rub while I waited all night for the E to wear off and I could call somebody from the rooms back home.

It turned out I wasn't on E. I don't know what it was. Maybe something derived from *chat,* the local leaf that's chewed for speed-like effects.

I flew from Addis to Bahir Dar. My taxi passed an Ethiopian cinema with slap-dash signs, hand painted on a mud wall, for BRITNEY SPEARS CROSSROADS and ROB SCHNEIDER THE HOT CHICK.

I stayed at the Ghion Hotel, on the shores of Lake Tana. I took a three-hour boat ride to the middle of the lake to see a monastery. Two men, in papyrus canoes, paddled slowly towards us. They were repeating something indistinctly, smiling.

They came closer. They were saying, "Money. Money. Money. Money. Money. Money. Money. Money. Money. Money."

In the monastery were paintings of Saints Gabriel and Mikael with Afros, lifting swords, and images of the damned, blue-skinned, swimming in the fires of Hell.

There was an old guy in robes, with a rifle that seemed to be vintage '40s, leaning on a pillar. He said: "I am the guard. Give me money." I gave him a few notes. He said again: "I am the guard. Give me money. I am the guard. Give me money."

That night, I pulled a chair down to the lakefront and played guitar to the darkness. Suddenly I was surrounded by excited waiters in green coats. Immediately, everybody wanted to be friends with the weird guitar-playing white guy.

One guy, maybe eighteen, sang me, with his voice breaking and faltering, a gruesomely sappy song he wrote for an unreciprocating girl. "Mike, I love her! Tell me what do I do?"

Later, I stood outside the gate of the Ghion, looking down the empty streets. One of the waiters, a guy named Lul, came out, on his way home. "Mike, what are you doing? Do you not enjoy? Come with me!"

He took me through the streets of Bahir Dar to a club where an Azmari was playing. An Azmari is a guy who sings and plays a *masinko,* the one-stringed fiddle, improvising verses about the patrons hanging out drinking. It sounded like an Islamic James Brown playing square dance music. Everyone in the place was laughing.

Lul kept asking me, "Mike! Are you fine?" Yes, Lul, doing great. A few more minutes. "Mike! Are you fine?"

The Azmari came over and asked Lul something.

"Mike," Lul said.

The Azmari sang, "Blah blah blah Amharic blah Mike! Amharic blah blah Mike blah!"

The audience roared.

"Blah Amharic Mike blah Amharic blah!"

The audience roared again.

Lul, what's he saying?

"He is saying words of praise for you," Lul said.

I went to buy Ethiopian music with another guy, Sirage, from the Ghion. The shopkeeper would disappear into the back, bring out a few pirated CDs, and I'd listen to them on cheap headphones. A bunch of Ethiopian guys crowded around me, amused and perplexed by the white guy buying an insane number of Amharic CDs. They murmured every time I rejected something.

I bought an armload. "Sure, if nine is good, ten is better," said Sirage, bewildered.

A copy of Jeff Buckley's *Grace* sat on a shelf behind the counter. Obviously pirated: a photocopied cover. I told Sirage, That's my friend. I explained how he drowned. Sirage bought the CD.

Sirage brought me back to his house for coffee and showed the CD to a neighbor. He told her a long story in Amharic, clearly the tale of Jeff's death, as she clucked, dismayed.

"She says she is sorry about your friend," Sirage said.

The next morning at breakfast Charlie Rich was playing.

Do you like this? I asked Sirage.

"Oh, I like country music for all my life," he said.

A black-and-yellow bird hopped on the table between my coffee cup and my eggs, hopped tentatively towards the sugar bowl, and, upon finding I wasn't a threat, dipped its beak in, snapped it back, munched the sugar furiously, then dipped its beak in again. I tore off toast fragments and put them on the edge of the table. Instantly, a tumult of twenty birds fluttered down onto the table, battling savagely.

That night it rained. In the restaurant, two girls in their late teens sat on the hotel veranda, looking out at the lake. They called me over to sit; we had a stilted conversation about their school and *injera*. I wondered if they were whores, but they were dressed conservatively, arms and knees covered.

"Mike, when do you sleep?" one asked.

Lul, waiting tables that night, came by. "Mike! Are you fine?"

We walked through the puddled streets of the town, Amharic pop blasting from the doors of the bars, to a place called the John Bar. A sardonic guy named Mulgeta and a minibus driver named Daniel were dancing. Daniel was a very sweet maniac. He had a dance move something like a boxer's version of the cabbage patch. He kept reaching out to me, dancing with me, shaking my hand, grabbing my arms.

In Ethiopia, you see male friends walking down the street, hand in hand, or draped around each other like only lovers do in the West.

Lul asked me if I played guitar for a living. Yes.

"Mike!" he said. "You are a *great man!*"

A chubby whore in tight white jeans and white jean jacket vied for my attention. She was grotesquely alluring: big-faced, her eyes circled too many times with dark makeup. She had long blonde extensions tied up on top of her head, sort of a superheroine's hairdo. The low-cut jeans and high-cut jacket exposed an appealing muffin top of hip flesh. I was transfixed.

I looked at her, and she raised her eyes, smiling and touching her mouth to signal that she wanted to me to buy her a drink. My heart beat faster. She motioned for me to come over, but I jerked my head away, talking to the guys from the Ghion. I was ashamed to want a whore in the first place, but moreover, ashamed to want this quasi-ugly whore. I headed to the bathroom; she followed, and cornered me. "What your name?"

Mike, I said.

"I, Hannah." she said, offering a very formal handshake.

It's nice to meet you, Hannah, I said, shaking her hand, but I have to go.

She seemed at a loss. "You want short?" she asked.

Back at the Ghion, I got in bed, lowering the mosquito netting around the mattress. There was a knock. In my boxer shorts, I opened the door to find one of the girls from the veranda.

"Do you sleep now?"

A plain implication.

Yes.

"Give me 20 birr for a taxi?" she said.

Sorry, baby, I can't do that, I said, Sinatra-circa-1962 suave. I gave her a peck on the cheek and shut the door.

I went back to the John Bar the next night. It was just me, my Ghion friends, the bartender, and Hannah there.

"Do you want to dance?" one of the guys said. "Dance with this one, she is known for dancing." He nodded to Hannah.

So I danced with her. Standing right in front of the couch on which my three friends awkwardly sat. She wasn't a great dancer, but she was sexy, and I was looking at her ass and into her huge made-up eyes. My heart galloped.

The sound system played 50 Cent's "In Da Club," the bass fuzzing in the bad woofer. Its most outstanding lyric: "Come give me a hug if you're into getting rubbed."

I took her back to the Ghion.

I asked if I could kiss her. I always thought the whores' code forbade kissing. She seemed perplexed that I would feel the need to ask.

I kissed her; she was missing a stretch of teeth on one side. Somehow this made her sexier to me. I took out my iPod and my headphones and dialed up "In Da Club," and turned up the volume loud enough that we could sort of hear the tinny buzz of the track.

We danced. I took off her clothes. I danced behind her, holding her hips. I leaned her towards the bed. My hand was on her pussy. "What do you want?" she said, mildly. Just to dance, I said, I just want to dance.

My cock got hard against her ass, and I rubbed it against her as she was dancing, and eventually I was sort of grasping at her back muscles, looking at her glossy flesh, and I slowed down because I didn't want to come so fast. I kissed her back and ran my hands down her sides. Then I came on her back.

We lay down. She was talkative, smiling. I asked her about where she was from—Addis—what she did there—she worked at, as it happened, the disco at the Concorde Hotel. She warmed up, in this unnervingly genuine way, to me. "You want to come to my sister house for coffee ceremony?" No, I said, I have to leave and go to Gondar. She kept talking, and saying nice, mild things, but I was agonizing, ashamed.

I told her I needed to sleep. She got up and dressed. How much do I pay you? She said, very casually, "What you think." This is a ploy to make a tourist overpay. I gave her an excessive roll of Ethiopian birr anyway.

At the door she looked at me sadly. "You don't like me," she said. "But I like you."

In Gondar, I splurged, and stayed at the Goha, the most expensive hotel in town: $37 a night. On a porch overlooking the town, two girls in t-shirts shivered in the mountain air. They pestered me with questions about my girlfriend—"Can we see her picture?"— and Dallas. Dallas? One of them had a relative there. She said she fantasized about winning the American embassy's visa lottery, so she could go live in Dallas. I told them that Dallas is the plastic-surgery capital of America. They didn't understand.

There was the sound of Amharic pop music in the distance, and dogs. Dozens of dogs, barking in the dusk.

A guide took me around the sights: the castles built by King Fasil-das, and a pool built by a king who converted to Catholicism, to baptize his people en masse. We stopped at the Falasha village: the Falashas are the Ethiopian Jews, who were airlifted to Israel in 1991. "There is nothing to see here," said the guide. He motioned to my *Lonely Planet*. "We only come here because it's in the book."

I flew to Lalibela. At the luggage carousel an Ethiopian guy wore a t-shirt saying GEISHA PERFUMED FAMILY JELLY.

The town was ancient; half the houses in the town were *tukuls*, cylindrical thatch-roofed huts. Robed farmers who had walked miles from the countryside to get to the weekly market sold bricks of salt, red honey glopped in clay jars, and the teff grain in numer-ous grades: brown, red, beige, the lighter-colored grain being more expensive.

A guy named Abaye took me to the rock-hewn churches. "The book says it took 40,000 people to build these, but it's not so," he said, in the same tone he used for dates, heights, widths, the sym-bolism of the number of points on the crosses. "These churches were built by angels."

A priest sat in each church: each blessed Abaye with a golden cross, touching his head with each point. Abaye kissed it, then pointed to it, and said, "This cross was made in the fourteenth century."

The churches are set in trenches lined with cubbyholes that were once the graves of aristocrats. Monks sit in the empty cubbyholes now, reading, praying, contemplating. One asked me to change US$1 into birr; he was tipped that by a tourist who took his picture. Children were begging. "1 birr," each said.

"Not 2 birr," said Abaye. "10 birr no good. Only 1 birr."

I gave out a lot of 1-birr notes. An eyeless man came up. "Hello. I am blind," he said. I was out of the notes. He kept staggering towards me. Terrifying. "Hello. I am blind. Hello. I am blind. Hello. I am blind."

At a restaurant, a kid named Andalam came and sat with me. He pulled out a sheaf of foreign notes—Eritrean, Kenyan, Ugandan. He said there was a foreign-currency-collecting contest at his school. "I need US$10 and $20 to win," he said, quite sweetly. Nice try.

I give him $1. "Who is this?" he asked. George Washington. "Father of George Bush?" he asks.

He asked me about 50 Cent. "Black American English is difficult for us to understand," Andalam said. "He sings, 'Gasharby, eezabirfay.' What does it mean?"

What?

"'Gasharby, eezabirfay.'"

Oh, 'Go shorty, it's your birthday.'

At the airport in Axum, all the clocks were stopped at 4:41. Not just one or two clocks, but ten, fifteen, throughout the terminal.

I arrived in Axum on a holiday: packs of preteen girls, in traditional Tigrinya white dresses, prettied up with hair braided and hands dyed red, took to the streets, not letting any man pass until he gave them a pittance. When I went to the bank to cash a traveler's check, I got a bunch of 1-birr notes to give out.

A pack of girls surrounded me, singing a traditional song, then devolved into a chant, in English: "GIVE ME MONEY! GIVE ME MONEY! GIVE ME MONEY! GIVE ME MONEY!"

Dozens of women in white dresses surrounded a church; they were walking up and kissing its doorway.

An old man approached me; he wore a woozily chromatic checkered shirt with a butterfly collar. "Give me 1 birr," he said.

You're going to give me 1 birr? I said. Wow! That's great! Thank you! Give me 1 birr!

An old woman behind him got the joke and cracked up. He persisted.

"I want a drink," he said. "Give me 1 birr."

Wow, that's *so nice* of you, I said. 1 birr for me?

The old woman guffawed.

I sat down beside the Queen of Sheba's reservoir. A group of teenage boys surrounded me. I was suspicious and grumpy, and I didn't want to be nagged for more dough; they asked me questions and I grunted monosyllables.

But they really just wanted to talk. I felt ashamed.

They were draped all over each other, hugging, holding hands. We talked about their school, the English soccer team Arsenal, 50 Cent, New York, playing music for a living, the difference between Tigrinyan culture and Amharic culture.

"I like George Bush," one said. I assumed he was misguidedly trying to be nice. I don't like George Bush, I told him.

"I also like George Bush," said another boy. "He is tough on terrorists."

I went back to Bahir Dar. I met a guy named Genanew, who gave up a job as a high school history teacher for a more profitable career as a tourists' guide.

He asked me about "the sisterly buildings." The sisterly buildings? Oh. He meant the World Trade Center.

I asked him about the war with Eritrea. "Eritrea think you can make a country with blood and iron," Genanew says, "but Ethiopia know you can make a country only with loving."

I met an Ethiopian guy staying at the Ghion named Hunachew, a man in his sixties who lived in Sweden for years. He moved back to Ethiopia because of an old injury that flared up in the Scandinavian cold. He was living a rich man's life—for Ethiopia—on his Swedish pension. He told me about the time he saw Jimi Hendrix play, in Malmö. I met his wife—his third; two Swedes divorced him—a young woman with traditional Ethiopian cross tattoos on her cheek and forehead. He talked about Aretha Franklin, the certainty of life on other planets, cyclical famine, his job as a clerk in the Physics Department of a Swedish university.

"My life today is nothing but reading, smoking, having coffee," he said. There was a paperback in front of him; an Amharic translation of Chekhov's short stories. Fat Amharic letters outlined a cartoon dandy with an undulating mustache and a pocket watch. "I've read them in Swedish and English already."

I went back to the Azmari bar with the guys I knew. There were two beautiful African American girls who had just come to Bahir Dar to teach English. They were from Brooklyn; they wore

groovy-Brooklynite-asymmetrical-sexy clothes and hairstyles. Lul
and Genanew were transfixed by them.

Lul held my hand. I tried to be OK with it. I failed. I reached
across the table, feigning the need to pick up a glass.

We went to a bar crowded entirely with men, except one tetchy
woman who came in to bus the bar and then disappeared again.
Daniel the driver ordered a wine—it came in a beer bottle—and
a Coke. He mixed them in a glass, laughing at my expression of
alarm.

I imitated Daniel Coke-and-Wine's boxing-cabbage-patch dance.
Everybody laughed. I pointed to Daniel, saying, "Coke and wine!"
and then the two of us would do the boxing-cabbage-patch together.

Being the rich man, I bought the drinks. Everybody got shit-
faced except me and Genanew. The dancing got wilder. Lul twirled
and reeled. A robust and tacky European disco version of John
Denver's "Take Me Home, Country Roads," came on. The packed
bar exploded.

I turned to Genanew and sang the bridge:

> *I hear her voice, in the morning hour, she calls me*
> *The radio reminds me of my home, far away,*
> *Driving down the road I get a feeling that*
> *I should have been home yesterday,*
> *Yesterday*

Genanew tried to smile as I gazed into his eyes and sang the
longing lyrics, but he looked alarmed.

A kid I didn't know, sitting near me, tapped me on the shoulder. "I HATE MOTHERFUCKING WHITES," he said. "But, I
think I like you." It sounded like he'd heard somebody say that in
a movie.

I got a lift back to the hotel. Everyone in the minivan held hands. Again, I tried hard to be OK with it. I opened the door to get out and received a tender kiss on the neck.

Daniel drove me to the airport. "Coke and wine!" I said. We danced the boxing-cabbage-patch together, me on the curb, he behind the wheel.

I had a day's stopover in London. I spent $700 there, on a hotel room, two cab rides, food, a day pass on the Tube, a ticket to a Luc Tuymans show at the Tate Modern, and a shirt. I spent about the same amount in almost a month in Ethiopia.

I was in Asmara, the Eritrean capital, the next Christmas Eve. Christmas carols, in English, played over loudspeakers in the tumult of the tight streets around the cathedral. Elegant old men in sunglasses—Asmara teems with them—in natty hats, threadbare suits, fat ties, leaning on canes, hung out on the corners and slouched on bus stop benches. I'd spent most of the last three weeks walking around Asmara, taking pictures of the fountains, the gas stations, and the houses—some curved, austere, Fascistic; some ostentatiously floral—that the Italians built. Excuse me, that the Italians *designed*, and the Eritreans built.

I hung out watching my friend Menges paint a fat red candle and "Felice Anno Nuovo" on a storefront window; pervasive holiday decorating makes Christmas the busy season for a sign painter in Asmara. I tried to get him to come to a Christmas service at the cathedral with me, but he had to go back to the suburbs, where he lived with his wife and three kids in a one-room concrete house.

I don't usually do Christmas things, but I was lonely. The cathedral was homely, and filled mostly with Westerners, people from the NGOs and the embassies. A choir of Eritreans sang "Silent Night" torpidly. I left.

It was now dark. I got in a taxi sitting at the curb; the backseat was already occupied by a woman in full Islamic-propriety cover-up: black *hijab*, black *abaya*, black veil. I didn't see her till I sat down. *"Yekanyeley,"* I said—skittery about offending a Muslim woman—realizing as I said it that it means thank you, not excuse me. I reached for the door handle, but she grabbed my arm. "Wait! Where do you go?"

"Just somewhere I can hear some music."

"You want to go to Expo?"

I looked at her eyes, the only part of her face visible above the veil. They were copiously mascaraed. She told the cab driver something in Tigrinya, and he started the car.

She pulled the veil off, revealing a pretty smile and orange lipstick. "Where are you from?"

America. New York. Questions about America and New York; was I working at the embassy? No. Are you a peacekeeper? Just a tourist. Do you go to Massawa? Yes, probably, soon. You like music? Yes, I'm a musician. What kind of music? Rock music. Like 50 Cent? Kind of.

She uncovered her hair: cornrows, tinted reddish. She kept asking questions. She pulled off the black robe. Her shoulders were bare; she wore tight charcoal acid-wash jeans. Acknowledging the stunned look on my face, she told a story about a man she said she didn't know, who had a knife and was inexplicably angry at her. It was confusing, except that, in her shoes, I'd veil my face and cover my body, too.

We reached the club, where we were the only customers. We sat in a sea of café tables and chairs; onstage was a Korg keyboard that nobody was playing, washed in dramatic blue light. A waiter came with a beer; I turned it down. She clung to my arm possessively.

I invented an excuse. She frowned, confounded, as I walked out.

The next week, I was in the dusty town of Keren, north of Asmara. I stayed in a steel cabin built on the top of a concrete-block hotel—the tallest building there, and entirely empty.

I was looking out the window when the power went out. The whole city suddenly went dark. A huge collective voice went AWWWWW!

The lights came back on. I could hear the city start to move around.

Then the electricity cut for a second time. Again, the entire town said, at once: AWWWWW!

On May 5, 2005—05/05/05, the fifth anniversary of my first meeting—I was serving jury duty in Manhattan. The first thing I started thinking about, perversely, was creative ways of smuggling drugs in there. A hollowed-out bagel, I considered.

I was made the chairman of a special grand jury exclusively hearing narcotics cases. There was a guy who recognized me from the old band and did a double take in amazement. My co-chair—sitting up at the head of the room, next to me, in the tall wooden Junta desk—was a girl who lived not in Manhattan but in Queens, but kept her legal address at her sister's apartment in Harlem for an indeterminate, sketchy reason. She sat beside me, reading the African American–target-demographic porn novels of the prolific eroticist Zane, with a poised smile.

We let one guy walk. He had rolled up, in his wheelchair, to a lady cop and tried to sell her sticks of Xanax *while she was handcuffing a guy.* She laughingly showed him her badge and he zoomed away in the middle of St. Nicholas Avenue, hands pumping madly on his wheels, trying to throw a handful of Xanax down his gullet.

I don't remember why we let him go. I do remember that we had to give each case a code name for reference purposes, and my dignified, porn-reading co-chair suggested we call this case "Scooter." Upon hearing it, the assistant D.A. suppressed her giggles.

My teeth were fucked up. I had a couple years clean, and eating involved moving food around in my mouth, chewing it only on one side: dental acrobatics.

I got a tip on a sober dentist. He used to suck on his own nitrous tanks; now he fixed the teeth of dope fiends while radiating a charming benevolence. He intoned, Buddha-like, that you should take deep breaths as he sank the Novocain needle into your jaw. Leaving his office with a numb, puffy mouth and complimentary floss, you felt like you were leaving a meditation center.

But he was profane when eloquence required it. "That motherfucker's getting ready to blow," he said, as I lay in his chair under the light, his instrument on a molar.

I needed teeth extracted, so he sent me to a surgeon, a guy in his secret society of sober dentists, on Park Avenue. The profane Buddha-dentist wrote a prescription altering what they'd use to put me under, upping the Valium content and eliminating the opiates.

But his guy was on vacation. They put me with another guy. He examined the prescription like I was messing with his style.

"Is this what you want?" he said.

Uh, yeah, please.

"Well, *OK*," he shrugged. He pulled a pad from the pocket of his blue scrubs. "Now, for afterwards, I'm gonna give you a prescription for thirty Vicodin . . . "

No, that's okay, no Vicodin.

He looked at me with an annoyed kind of puzzlement. "Well, I have to give you *something*." He paused. "How about I write you one for five Vicodin, just in case you're in pain?"

He's a dentist, and I should listen to him, and after all, he's compromising, right? I went under, the teeth got yanked, and I walked out of the place in a wooze with the prescription in my fist.

My girlfriend came over to tend to me. She was a tiny Bengali girl, a grad student at Columbia, thirteen years my junior. I wasn't in pain, but I gulped the first pill and the wonderfulness came over me. The sleet outside was suddenly imbued with beauty and melancholy.

She went to the bodega. I lay on the couch, staring at the pill bottle.

What's up, player? the pills said.

Spooky rockabilly played on WFMU: echoed twangs. Isn't this stately grey day, the music, the girl who loves me, good enough without being high?

What's up, player? the pills said.

I popped two more before she came back. I didn't tell her. I became expansively self-revealing that night, showing her yearbook pictures and telling her sad tales of my teenage years.

I popped the last two pills.

"Are you supposed to be doing that?"

I'm doing what the surgeon told me, I said.

I realized at some point that I had been scratching my nose for five hours straight. A terrible sign. I drifted off.

Hours later I woke in a panic. I had had a microseconds-long dream in which my tiny girlfriend turned into a jackal and was gnawing my face off.

Her eyes clicked open to find me looming.

"How are you feeling?" she said, very quietly.

I lay awake the rest of the night. In the morning the tender sleet had turned into a dismal curtain, the radio into a resentful drone. It was what life was two years before: a terrible grey grind, just an interval to suffer until the next time I got high. The desolation, two years gone, took twelve hours to come back nearly at full power.

I had to audition a drummer that day, a guy I played with in college, a jazz fusion guy who, back then, was exasperated by my elementary musical notions. Now that I was a rock star, he had this kind of nervous, forced niceness. We went through a few songs—I freaked him out by not explaining what I wanted, which is what I always do—in between, he'd ask, manically, How was that? Did you like that?

Inside, I was wretchedness itself.

I caught up with friends in the rooms. I hugged them, I told them. The day before, as I popped the first pill, I wondered if, after my medically sanctioned relapse, going back to the abstinent life would be depressing. Actually, I was deeply grateful for the reminder of what a life spent needing to stay high was actually like.

A guy who sat with me in that meeting and told me his own tale of a creepy painkiller episode passed away a few years later. He was out on Long Island, helping a friend get clean. He went surfing and was stung by a wasp, had an allergic reaction, and died. I learned about it in Cambodia: I was sitting in a restaurant with wi-fi, and my friends had posted all these videos of him. He was, I suddenly learned, a pioneer skateboarder in New York—I knew he skated, I knew he built skate parks, but he never mentioned that he was quasi-famous. Huh. Weird. Why's everybody putting all these videos up?

Oh, no.

I had a dream a few months later, back home in New York. I went to a meeting and saw him there. "You're not really here, are you?" I asked.

"No," he said, smiling.

I did an interview with a punk-rock-porn-pinup website: tattooed women give the camera slatternly looks. The guy who ran the site was a fan of mine; he gave me a free lifetime membership. I parlayed my minor rock-stardom to befriend a couple of the models; I photographed one of them on my roof for the site.

I learned that when photographers say they don't notice the naked sexiness in front of them, they're not just telling a lie to be infuriating: I was panicked as I shot her, trying to take decent pictures. I tried hard to make her laugh; her default setting was a robotic porny face with sucked-in cheeks and lightless eyes, an unintentional lampoon of sexiness. So I made stupid jokes and imitated the barking Japanese photographer in *Lost in Translation,* and she laughed, goofily, with a big horsey grin.

She was missing the top part of her left ring finger, from the knuckle up. I asked her how she lost it.

"It's a body modification," she said.

You mean, in the same category as tattoos, piercing?

Her ex-boyfriend held her hand down while her current boyfriend whacked it off with a hammer and chisel. Afterwards, she wallowed in a pit of opiates for a year; ghost pain maddened her. She knew the finger was gone but she *felt it there* and it *hurt.*

She'd been abstinent for a year, but I felt that addict energy, that force of denial, emanating from her. I brought up the rooms with careful offhandedness. She bristled.

After the shoot, we sat at a café going through the pictures on my laptop. I begged her to not make me throw away the pictures with the horsey grin. I tried not to say that her porny-face looked un-human.

She leaned pliantly into me. I could've turned her around and kissed her. But she was an addict; I couldn't take advantage of her.

She was at my house days after I had broken up with someone, and I let her go down on me; I didn't come, because I was so freaked out that I was getting sexually involved with somebody I should've been helping into the rooms.

Years later, she started going to meetings. She found a meeting she loved in which she was the lone girl among a bunch of elderly blue-collar dudes. A tattooed, quasi-porn goddess among these loving, funny, profane old men.

She married a guy, got pregnant, and moved to a farm. She put up pics on the site where her belly stretched the tattoos to comical shapes.

She had made an arrangement with a distinguished tattoo artist; she gave him the chopped-off finger in a jar, and he inked her for free. His shop looked like the interior of an H. R. Giger painting, grotesque organic forms covering the ceiling, but he was a rather aw-shucks kind of a guy.

He called and told me that a friend of his, another model from that site, was in and out of the rooms in Minneapolis, getting clean and then shooting dope again. She was a fan of mine. As it happened, I was off to Minneapolis to spend a month or so working on a recording.

So we met. She came to my hotel, after a job dancing for a bachelor party, and drove me to a meeting. She drove a sumptuous Jeep: dancing is lucrative, and, not incidentally, hard to walk away from.

She was fidgety. When she drove me home, she gave me a recovery book called *Twenty-Four Hours a Day*, in which she had written:

> You have an amazing energy, and you're a beautiful man with an amazing voice (I mean that in a few different respects). I hope you keep in touch, and I can call you a friend. Live in Love, Erika.

She texted me while I was in a cab in Brooklyn to tell me she had a crush on me. She said it obliquely, in such a way that I could simply choose not to answer. Which is what I did, just ignoring it, rather than saying: You're beautiful, but I can't get involved with you. Your feelings are, as should be expected, pretty wild at the moment: no drugs to regulate them. You don't know their powers yet. I don't want to mess up your recovery.

The next time I was in Minneapolis, she had relapsed, then come back, and had about a week clean. We went to a meeting, then she came back to my hotel room to watch TV. I let her talk her way up to my room. But I wasn't going to try anything.

We lay on the bed watching *The Wire*.

"I'm going to cuddle you," she said.

Okay, I said.

She lay at my side, with her head on my chest, that position that feels like she's a battery and you're the recharger.

I came back a month later and texted her. No response.

She's relapsed again, I figured.

I left her a voice mail, saying nothing about it, just, Hi, I'm here. She could call if she wanted.

The hotel's internet was malfunctioning. When it was back up, I logged on and found everybody she knew eulogizing her in the comments on her page. She had overdosed and died.

Her last blog was a day or two before her death. She described a dream in which she is running from something and comes to a house. She opens a sliding door to enter and suddenly realizes it is the house of somebody important to her. She finds him there, in a suit and tie, wearing a corsage. She leaves, running through the trees in the snow, and suddenly the guy's there again, but there are two of him. They peel off in two directions, and she doesn't know who to follow, so she follows neither.

I found out a few things about her after she passed. For one thing, she was married.

A year later, I texted her old number: I'm still thinking about you.

A text came back. *Who is this?*

I typed embarrassedly that I had the wrong number.

Are you sure? came the response.

Twenty Four Hours a Day is sitting in a pile of half read books by my bed. Sometimes I open it up to look at her handwriting.

That final blog is still there on her page.

I was stopped for speeding as I drove out of Athens, Georgia, on a local highway. One cop was missing half his teeth. But he was cool—I was cheerful, didn't argue. Apologetically, he searched my trunk and guitar case, and went through my pills—finding out that I didn't have the prescriptions on me, he had to call in and describe each of them to the station house ("How many anti-depressants do they have you *on?* Have you thought about just changing your diet?").

I waited behind the car, talking to his partner, a guy with a grey mustache. He said he used to be a nightclub bouncer, twenty years ago, and doesn't drink now. "I had two libations the day before I put on this badge," he said. "When they legalize marijuana, I'll start smoking it," he said.

When, not if?

"They'll legalize it as soon as they figure out how to tax it."

He said it's not addictive. I said I agreed it should be legal, but I know lots of people completely crippled by it, they wake and bake, can't get their lives together. Creative people that think their creativity depends on weed, but don't seem to notice when their art dries up and dissipates. Haven't you noticed that you can have a glass of wine for a mild buzz, but if you get stoned, you're going to get *wasted?* They don't grow weed that gives you a glass-of-wine feeling anymore. It's all turbo-charged Amsterdam shit. If you want to just get a little purr on, you have to, like, use tweezers to meticulously pluck a single tiny leaf off a bud and put that in the bowl. The gateway drug thing may or may not be true; some people get fucked up just hanging out in front of the gate for the rest of their lives.

"Marijuana is *not* addictive," he said, with some hostility.

He told me he had a '68 Fender Stratocaster once owned by Minnie Pearl.

I put up a notice on my blog that I was looking for a bass player. This one guy sent an MP3 of an esoteric free-jazz jam from which I could discern almost nothing about his playing. His e-mail read:

*My name is Andrew Livingston. I have a Ph.D. from Brooklyn College
in composition. I live in Brooklyn with my wife and child and dog. I'm
diabetic. Sometimes I cry at commercials.*

There's no way this is the guy, I thought, listening to his MP3.
But *man,* I wish this guy could be the guy.

I went to his place. He was wiry, wore octagonal Ben Franklin
spectacles, and was dressed like a homeless golf coach. He was a
deft and responsive player. He was indeed the guy.

After our first rehearsal with the full band, we were taking the
F train downtown, and our drummer turned to him and said,
"You don't look like an Andrew. You need a nickname." Rubbed
his chin. "Scrappy." More chin rubbing. "No, *Scrap.*"

Thus was Andrew "Scrap" Livingston named. I've been touring with him for years—sometimes he plays the upright bass,
sometimes cello, sometimes electric guitar (I lent him a solid-body
Silvertone that was lent, in turn, to me by Molly Escalator years
ago, when we were going out).

"Aw, word, B," he'll say, in his Mississippi drawl, to assent.
"That's how I'm living today."

His self-description in an online profile reads: "I like many
things, and mini things. I like to check my blood sugar. I like to
speak when it's appropriate."

He's preternaturally gentle. As there is a Theoretical Wayne,
so there is a Theoretical Scrap. He was a Dallas street kid as a
teenager, shooting dope, driving around with a gun in his glove
compartment. He once nodded out and fell asleep while placing
an order at the drive-through window in a Whataburger.

He concocts nicknames. He calls our friend Daniel Old Tin
Rummy. He calls our drummer McBible. He calls our electric

piano player Benjack Ladstack. He calls his best friend from Mississippi Tumpy. He calls his daughter Larry. He called his daughter's mother Funticus, which perhaps bespoke the fate of the relationship. None of these have any discernible logic to their etymology, except my nickname, which is Foss: my middle name is Ross, but there's a typo on my Social Security card.

He uses the word *friends* instead of *things*: "We should move these friends over there." Or, "I think I'm gonna eat those friends for lunch." I've heard him call chicken carbonara "chicken carbon-friends."

He calls a street a "scrump." He calls Starbucks "Whorbitron's." He calls cigarettes "dodecahedrons."

If you ask something like, Do you think we can make it over the Throg's Neck bridge before rush hour? Or, Can we stop for chicken sandwiches? He'll answer, "We can do all things through Christ."

Examples of Scrap utterances:

"If we were cartoon characters, don't you think I'd be a moth?"

"This doughnut is right in the eyes of the Lord."

Upon being asked what he's doing: "I'm just learnin' about my body."

"You can turn a spider into food, but you can't turn food into a spider."

While driving: "That guy yielded! If he needed a mechanical pencil, I'd be like, Hey, take mine."

"There might be people here that look like Steven Spielberg. I don't know much about Connecticut, but I know that."

"If a unicorn is more than a pentacorn, maybe they just call it a multicorn."

"If this airport turned into a straight-up dance party, I'd be stoked."

Several times daily, unpredictably, I'll say "goddamn it!" out loud. Sometimes under my breath, sometimes audibly. Sometimes in public: on the subway, in a store. It's because I'm flogging myself, internally, for something I've done: last week, two years ago, ten years ago, when I was fifteen. In my head, it's all still in the present.

Sometimes I'll yell out, MOTHERFUCKERS! Plural. Not that I know who the motherfuckers are.

I tried to type out a shopping list of grievances against myself to put here, and I couldn't. Even seeing each episode as an absurd banality—how can I be angry at myself for a faux pas committed as an eight-year-old? How can I not have sympathy for myself committing shitty behavior under duress? How can I hate myself for writing some corny, contrived lyric that I *didn't even use in a song?* How can I punish myself, relentlessly, for things I *thought about but didn't actually do?*—I couldn't sit through the singe of discomfort long enough to type out the incidents.

On the way out, the *goddamn it!* or the *motherfuckers!* is the voice in my head saying, *How dare you* _____? By the time it's out in the air, the *goddamn it* boomerangs: it's my voice, saying, Fuck you, voice in my head, for constantly torturing me for my mistakes.

My shrink told me the diagnostic term for this voice is an *introject.* The introject is like a malevolent district attorney, forever presenting evidence against me. Each piece of evidence goes *bang!* as he throws it on the table.

Just being able to know that this voice is a *voice* is a victory. In shrink-speak, my introject the evil D.A. is ego *dystonic,* rather than ego *syntonic.* Ego syntonic, which it used to be, means, basically, that I didn't recognize it as a voice in my head at all; whatever ancient trespass popped into my mind, I saw it as something that occurred to me innately and reasonably.

I was driving around with Scrap. *Goddamn it!*

Startled him. "What's wrong?!"

Just punishing myself for something that happened years ago that I can't do anything about, I said.

I went up to Schenectady to see Luke in a touring production of *South Pacific.* I said I was writing a memoir. "Yeah, *I know,*" he said, glaring at me in worry and consternation. My editor—the guy editing this very book—used to play bass in a band with him.

In his prestigious grad acting school, he played the leads in all the productions: the directors didn't operate on an elementary-school-soccer-team everyone-should-get-to-play system. He was the best. When he graduated, he went from *Hamlet,* and Berenger in Ionesco's *Rhinoceros,* to trying out for minuscule roles as Latino hoodlums: "I'll cut you, ese!" Some of his classmates became movie stars or took iconic TV roles. He worked as a bellhop between parts in Spanish-language cable commercials. Now he does some Broadway and touring musicals. Twice, he's been replaced by ex-contestants from *American Idol.*

He seems bitter. Maybe I'm projecting: it's just my guilt for being more successful than he is (am I? I have no idea how much money he makes). We were born a week apart. One year I gave him the June 1970 issue of *Life*—Richard Burton and Elizabeth Taylor in evening wear on a rocky beach—as a birthday present. The current issue in the month we were born—it was probably on a chair in the waiting rooms of the hospitals we were born in. The year we both turned forty, I wrote him and didn't hear back.

When I was in school, all my friends were artists. As I reached my thirties, they began to drop away; they weren't able to make any money doing what they used to dream of doing. I feel embarrassed, not lucky: when I see them, I play up the hard part of my job—demanding travel, persistent rejection—but a claim of hardship is absurd.

People who got successful doing what they want to do tend to disbelieve in luck. Got here by working hard, we say. I did, indeed, work like a motherfucker. I credit myself, in particular, for sticking it out with Soul Coughing until I had enough of a career to go out on my own. But maybe I was just fortunate to be the right kind of insane.

A shrink friend of mine from the rooms had a good definition for *fear of success*. There was a poetic, elderly crank in the soap-opera-star meeting, given to wearing berets, who drank himself to death. He had relapsed repeatedly, always coming back to much affection. The story about him was that he was a brilliant painter who never caught a break. Not true, my shrink friend said. Breaks came, but he didn't take them. If he took them, he'd cease to be an undiscovered genius and become just a very good painter.

(I'm afraid of that right now: I've loudly vowed to write a book for years. I'm also trying to avoid the paralysis that begins with, *Now, just exactly how much better is Nabokov than me?*)

Prosperous artists *tsk-tsk* at the talented but hapless, and almost invariably diagnose a fear of success. To acknowledge that there may be such things as fortune and flukes is terrifying.

My former bandmates turn up from time to time. Usually on old Soul Coughing internet bulletin boards. The bass player posts that I never actually had a drug problem; I made it up to be glamorous. "Ask Doughty how he wanted to be Lou Reed when he grew up," he typed.

I did a song with the techno producer BT, using some fragments from a song I brought into Soul Coughing that never turned into anything interesting. But because there was a rudimentary recording of a Soul Coughing version of the song, they called my publisher and my lawyer and I had to pay them.

The sampler player talked to my manager. "I bet Doughty told you he was a drug addict, too," he said.

Sometimes, when my bandmates say it—as with the songs they say I didn't write—I'm convinced that they're correct, I'm lying, and I have to go look at the two Post-Its that I put at the beginning of this book to convince myself that I'm not a hoax.

I never used a needle. I always had an apartment, and money. I never ran out of drugs—I was assiduous about that, because if I were to run out of drugs that would mean I had a *problem*. I have more than a few friends who've been to jail; I've never been arrested, except once for turnstile-jumping in the subway, and when I went to court, I was told that I was not, in fact, arrested, but *detained*. I have no record of bad-assery. Sometimes, this makes me feel like it doesn't count.

(You learn something about bad-assery in the rooms: it's not actually badass at all. Scared and pathetic people, whether with guns, or having guns pointed at them, or being thrown in jail, do not feel like badasses. They feel even more scared and pathetic than we on the outside can imagine.)

Long after the band broke up, the sampler player met Lou Reed in a studio. It turned out that Lou Reed was a Soul Coughing fan.

"Oh, thank you," said the sampler player, "but the band was more than *just me*, you know."

Someplace on the internet, the bass player was asked if there would ever be a reunion. "Not unless one of us dies," he replied.

There's much to be said for having a life.

On good days, living is about acceptance. If I win the lottery, I'm a millionaire; if my leg gets chopped off, I'm a one-legged man. They're not all good days, but the good days are very good— sometimes the days are very good when things are very bad, if that makes any sense.

I prefer where I'm at to where I was; the general serenity and satisfaction of my life is better than the brief surges of euphoria that were all I used to have. I wouldn't want to go back to the drugs even if they concocted a pill that would allow me to use casually, like a non-addict does. (The joke goes: If there were a cure for alcoholism, I'd go get *wasted!*) But I don't discredit the drugs. I wouldn't be where I am now if I wasn't where I was, then.

(I don't *recommend* drugs, either: if you have the addict thing, you're more likely to die, or live a sad grey life, than get to where I got.)

I do stuff, the way I used to envy Molly Escalator's ability to do stuff. All the travel I've done. I learned how to speak German, just for the joy of it. (I'm of the minority opinion that it's a beautiful language; more people might dig it if we heard it anywhere other than being *yelled* in movies; even French sounds ugly yelled.) I went to a meeting in Germany and spoke, although what came out probably sounded like: "Drug is no happy, I make bad! To stop, many times meetings, I go fine! Good the life-ing is!"

I struggle with a notion of god-consciousness. I need both reverence and irreverence. I chafe at the word *god,* and I chafe at self-important atheists. I don't believe in God-the-dude, who *lives somewhere,* but I don't pray to a gaseous ball of energy, either, but to something with compassion in the way a human being has compassion.

A guy in the rooms said, "I call it *god* because it's easy to spell."

By pray—and I wish I could express the act with a word other than that one—I mean, mostly, speaking out loud to the darkness. Sometimes, just thinking *at* the darkness. Some people like the on-the-knees gambit—it's been recommended to me, and I've tried, but couldn't get with it. (Do you lean back on your ankles? Or sit up, *Dorf on Golf* style, putting the weight on your knees?) Scrap and I go to meetings out on tour; sometimes the Lord's Prayer is said at the end of them, rather than the serenity prayer, and it fills me with resentment: I won't say it. Scrap sighs at me, annoyed, like, *Come on, man, it's not a big deal, just accept it as its own thing.*

Sometimes, in a freakout on the subway, in a theater, in the park, I'll type long stream-of-consciousness prayers into my phone.

And it works. Atheists, your points are often impeccable—but, for me and a bunch of my friends, at least, it works. Or, maybe I should say, it *can* work. You want data. I don't have any. You might want me to quantify the effects of prayer on—what?—pulse rate, income level, serotonin secretion, indices of satisfaction. You probably can't take me seriously if I don't have a solid hypothesis on who/what/why god is, a firm set of givens, but that's not possible for me—my version of god is one thing one day, another thing the next, yet another thing an hour later. My faith in the usefulness of prayer fluctuates from the prompting of cosmic intervention to a very slight easing of stress. Even to call myself agnostic is to presume a lot more sense and rigor than I could muster.

Key to me is what the rock legend said: *You're like a flea contemplating the Empire State Building.* What's there is too vast for a human being to get his or her head around. The only shred of a rational justification—and I mean justification *to myself*, I'm not presenting an argument here—is this: if you believe in evolution, and thus believe that dogs aren't as smart as pigs, which aren't as smart as dolphins, which aren't as smart as humans, you *must* believe there's an evolutionary step—millions of years down the line—beyond the current state of humanness. There *must* be things we aren't sophisticated enough, as animals, to comprehend—to perceive, even.

(To believe we're the pinnacle of evolution—that no facet of reality could elude our understanding—might be thought of as along the lines of the book of Genesis: god made man in his own image. God gave man dominion over the animals.)

This is deplorably shoddy proof of a personified, interventionist deity; what it more likely proves is that even the most expansive, nebulous, and mysterious idea of god-consciousness depicts what may be the true nature of the cosmos with less accuracy than a three-year-old's finger painting of a mountain. What I'm trying to say is that we're all—from cub scouts to Nobel laureates—viewing existence through our humanity. Which is to say: in metaphor. Some of our metaphors—and our metaphorical systems—are much, much more sophisticated, and meticulous, than others.

Yet. Half an hour ago, I spilled a cup of coffee. My automatic thought: the universe is directly intervening, to tell me I don't need more caffeine.

I believe in the twelve-step thing about making amends. *Making amends* doesn't mean to apologize, and it doesn't mean obtaining forgiveness. I go to somebody I've hurt and express that what I did haunts me. I once wrote something mean and vengeful about that *Spin* reviewer who scorned my voice; I wrote an e-mail telling him of my remorse. He was receptive, not to mention surprised. There are other people who haven't even returned my call. All I'm able to do is put it out there, and let go of whatever I want to get back. I wrestle with making amends to people who've hurt me.

How do I express my regrets to someone who's done something worse to me? How do I just take responsibility for what I've done, and move on?

My closeness to the rooms waxes and wanes. I'm often ambivalent in the real sense of that word: I believe as much as I disbelieve. I'll blow off meetings even though I know that just going and sitting in one will make me feel better. Sometimes much better, sometimes a little bit better, sometimes just a speck better, but always better.

I have friends. I recommend having friends. Were they in trouble, I'd help them, and I wouldn't hesitate to ask for help myself. The question, How are you? posed to someone in recovery gets an actual account of how one is, and one actually *hears* what the other guy is saying.

This stuff sounds corny, right? I don't want to be corny. But it's all true.

I'm typing this to you from Los Angeles on Labor Day. I broke up with my girlfriend last month, during a vacation to Cambodia (my advice to you is, should your relationship implode, don't be 5,000 miles from home). Since coming back, I've been spending money madly, trying to alter my feelings via consumption. I paid to fly out here business class; I'm staying in a pricey hotel. The business class flight didn't make me feel better; there was a movie star sitting a row ahead of me; I sat there feeling like I didn't measure up to the movie star, who held hands with a handsome boyfriend and was thus mocking me as boring and unlovable. The expensive hotel room isn't doing it for me, either. I need a bigger room, I need to spend more money. I need to throw more material into this weird hole in myself.

The night before I was doing a track with a producer who smoked weed continually. The kind that you get at dispensaries in California, in pharmacy bottles, with their varietal names—*White Widow, Northern Lights, Pancake Throatjam*—printed on the labels. As a friend to the demimonde, I can't fault the racket, but I don't buy the medicinal-value thing, other than helping chemotherapy patients gain weight by giving them the munchies.

I'm feeling jumpy. I skipped out on the men's meeting in Greenpoint, Brooklyn, I go to on Saturday nights, my mainstay of late. It's filled with groovy art dudes, and the occasional Polish guy from the neighborhood's enclave. Groovy art dudes intimidate me, even though I am one, because I feel their very existence proves me to be a sham. This meeting, because it's only men, no women to impress, is particularly soulful and honest; hearing the groovy art dudes open their hearts, express their insecurities, is extremely moving to me. But I skipped it, and now there are uninvited, unwanted feelings knocking around me.

I spent the morning moping in the hotel bed, watching Jerry Lewis lumber around exhaustedly on the set of his telethon, but I got smart and dialed up a meeting on the internet. There was one ten minutes away, at a university, in a nondescript student union. I went up to the floor with the meeting on it; there was a student in the elevator with me. She wore a yellow t-shirt that said *Life, Pot, Microdots*. So, likely not looking for the meeting, I judged. I walked up and down the hall, peering into the sterile meeting rooms.

"Are you looking for . . . a meeting?" the microdot-shirt girl said.

What . . . *kind* of meeting? I said. She must be looking for something else.

"A twelve-step meeting?"

Oh! It's supposed to be in here, I said, pointing into Room 3508. You a friend of Bill's? (I alluded to it earlier; a code for twelve-step people.)

"No? . . ." she said.

I took a closer look at her face. Yellowish-grey.

"My first meeting," she said.

It was just the two of us sitting in the empty conference room, with its institutional chairs and dry-erase board. I was panicky—suddenly I'm responsible for helping this girl, by myself.

I smiled. So what happened?

She shook her head, didn't want to talk about it.

Once you get your shit together, you stay in to help other people. It keeps you clean. It astonishes me that I get one of the best feelings in my life when I encounter a stranger, suffering from the same thing I suffer, who needs help. It was not ever thus.

You sure? I said.

"I had a really bad night," she said. I was filled with tenderness. I could've sobbed out loud.

The door opened, a woman walked in. She had a gee-whiz-dadgum-jim-cracky! sort of demeanor. She, too, was passing through Los Angeles, and found this place on the website.

So, apparently, they'd canceled the meeting because of Labor Day. We had one anyway. The gee-whiz lady knew the preamble by heart; she recited the twelve steps. Impressive. I cringed every time she said "god"—this new girl's got to think that's creepy, I thought, all the god god god over and over.

I spoke. I talked about this misguided hole-filling excursion. I talked about how amazing it was that wherever I was in the world, I could find it—Bangkok, Berlin, Buenos Aires, Detroit, Des Moines—*something* would happen to me in a meeting, something in me would settle. I talked about how the god thing had baffled me, how Homer Simpson was my spirit-animal, how, even now, in a life buttressed by prayer, I was truly ambivalent about god: I believe as much as I disbelieve. It's considered tactless to address someone directly in a meeting—the term is *crosstalk*—so I tried to say it from my heart, not to aim it at her.

The gee-whiz lady spoke. Eleven months ago, she woke up, bruised and cut, outside a bus station, not knowing what happened. She was more orthodox twelve-step than me—I guess that's more common to people relatively new to recovery—and was into slogans: *Keep coming back, Progress not perfection, One day at a time!*

And that terrible cliché: *Today is the first day of the rest of your life.*

But you know what? Hell yes it is.

We turned, hesitantly, to the new girl. "OK," she said. Tears came to her eyes. She'd woken up rough that morning, in an inexplicable place, had to walk home—in Los Angeles, where walking is either an eccentricity or humiliation. Her sister forced her to come to the meeting. She was flying to _____ soon, how could she do that without drinking? She was a keen atheist. She had to tell her dad about something terrible—she didn't say what—something she wrecked or negated.

After the meeting, I talked to her in the elevator. I imagine this is strange to hear, I said, but you've helped me so much today—you don't even know. I heard myself in you, and I remembered. If you want to get into this, go out and find people you identify with; find people who make you feel that you *want what they have.* I found freaky art people whose lives and hearts and minds I wanted. Maybe you're looking for someone exactly like you, or somebody unlike you, I don't know, but there's as much variety in the rooms as there is in the world, *keep looking.* I have a dozen friends who got sober at your age—or younger!—there's a meeting in New York called *Never Had a Legal Drink*. You don't have to believe in god, the rooms are full of atheists—I *am* one sometimes—I heard about a meeting in San Francisco called the *Fuck God, No Readings* group.

Good luck, I said as the elevator doors opened. A ludicrous thing to say. There's no luck involved in this.

"Good luck to you, too," she said.

She walked out of the elevator and into the rest of her life.